# Cornerstones of Peace

# Cornerstones of Peace

*Jewish Identity Politics and Democratic Theory*

Marla Brettschneider

R | Rutgers University Press
New Brunswick, New Jersey

**Library of Congress Cataloging-in-Publication Data**

Brettschneider, Marla.
    Cornerstones of peace : Jewish identity politics and democratic
theory / Marla Brettschneider.
        p.   cm.
    Includes bibliographical references and index.
    ISBN 0-8135-2215-3 (cloth : alk. paper). — ISBN 0-8135-2216-1
(pbk. : alk. paper)
    1. Jews—United States—Politics and government.   2. Jews—United
States—Attitudes toward Israel.   3. Peace movements—United States.
I. Title.
E184.J5B7413   1996
320.5'4'0956940973—dc20                                                    95-16068
                                                                                          CIP

British Cataloging-in-Publication information available

Manufactured in the United States of America

אבן מאסו הבונים היתה לראש פנה

The stone that the builders rejected has become the
cornerstone.

Psalm 118:22

This book is dedicated to my parents,
Solomon and Phyllis Brettschneider

and to the peace and democracy activists/thinkers.

What can we learn?
What can we do?

# Contents

# Acknowledgments

This book began in 1989 as my Ph.D. dissertation in political philosophy at the New York University Politics Department. Most of it was written originally in Jerusalem during the winter of 1992, completed and revised over the years from Bleecker Street to Bloomsburg . . . and anywhere I could bring my laptop computer.

In many ways this book was a collective, even communal, effort. It would be impossible for me to thank by name all of the individuals and groups—friends, family, colleagues, comrades, and supporters—who made this work come to be. I am grateful for the help from the many organizations that offered their resources, and the many, many people who invited me into their homes, gave me access to their personal files, shared their stories and their visions, and answered my continuous streams of questions. Some of these individuals and organizations are noted directly in the text, though most are not. If it were not for the intensely interactive nature of my research, and the steady and bountiful support I received, I don't know that I could have accomplished this enormous task.

I would like to thank, in particular, the following individuals who read versions or sections of the manuscript and provided sometimes tough, but always welcome and helpful, feedback: Martha Ackelsberg, Reena Bernards, Dennis Fischman, Sherry Gorelick, Cindy Greenberg, Barbara Hinckley, Jane Mansbridge, Lori Marso, Beth Martin, Patricia Moynagh, Egon Mayer, Bertell Ollman, Mark Rosenblum, Elissa Sampson, Gerry Serotta, Phillipa Strum, Susie Tanenbaum, and Deborah Waxman. H. Mark Roelofs has always been a friend and mentor. Martha Heller at Rutgers has been wonderful, believing in me and somehow enabling me to do the rewrite I had been tormented by for more than five years. All the people at Rutgers have been great, including Judith Waterman and Adaya Henis. The discussants and other colleagues at various academic conferences where I presented papers from this text—APSA, NEPSA, WPSA, NYSPSA, PAPSA, NEISA, USD—and the participants in the activist research workshops were always helpful. I would also like to thank my parents: Their lives and our never-ending political debates have contributed more to my thought than they probably realize. My sisters and grandmother are an endless source of laughter and encouragement.

I am thankful for the financial support from the Lynde and Harry Bradley Foundation, the Amy Adina Schulman Memorial Fund, and a Pennfield Fellowship, as well as from the administrations and politics departments of New York University and Bloomsburg University. Christie Shuman and the work-study students in the Bloomsburg University Political Science Department, as well as Nancy Weyent in the Library, gave me much needed technical assistance. The folks at Bretmar always came to my aid and added greatly appreciated levity to this serious project.

Of course, responsibility is mine alone.

V.
1995

# List of Abbreviations

| | |
|---|---|
| AFSI | Americans for a Safe Israel |
| A-ICLC | American-Israel Civil Liberties Coalition |
| AIPAC | American-Israel Public Affairs Committee |
| AJCommittee | American Jewish Committee |
| AJCongress | American Jewish Congress |
| API | Americans for a Progressive Israel |
| APN | Americans for Peace Now |
| CAJE | Conference on Alternatives [now Advancement] in Jewish Education |
| CJF-GA | Council of Jewish Federations–General Assembly |
| IJPU | International Jewish Peace Union |
| FLI | Friends of Labor Israel |
| JAC-PAC | Joint Action Committee for Political Affairs |
| JDL | Jewish Defense League |
| JPF | Jewish Peace Fellowship |
| JPL | Jewish Peace Lobby |
| JWCEO | Jewish Women's Committee to End the Occupation |
| NJCRAC | National Jewish Community Relations Advisory Council |
| NIF | New Israel Fund |
| NJA | New Jewish Agenda |
| NAJSA | North American Jewish Students Appeal |
| PZC | Progressive Zionist Caucus |
| RZA | Radical Zionist Alliance |
| SZU | Socialist Zionist Union |
| UJA | United Jewish Appeal |
| WJC | World Jewish Congress |
| ZOA | Zionist Organization of America |

# Introduction

> The large hall was overflowing with people. A combination of pride, fear and tension weighed heavily in the air. She took her place at the floor microphone and began to address the panel of speakers. She said, "My name is Ester Leah Ritz and I signed the 'Letter of Forty-One'." As she went on to make her statement, many in the room booed her angrily... but many clapped for her too.

Ester Leah Ritz is a well-known and highly respected member of the American Jewish community.[1] Her Jewish and Zionist credentials are impressive; she is past president of the Jewish Welfare Board and of the Milwaukee Jewish Federation, board member of the Council of Jewish Federations, and on the Board of Governors of the Jewish Agency. Ritz made this declaration at a presentation by an Israeli general on the issue of Israeli security at the 1989 Council of Jewish Federations—General Assembly. The CJF-GA is a week-long gathering of approximately four thousand North American Jewish leaders, professionals, and activists, including students. It is the crowning annual event of mainstream North American Jewry. At such events there can hardly be a topic that commands more seriousness than the security of Israel. In fact, by the 1980s the security of Israel had become a central concern of the organized American Jewish public and was a defining criteria in evaluating one's pro-Israel loyalties.

Central to an understanding of American Jewish identity is this idea of being pro-Israel. Over the years of Israel's statehood, beginning in the early Labor-dominated period and particularly since 1967, an unstated yet very specific understanding of being pro-Israel emerged in the United States. As an aspect of communal responsibility, the American Jewish community has been expected to be pro-Israel by acting as defender of the Zionist[2] idea by uncritically supporting, promoting, and defending the Israeli government.[3] Traditionally, major American Jewish organizations, such as the United Jewish Appeal (UJA), the Conference of Presidents of

Major Jewish Organizations, and the lobby group AIPAC (American-Israeli Public Affairs Committee), have been essential participants in the development of this attitude toward the state of Israel found at the heart of American Jewish identity.

Fundamental to the American Jewish community's dominant pro-Israel understanding, however, was the climate that developed in which politics—serious public discourse necessary for ongoing identity formation—was stifled. Those who took issue with such an undifferentiated pro-Israel/pro-government vision, whether publicly or internally and regardless of their commitment to Israel and to Jewish life, were labeled "anti-Israel," berated and turned upon by the organized Jewish mainstream. By the 1970s, as the mainstream organizations began to wield unprecedented power in Washington, D.C., the litmus test for the stance constituting such an attitude reached hegemonic proportions.[4] The most powerful people within the community, and many outside it, such as journalists and politicians, were castigated for not falling into line. Whether members or not, many had come to feel that on issues relating to Israel, the American Jewish community had become a closed political space, an arena where neither dissent, nor even debate, is tolerated.[5]

But no ideology, however dominant, is without its contradictions: Despite the intensely entrenched and monolithic public definition of American Jewish pro-Israel identity, there has always been an internal loyal opposition. It seems that every idea, no matter how dominant, is never without contradiction, a past, and the seeds of its transcended future. Every unity, each group-self—including tightly knit and highly cohesive communities such as those found among American Jews—will struggle, be rooted in history and develop over time.

While exploring the roots of diversity within the American Jewish community, this work focuses on the decade of the 1980s[6], as it was in this period that the internal contradictions of the community's pro-Israel identity politics came to a head.[7] With the Likud in power and the policies of the Israeli government growing harder to justify, American Jews became increasingly uncomfortable with a central aspect of their identity: living up to the call of communal responsibility to support kin in Israel through support of the state's elected leadership. After the war in Lebanon, news of the massacres at Sabra and Shatilla—and later the Intifada—this traditional pro-Israel identity became untenable. In the past decade there was an explosion of new Jewish groups (many of them small and therefore effective in reaching diverse, particular constituencies) intent on challenging the mainstream pro-Israel attitude developed and guarded through the activities of the dominant large-scale organizations such as AIPAC.

The coordination of the Letter of Forty-One was one brief, yet powerful, example of the new 1980s mode of challenging the American Jewish community's pro-Israel identity, and it reflected a new vision of a more democratic, inclusive communal politics. The letter was presented to then Israeli Prime Minister Yitzhak Shamir upon the occasion of his address to the 1989 CJF-GA in Cincinnati. While expressing respect and loyalty, it was a letter of dissent from the policies of the Likud-led Israeli government concerning the situation in the Occupied Territories and as such represented a direct challenge to the then prime minister of Israel. The letter was signed by forty-one people known as outstanding American Jewish leaders, famous rabbis, creators of Jewish public opinion, and coordinators of what was known as the pro-Israel lobby. Chairs and presidents of the most powerful Jewish organizations in the United States were represented: AIPAC, UJA, the Conference of Presidents of Major Jewish Organizations, national and local Jewish Community Relations Councils, CJF and local Federations, the American Jewish Committee, both the National Foundation and the National Federation of Jewish Culture, the National Council of Jewish Women, the Jewish Agency, major Jewish philanthropies, the Jewish Welfare Board, the National Conference on Soviet Jewry and Operation Exodus; the list goes on.

The Letter of Forty-One was also well publicized in the press.[8] Given the powerful expectations of the pro-Israel hegemony, the letter is worth quoting in full:

Dear Prime Minister Yitzhak Shamir:
Shalom
    We join with all those attending the 1989 General Assembly of the Council of Jewish Federations in warmly welcoming you to Cincinnati. We are honored, again, by the presence of the Israeli Prime Minister as we gather here to consider the great issues facing American and world Jewry.
    Surely the principal concern of all Jews is the safety and well-being of the State of Israel. You will find no differences among us on our central objectives: assuring the security of the Jewish state and continuing to strengthen the special relationship between the United States and Israel.
    Yet just as public opinion is sharply divided among Israeli citizens on how peace and security can most constructively be pursued, so American Jews too hold diverse views. We have differed on how best to move toward implementation of your government's proposal for elections in the West Bank and Gaza. More basically, profound differences exist with respect to the principles of land for peace with secure borders, a principle that some reject outright, but, we believe, most American Jews do not reject.
    We recognize, of course, the danger that Israel's enemies may try to exploit

such differences, and so we say as clearly as possible: let no one, friend or foe, mistake our differences with regard to particular policies as signifying any attrition whatsoever in our support for Israel's people and their right to a national life free of terrorism and war.[9]

At the same time, when you are presented to the General Assembly and all rise to greet you with every courtesy that is due the Prime Minister of Israel, we respectfully ask of you this: Please do not mistake courtesy for consensus, or applause for endorsement of all the policies you pursue.

Mr. Prime Minister, we understand the limits of our role. Neither American Jewry, nor the U.S. government can impose a solution or a process on you and the Israeli people. Only the Israeli people and their democratically-elected government can make final judgments on these matters. But we owe you more than courtesy and expressions of respect. We owe you honesty and clarity as well, and it is in this spirit that we write this letter.

The decade of the 1980s was drawing to a close. On the day of Shamir's speech thousands of American Jews clapped, but for the first time in history it was made clear that such a response did not symbolize monolithic support. The members of the American Jewish community who were present that evening stood together as one, paid communal respect to the current representative of the Zionist dream, and still affirmed their passionate—yet not necessarily divisive—diversity. Fundamental aspects of Jewish identity and communal politics had begun to shift significantly. It was a magnificent moment. On that same night, at the front of the great hall and also without precedent, a group of Jewish students registered their loyal yet risqué opinion. Against the background of other students' songs of Jewish strength and unity, a group of progressive Zionist student activists held up a banner before Shamir that read "For Israel's Sake REALLY Seek Peace." Despite the earlier threats that had been made against them, there was some confusion, but no one was arrested.

The Letter of Forty-One was filled with the correct code language of the pro-Israel hegemony framed by AIPAC (for example, the "special relationship" between Israel and the United States). Still, to many American Jews, the letter, and especially its publication in the press, was an outrage. American Jewish common lore (created earlier by many of the signatories themselves) maintains that loyalty is expressed with undivided support, that criticism belongs to the self-haters. We must show a united front, we are *am echad* (Hebrew for "one nation"), unanimous in our uncritical support for Israel. Dissent is equivalent to opting out of the community; and whatever dissent there may be, we are not to expose it. We do not air our dirty laundry in public: *Lo lifney ha-goyim* (Not in front of the Gentiles). Those who do are just giving ammunition to the enemy (those who hate the Jewish people and seek the destruction of the state of Israel). As the 1977 annual report of the Conference of Presidents of Major Jewish Organizations clarified so boldly, "Dissent ought not and should not be made public . . . because the result is to give aid and comfort to the enemy and to weaken that Jewish unity which is essential for the security of Israel."[10]

Until this point, when rank-and-file Jews expressed these dissenting opinions, they were virtually disinvited from the Jewish community. When Jewish leaders tried to do so, they were delegitimized. When Jews with such opinions had tried to come together organizationally in years past, their group was destroyed. Thus, when Ester Leah Ritz signed the Letter of Forty-One, and stood up in a filled room to take responsibility for her action, she was defying all convention. What were she and the other leaders who put their good names on this letter doing? What was happening to the pro-Israel hegemony? What was becoming of a core facet of American Jewish identity? Which other Jews had come before these *machers* (Yiddish for "makers," or influential people), stood up to the community and had worked for years to make such an action by leadership possible at this 1989 CJF-GA? Even under the weight of the dominant pro-Israel idea, and despite its enormous power, why were so many Jews so happy about, and others thankful for, this gesture?

These questions reach the heart of the American Jewish experience; in exploring answers we will travel through a complex historical world of communally defined ideas, identity, and group politics. When we look at pro-Israel identity and American Jewish politics into the 1980s we see dominant organizations playing in a big-league Washington, D.C. ballpark; we also see a host of smaller organizations challenging both policy and the very rules of the game. What I am talking about is democratic process. In order to understand the political life of the American Jewish community and the struggle involved in changing its pro-Israel identity, we will need to understand the rules of the major game—in order to understand the work of those groups trying to change them. To do so I bring to bear a grand and ever developing tradition of American democratic thought. What can Jews, and all activists, learn from democratic theory? What does the experience of the Letter of Forty-One add to the debate among democratic theorists on the nature of the "self" in understanding group identity? With the involvement of these new groups, Jewish political activity in the 1980s increasingly affirmed that a vibrant and thriving community committed to democracy must be a place where members can reevaluate their community's sense of self and its historical mission, and take action. These groups have been reformulating communal pro-Israel identity politics by reclaiming it as a collective multilayered process, teaching democratic theorists essential lessons about working with diversity.[11]

As such, this book is a work in applied theory and should interest scholars, Jews, and other activists. I hope to add a discussion of Jewish communal politics to a newly emerging democratic theory in the multiculturalist tradition. This work is one of a growing number that seek to develop our understanding of politics beyond the governmental, and in the realm of communities.[12] The increasingly sophisticated attention to diversity within democratic theory calls for a reinterpretation of the oneness of our communities in terms of the multiplicity of our lived identities. Scholars and activists have been exploring our experience as members of American subcommunities, playing at the dialectic of sameness and difference to reimage who we are as a nation and how we may relate to each other in creating a politics of inclusion and social justice. More and more we are all able to conceive of ourselves both as Americans and as members of various nondominant, subidentity groups such as Jews, women, Latina/os, queers, African Americans, working class, and so forth. Receiving less attention, however, is a discussion of the struggles and contradictions in our identities within these subcommunities. As we have been developing a fluency in seeing the United States at large as a complex multicultured society, we too often have treated individual identities as static. We still often see Jews, women, and other subgroups as monoliths, as we once saw the whole country to be. This work contributes to a growing tradition of new democratic theory by applying multiculturalist concepts to a discussion of identity found today within communities, and in particular within the American Jewish community.

We also need new democratic theory because many of the problems activists and community members experience in concrete, daily politics are found rooted in the very philosophical foundations of our system. Large, mainstream Jewish organizations such as AIPAC have been very important to Jewish life, but it is also imperative to understand the systemic pressures on such groups as Jews seek to engage in constructive criticism and to build a stronger, more vibrant community. The new dovish pro-Israel and Middle East peace groups of the 1980s[13] were critical of dominant groups and of a communal political climate that stifled internal debate and presented the Jewish community as monolithic and narrowly self-interested. Mainstream politics in the United States, however, has long operated within a paradigm in which atomistic, competitive, and self-interested behavior is most likely rewarded. This is the dominant political mode in the United States. Our system of pluralist democracy,[14] based on the antagonistic activity of interest groups, is generated from a historical tradition of Liberal theory.[15] A serious player in politics must understand the underlying ideas, the very rules of the game, especially in order to change the rules or to create a different game. This is why we must understand the theoretical premises manifest in the current system, which the new pro-Israel groups are working to transform.

Therefore, in order to understand the concrete reality of our own political predicament, we will examine the origins of this Liberal theory particularly found in the writings of the seventeenth-century English philosopher Thomas Hobbes. Hobbes's writings formed the theoretical bases that justified the burgeoning Western Liberal order, the dominant framework within which we still operate. Particularly in *The Leviathan*, Hobbes confronted his native England, a society in crisis, in the midst of a bloody civil war, and Europe generally toward the end of the terrifying witch craze. In *The Leviathan* Hobbes describes the crisis as if it were a state of nature, a time before government, and characterizes the fundamental problem with five chilling words: Life in the state of nature is "solitary, poor, nasty, brutish and short." He finds the root of this crisis in human nature itself: Man[16] is isolated, fearing, and dominating. Hobbes's thesis is well known: Such a foundation has led man to the societal condition of a state of war of each against all.

To Hobbes, this situation is intolerable; who wants to be at war with each and all? He thus posits a further feature of human nature: Man desires peace.[17] However, what Hobbes means by peace is something very specific that also has left its mark on politics and on our contemporary understanding of the political groups that are vying for hegemony in the development of identities. As Hobbes was writing to justify the new bourgeois system, which was inextricably linked to the emergent European technological revolution,[18] his measure of evaluation became an aspect's "use value." Thus, Hobbes refers to man's yearnings for peace in terms of a desire for a "commodious" life, where everything becomes a potential resource, a commodity, available for use.[19] Things are evaluated on a quantitative scale that ignores the qualitative considerations of their social relations. When Hobbes wrote of a social contract, a group agreement to move out of the state of nature and into civil society with government, his goal was to create a certain kind of peaceful society: the longed-for commodious society of blossoming bourgeois aspirations.[20] Thus, when we surrender our natural rights and freedoms to the sovereign to secure order out of chaos, our lives will still be solitary, poor, nasty, and brutish—they will just be a little bit longer.[21]

The problem for the 1980s pro-Israel groups and for all of those seeking deep change is that we largely continue to think and act within this Hobbesian framework today. The central tenets of Hobbes's understanding of human nature are still with us in concrete politics and are directly represented in contemporary scholarship on political groups and group-based identity formation in democratic theory.[22] There is one slight variation: What Hobbes assumed for male individuals is translated into the assumptions about groups.[23] Where Hobbes saw men as isolated, contemporary thinkers assume an atomistic autonomy of independent groups. The unity of the atomistic Hobbesian self underlies the assumption of a monolithic collective identity. Where Hobbes saw men as fundamentally fearful, and thus able to rely on and therefore think about only themselves, democratic theorists tend to assume narrow self-interest as a fundamental characteristic of political motivation. In this formulation, difference must therefore be stifled as a threat to the strong self or community. Where Hobbes saw men as dominating, scholars assume competition as the normative principle of intra- and intergroup relations. Mutual aid and collective responsibility are given short shrift as aspects of the political process explored in contemporary democratic theory. As Hobbes wrote to promote a social order that would remain brutish but would guarantee man's basic existence, American democratic theory, in its dominant pluralist formulation, also neglects to challenge the supposed brutish nature of the political arena. Pluralism merely promises that while some interests will be subordinated at times, no one group will lose or win the war all the time. This construction of the political process has no room for the concept of fundamental social change.[24] This is the world in which pro-Israel groups find themselves struggling.

Through philosophical analysis and the empirical discussion of Jewish communal politics, this book challenges such common expectations of individualistic, selfishly-interested, and competitive political actors. The vision of the activists and many others in the American Jewish community reminds us that we can indeed expect more than a brutish political existence. In demonstrating this I am concretizing a Rousseauian conception of the self in a contemporary dynamic, drawing on Rousseau to ground the as yet emerging multiculturalist theory of identity politics.[25] The establishment of the Hobbesian Social Contract produces no great change in man, and the chaotic situation in the state of nature is found replicated everywhere in Liberal civil society.[26] This, however, is not necessarily the case for Rousseau. Despite both the contradictions in Rousseau's writings themselves, and the debate over their interpretation, it is clear that to Jean-Jacques Rousseau, the establishment of the Social Contract produces a remarkable change in man.[27] In the passage from the state of nature into civil society, man develops a more noble sense of self and his freedom is made moral.[28] By entering into the Social Contract, man begins the process of maturation in which he is no longer merely a childish ego, but learns freedom in responsibility: He becomes a citizen, an equal member who in his duties and obligations is free. From then on, the civil self participates in an ongoing communal deliberation, the ever changing enunciation of the general will. In the Rousseauian change to civil society, in contrast to the Hobbesian version, the identity of the self becomes developed as a construct of relations, changeable and connected. This vision is at the heart of multiculturalism and will help us to understand the kind of community toward which the newer brand of pro-Israel groups are working.

In order to represent this contemporary dynamic within the American Jewish community in its more Rousseauian spirit, to highlight the inadequacy of democratic theory based on Hobbesian individualism, and to demonstrate that there is a better way to understand groups that more closely reflects their struggles, it becomes essential to use the dialectical method of Marx. At base, Marxist dialectics provides us with a way to see phenomena in their multiplicity, dynamism, and connection.[29] Its attention to the process of abstraction will be particularly useful. A major factor contributing to the inadequacy of the Hobbesian conception of the self, as with the limiting pro-Israel identity that the 1980s groups faced, is found simply in the process of abstraction. Hobbes draws steel boundaries around individual men at a particular point in their mature life. Whatever is found inside the boundary becomes the Hobbesian "self." Contemporary theorists draw similar boundaries around individual groups, abstracting out their history and their connection.[30] This is the way that many people will interpret what is happening within the American Jewish community. Instead, a more dialectical approach assuming change and interaction will be a necessary component of multiculturalist theory and will give us the language to articulate the vision of the 1980s pro-Israel groups.

The analysis presented here is made possible through a different process of abstraction indebted to feminist contributions to the contemporary discourse on the self.[31] If the goal is to understand the Jewish community and actual groups in the political process, the boundaries of analysis will need to be drawn more fluidly. The abstractions to be used here will include history, and the internal relations among groups and of groups as subentities of a larger whole. When a group is looked at in this way, its contradictions at once become visible. Such an analysis will show that a self, a single unit, is always multiple. It will show that what appears as agreement involves dissent, and that within a dominant conception there is often a counteridea that not only opposes the original thesis, but transcends its very construction.

That this concrete example is taken from the American Jewish community is important. Hobbes is nowhere more alive and well today than in the United States. However, despite the pervasive feeling of a triumphant Liberalism, such Hobbesian influence is not now, nor has it ever been, complete. A helpful way to demonstrate the inadequacy of Hobbesian thinking is to explore a more desirable alternative, and the best way to assert that there is and can be alternative ways of life and congregation is to explore where such alternatives already exist—even if they exist in constant struggle with Hobbesian expectations. To this end, the American Jewish community provides a fertile base.

The current issue explored in this work is grounded in a rich history of Jewish political consciousness.[32] It reflects the development and struggle of a community that, for thousands of years, has lived the Platonic dialogue concerning the nature of justice and the well-ordered society; it is a community that has lived the Hobbesian experience of fear and the dire longing for security; it has lived the great philosophical tension of concern to contemporary multiculturalists—that of affirming the member and fulfilling the collective. It is true that in many ways the contemporary Jewish community is like so many other communities, lesbian and gay, women, people of color, working class, the disabled. These are communities struggling with similar questions. They too are searching for a way to secure self-esteem and (for many of these groups) the richness of their own cultures in a broader environment in the United States still perceived as upholding a Liberal consensus.

Attention to multicultural studies helps us all confront the destructiveness of the dominant paradigm, even as it may affect us differently. Even those who seem to be the epitome of the dominant image, white-straight-able-middle class-Christian-male (or any of us who share one or a combination of such characteristics) must confront the dominant paradigm. We all suffer, albeit in particular ways, from the alienation to which Hobbes was responding. However, Hobbesian Liberalism only succeeded in institutionalizing this alienation. To listen to the story and the struggle, the wailing and the song, of this particular community, the contemporary American Jewish community, is part of a process of learning to listen to the many other communities struggling with similar questions of identity and affirmation. A contemporary form of such struggle is toward clearing a path to an individual, communal, and intercommunal process of justice and meaning. This work explores one version of such a struggle.

Thus, through applied theory we find a realm beyond Hobbesian philosophy and lobby-group politics. The empirical findings in the life of Jewish communal politics challenge traditionally Liberal group-based theory and contribute to an understanding of political groups and communities that affirms diversity. Here scholars and activists will develop a vision of politics as a process in which individuals and multilayered groups struggle to understand themselves and their social relations, where they come from and where they want to go. Listening to the activists we will find the political renamed as the space where individuals and their intersecting groups come together to interpret their needs and pursue their fulfillment; dream of their futures and seek to realize those dreams; stand publicly and be affirmed, encouraged, treated with dignity, and listened to. In the process of articulating a multiculturalist democratic theory, politics, as we will see, comes to include those steps by which a community engages in a historical process of self-identification.

There are four major sections to this text. Each section opens with a brief discussion of one of the theoretical principles at stake in the challenge posed by the 1980s groups. The theory serves as a framework for a historical discussion of the developments of the pro-Israel politics of the American Jewish community.

The first chapter reconceptualizes our understanding of the unity of the self as derived from pluralist democratic theory. The theoretical application here works through a broad historical overview of the American Jewish community seen in terms of its actual diversity. An in-depth look at an American subcommunity challenges the assumption of natural and unchanging identity by exploring how this community has developed a sense of its self over time, and by acknowledging that this sense has been envisioned and expressed in multiple ways.

The second chapter takes up the challenge of diversity politics. When multiple views within a community are noted, they are often seen as selfish interests, contradicting the interests of the whole. A more specific exploration of organizational politics focuses on two groups formed to challenge the mainstream paradigm: Breira in the 1970s, and the formation of Americans for Peace Now to meet the new era of 1980s communal politics. A look at the fate of these two groups suggests that diversity does not necessarily threaten a community. Subgroupings are the lifeblood of internal politics when politics is understood as a process of social creativity through which a community's history is constantly reinterpreted and its future reenvisioned.

Chapter 3 addresses the complexity of intergroup relations challenging the expectation of competition. In Madisonian fashion, we assume that factions motivated by self-interest will compete. Most democratic theory does not address the ways that relations among groupings may function as networks of mutual support. In the application, the vibrant mid-to-late 1980s come alive in a discussion of the complex webs and coalitions formed and constantly renegotiated among the dozens of new groups organized at that time. In this and the next section I rely more heavily on interview responses with those involved in the groups and find that despite some competition and concerns over turf, this period of identity politics within the American Jewish community suggests a network model of political struggle for democratic theorists.

The final section asks how we can appreciate social transformation by revisioning our measurements of political success. By the late 1980s and into the early 1990s, the activities of pro-Israel groups from across the political spectrum shifted. With a conceptual understanding of the history of Jewish communal politics, the 1992 elections of a Labor government in Israel after fifteen years in opposition and a new administration in the United States with high-profile alternative American Jewish leaders, begins to make sense. The conclusion contributes to the articulation of a democratic theory beyond Liberal assumptions of isolation, domination, and competition, and presents a new vision of politics as it is and as it may be.[33]

# Chapter I

# Unity

## Unity and the Constitution of the Self

A broad study of the historical development of the hegemonic pro-Israel attitude of the American Jewish community, and of the simultaneous development of the counterhegemony, is essential, as it demonstrates both the significance of difference in a collective and the reality of process in a given entity.[1] A focus on this tremendously cohesive community shows that any singular unit, any group "self," is also, at once and always, multiplicity, movement, and connection.

Jewish communal participants and other activists struggling with the pros and cons of encouraging unity should find it interesting that popular academic democratic theories make a number of consequential assumptions about the nature of unified groups and the constitution of the interests that necessitate them. In 1951 Truman warned his fellow scholars of the "pitfalls" of common classifications of politically active groups. He wrote of three dangers: implying a "certain solidity or cohesion," ascribing "*a priori* interests" to groups, and emphasizing a particular point in time while neglecting "dynamic changing content" (1951, 63–64). Despite such warnings, and similar ones given earlier by Bentley (1908, 213–214), group-based democratic theorists have not avoided such pitfalls. It should be noted that scholars have also not avoided the pitfall of seeing groups in isolation from each other.

When scholars look to the role of groups in the political process of a community, they commonly see disassociated entities.[2] The singularity of a group's makeup, its undivided unity, is assumed.[3] Traditional theories cast identity, often understood as interests, into a static and ahistorical role, perceiving it as natural to a group.[4] This traditional characterization often found in political science literature grows directly out of the Hobbesian conception of the self—of the constitution of the individual male, the perception of his needs, his relation to others and to his environment as he seeks to fulfill these needs. After Hobbes and Locke, some Liberals certainly have attempted a more nuanced explication of the self.[5] However, groups are seen to have natural, identifiable, and unchanging needs because scholars and citizens have been so influenced by a particularly Hobbesian understanding of men themselves as isolated, ahistorical, and static.

One of the most impressive of Hobbesian conceptions comes from the *Rudiments*. Here Hobbes writes, "Let us consider men . . . as if but even now sprung out of the earth, and suddenly, like mushrooms, come to full maturity, without all kind of engagement to each other."[6] There is no more chilling description of the Hobbesian Liberal self than these totally disassociated mushrooms, which materialize instantly and fully formed. Hobbes does not see men in terms of their development over time. He does not see the self as grounded in its own peculiar history, which makes it unique. He does not see a self that always acts/reacts/interacts in the world that is constantly changing, as it itself ever is. Further, Hobbes sees these ahistorical static beings as atomistically complete units in themselves; they are without any connection to others, and are defined as autonomous by their impenetrable boundaries. Each self exists in isolation, completely alienated from any communal and interpersonal experience.[7]

Communities and independent groups are then understood in terms of their singularity. One cannot break down this undialectical whole.[8] Take, for example, group scholars' treatment of the tension between agreement and disagreement in the political life of a community. Political actors are in line with group scholars when they consider a group to be an arrangement of agreement, where, for example, to Truman, the "shared attitudes" actually "constitute the interest" (1951, 33–34). For traditional, non-dialectical thinkers, it therefore cannot also embody disagreement. The fact that members of an organization or community may have differing views, then, presents these people with a problem: They cannot find a way to reconcile the "many" subopinions with the "one" taken by the group as a whole. This contradiction is irreconcilable.[9]

Many activists, such as those involved with the alternative pro-Israel groups, object to the way that the aspirations of their communities are characterized in the mainstream. The interests that the singular, isolated groups represent are seen statically as natural and ahistorical.[10] The Liberal mushroom-men are born fully mature, their sense of self—their interests—completely developed.[11] Much contemporary American democratic theory attempts to make sense of "Jewish interests," "African-American interests," the "interests of Labor" or those of the "disabled."[12] It has no conception of the politics of interest development: how a community comes to see itself as a group, how it identifies, understands, and articulates its needs and develops the strategies to have these needs heard and met within a larger context. Many of these theorists have little conception of this process whereby a community engages in a dialogue unique to its own history, understands itself, and acts. The history of American Jewish pro-Israel identity shows, however, that there is no such thing as a static set of Jewish interests or a rigidly perceived identity in this static manner and that groups are not necessarily atomistic entities defined by thick boundaries.

## A Jewish Historical Dialectic

Especially for those not familiar with Jewish history and communal struggle, it is easier to comprehend the dynamic of the recent changing pro-Israel attitude of American Jews when it is viewed within a broader context. Such a dynamic is but one example in a history alive with such wrestling. A dialectical approach compels us to explore this dynamic as it is found both in great historical Jewish memory and in the pain, tension, and feeling of danger that currently is experienced in the community.

There are two common yet somewhat contradictory understandings of the experience of Jewish community. One takes a broader historical perspective:[13] It sees the major changes, shifts, and internal struggles within the community as it understands the identity of the Jewish self, both individually and collectively. This understanding of Jewish community remembers the dialectic of its history: the multiple stories of the Bible, the struggle between tribes of ancient Israel, and the tensions between the prophets and the people Israel. It remembers the Talmud[14] as a quintessential testimony to the dialectical process. Religiously, it remembers the development of the Reform movement out of orthodoxy, followed by the Conservative, Reconstructionist, and Havurah movements. Its communal history includes the Bundist/Zionist/National Status debate.[15] In short, it knows the Jewish communal experience as that of historic, dynamic exchange.

Another understanding of Jewish collective experience grows more out of the communal life of our present. Here Jews do not see communal life as a complex process of visioning. Instead, Jews feel the tremendous weight of either/or thinking, experiencing, in the daily involvement in the life of the community, the Buberian development of a "monological us" of a narcissistic community. Here, as Arnett warns, difference is distorted into polarization (1986, xiv). In his *The Hidden Human Image*, Martin Buber's biographer Maurice Friedman discusses "the widespread tendency to polarize the concrete reality of our situation into a set of catchwords." Friedman writes of "a life-destroying, life-denying Either/Or that demands one be 'for' the Establishment or 'against' it, 'for' the Free World or 'against' it, 'for' Black Power or 'against,' 'for' the state of Israel or 'against,' 'for' America or 'against' (382). As Arnett asserts, the community dies in its labeling of everything either "pro" or "anti" (1986, 15–30).

Often, in the present self-understanding, critical Jews, or often even those merely open to hearing critique, are made to feel like traitors. Due to the push for unity, dissenters are silenced. Those who insist on listening to the silenced and who themselves insist on bearing witness feel the pain of being seen as outsiders, as political theorists suggest: Disagreement is beyond the conception of a group. At such times, dissenters can take heart from the more historical understanding of Jewish community. Critical Jews can learn to invoke the power of a dynamic history so that we may stand up to the dominant forces in the community of today. Drawing on the strength of our historical self, we say that we will not be silenced. We affirm that we may not even be right, but we reject the either/or conception of self: If we agree we are invited into the community, but if we disagree we are labeled self-haters. We do not accept this disconnection, but continue to engage until people begin to hear and we are invited back into the fold. At such times, we regain our identity as a living community that must ever anew embrace the dynamic process through which we understand ourselves.

At present, the American Jewish community is experiencing a significant existential shift. The communal conception of self is in crisis. The findings of the 1990 Council of Jewish Federations–National Jewish Population Survey have hit the American Jewish community with the devastating force of a hurricane. The statistics have served to confirm a reality that many people had only feared was true. Assimilation is at an all-time high, intermarriage is over 50 percent (in major urban areas it reaches into the seventieth percentile), Jewish illiteracy is abominable, and so on. Many large mainstream organizations find themselves in trouble and concerned for their futures. At the same time, however, there is an increased involvement of many Jews. Following the "advocacy explosion" of the United States at large in the 1960s and 1970s, there has been an explosion of new Jewish groups, particularly Israel-focused groups. As the hegemony crumbles and mass disassociation occurs, there is a simultaneous trend in the opposite direction. A flood of previously unaffiliated Jews is entering into Jewish communal life intent on experiencing more authentic politics. Longtime Jewish-identified Jews are reinvigorated and are participating in Jewish renewal. Together they are demanding the exploration of new paradigms, new relationships in the community, and a new communal politics.[16]

Judith Plaskow writes beautifully in *Standing Again at Sinai* of one aspect of this transition, revealing the pain of being on the "wrong" side of the either/or dichotomy. Jewish leaders traditionally have told Jewish women that feminism is foreign to Judaism and that they must identify themselves primarily either as women or as Jews.[17] Their struggle for inclusion has become the paradigm for a multiculturalist movement within the American Jewish community and offers much to the recent discussion of multiple identities. The presentation of the false choice, Jewish or feminist, merely served to silence the contribution of women in the creation of Jewish community. Plaskow, like Buber and his commentators Arnett and Freedman, writes that the either/or mind-set sunders being. Plaskow wants to bring her feminist self into her life with Judaism not simply to cause trouble, or out of a conviction that Judaism is essentially redeemable. The joining of, or actually acknowledging the internal relations between, her Judaism and her feminism is necessitated by needs dwelling in a deeper place in her modern Jewish self.

Plaskow moves "toward embracing a whole Jewish/feminist identity" out of a "sense that sundering Judaism and feminism would mean sundering my being" (1991, xiii). In this move she shows us the multiple part of the one. Plaskow's synthesis of selves transcends our Hobbesian conception of our self as a singular identity, and as defined by impermeable boundaries so that aspects are either "in" or "out." In doing so, Plaskow demonstrates that it is possible to live with a sense of self that transcends the either/or choices with which we seem to have been presented. She writes that "feminism impels us to rethink issues of community and diversity, to explore the ways in which one people can acknowledge and celebrate the varied experiences of its members" (1991, 9).

Plaskow has been through "a gradual process of refusing the split between a Jewish and feminist self." She explains,

> I have increasingly come to realize that in setting up Judaism and feminism as conflicting ideologies and communities, I was handing over to a supposedly monolithic Jewish tradition the power and the right to define Judaism for the past and the future. Judaism was a given that I could fit myself into or decide to reject. It was not a complex and pluralistic tradition involved in a continual

process of adaption and change—a process to which I and other feminist Jews could contribute. Like the wicked child of the Passover Seder, I was handing over Judaism to 'them,' denying my own power as a Jew to help shape what Judaism will become. (1991, xi–xii)

She writes, "I am no longer willing to relinquish that power." Instead, she rejects the self-conception of definition through rigid boundary and reaffirms the dynamic model of the self. She reminds us that Jews have lived through historic periods demonstrating the possibility of this understanding of self. Even the profound change into Rabbinic Judaism (another one of the current hegemonies of Judaism currently being challenged) "was perceived as a transition rather than a break only because the Jewish community willed it so, and undertook to reinterpret the past to meet the needs of a radically different present" (1991, xiii). Such a memorial reminds us that the Jewish community has experienced major periods of transition which support an understanding of the collective self as changing and changeable.[18]

In *Standing Again at Sinai* Plaskow is asking the community to hear the silence, in particular the silence we can hear when we attend to the absence of women's contribution to Jewish life. She does not claim, despite her commitment to present feminist trends, that this current feminist movement is "correct." She asks only that those involved be acknowledged as participating in the creation of one of the various forms of Jewish self-understanding and whose relevance to the community be allowed to stand the test of time. Plaskow offers this: Allow the activity of contemporary feminist movement participation in the very imagination of the Jewish community, and together let us see what form the community will take. This can only be done if we stop the silencing.[19]

This was the very call made by the new pro-Israel groups of the 1980s, and it continues to be paradigmatic of groups that feel excluded from definitions of "legitimate" Jewish identity. Therefore, it is important to note that Plaskow is no John Stuart Mill. She is not arguing here for a free marketplace of ideas, or a Liberally understood pluralistic Jewish community. The call for a free marketplace of ideas merely demands that everyone be allowed to put forth their opinions. It is justified by the, as yet, unproven notion that over time the good ideas will get sifted out from the bad ones, and we will end up with truth. Plaskow's call may sound similar, but it is significantly different. Mill's marketplace is populated by the Hobbesian atomistic individuals; Plaskow's arena is a community grounded in history. She is not merely demanding the freedom to speak, we can be screaming and still be silenced if no one is listening. Plaskow adds a dimension desperately needed in our individualistically based, Liberally bound discussion of freedom and democratic process. She demands that people listen—with love, respect, and encouragement. Plaskow is talking about deep and genuine engagement of members of a community with each other. In doing so, Plaskow, a theologian, has presented one of the clearest alternative visions of a multiculturalist communal politics.[20]

Plaskow's pain, struggle, and request are shared by many who feel outside the dominant paradigm of Jewish identity with its steel either/or self-definition. She does not ask merely to be let into the fortress, but writes in such a way that we see the fortress walls themselves dissolve before our very eyes. As this happens the world does not fall into Hobbesian anarchy with the prospect of violent death facing us around every corner, with the destruction of the Jewish community; but we do plunge into another form of Hobbesian anarchy, where selves are embodiments of their histories and ever changing with history itself.[21] What dies in the process is not the self, but the separative self,[22] a monster of distorted inhumanity. What we see when the fortress walls dissolve (or crumble) is the end of the hierarchical separation between lord and peasant, and between all those in and out, heard and silenced, subject and object, members and demonized enemies, pro and anti. Amidst the rubble we find a community engaged in an authentic[23] politics of engagement, and individuality in its internally related position—at once its particular self and a piece of the world of which it is a part.

In the past generation there have been other foci of Jewish renewal, related to this feminist movement, setting the stage for pro-Israel identity exploration. Again, those involved asserted that their questions came out of genuine love and pain over being Jewish, however distant some had felt from the organized community in the past. They demanded that their questions be taken seriously, that being Jewish meant, in all its connotations, "God wrestling."[24] What we saw was new poetry, ritual innovation, *tikkun olam* (commonly understood as healing, repairing, and transforming the world) reignited, new histories evolving, and a new relationship to Israel in the making. These people set out to reform existing institutions as well as to create new, more open ones.

In 1969 a group of committed students protested at the annual Council of Jewish Federations–General Assembly, and demanded inclusion. As a result, the North American Jewish Students Appeal was created.[25] This is a collective fund-raising venture for independent Jewish student groups and grassroots projects across the continent. Along with its constituent

organizations,[26] NAJSA encourages and supports student-run and -initi-
ated movement (the more well-known "student" organization, B'nai
B'rith's Hillel, though helpful to student movement, was actually non-stu-
dent-staff run[27]). These students have since graduated and gone on to be
new leaders in the larger community.

The late 1960s and 1970s saw the birth a host of Jewish social action
groups and of the Jewish feminist and lesbian and gay movements.[28] It
was also the period of the birth of the Havurah movement, which involves
grassroots ideology in the democratization and empowerment of religion.[29]
In 1976 the first Conference on Alternatives in Jewish Education (CAJE)
conference was held.[30] CAJE was formed to pursue alternatives in Jewish
education that would be relevant to the changed lives of North American
Jews. It is an outstanding success story of 1960s student activism, which
aimed at real and creative change.

Another major development in the North American Jewish Community of the 1960s was the new level of attachment to Israel, due particularly to the 1967 War. By the 1973 War this attachment became increasingly
solidified in the community's involvement in the non-Jewish political
arena. The American-Israel Public Affairs Committee (AIPAC) rose to
dominance in the world of Middle East foreign policy-making in Washington. This new institutional commitment to Israel solidified the emergent mainstream pro-Israel ideas. Thus, the radical and more democratic
changes in American Jews' relationship to Israel that would parallel those
mentioned above in religion, history, and education, social activism, and
so on, came later.

By the 1970s Israel became a central focus of American Jewry, to the
extent that many characterized it as an obsession.[31] However, surprisingly
little has been written about the pro-Israel attitude and organization of
American Jews, either in the literature of political science or within Jewish studies.[32] In relation to the power attributed to the so-called Jewish
lobby, and the undeniable hold that the pro-Israel hegemony has over
much of American Jewry and over some American politicians, hardly any
serious analysis is to be found of such a phenomenon. Instead, over and
over, especially in the interest-group literature, there are merely references
to the "Jewish lobby" or the "pro-Israel lobby."[33] The brevity of these references suggest a singular understanding of what the American Jewish
community, when understood politically, is all about: an isolated, greedy,
and competitive group.

It is important to challenge such an understanding. As interests and the
self traditionally have been seen as identical,[34] challenges to the boun-

daried atomism of the self and to the naturalness of interests are thus inherently related. Just as interests are fluid, historical, and in movement generated by their inherent contradictions, the self, our very identity, also is changing, permeable, related. We will explore the presumption of that monolithic notion of "Jewish interest," the powerful generator of the infamous pro-Israel lobby, which has set the terms of identity exploration within the community. Once this is accomplished, we may confront the reality of the boundaried atomism of the isolated Liberal self. It is then possible to find a new kind of autonomy to inform democratic theory when groups are seen as autonomous yet intimately related both to each other as well as to a larger whole.

## The Pro-Israel Idea: A Unity with Differences

Each idea, or aspect of communal identity, has emerged historically and is in constant process on its way into the future. Each self, singular or collective, contains internal contradictions that shape the contours of its evolving identity. American Jewry and Jewish communal politics take shape in a starkly different fashion from the monoliths of Hobbesian group thought. First of all, the pro-Israel idea is a recent phenomenon among American Jewry. Its establishment and rise to dominance were the result of counterhegemonic activity against a decidedly hegemonic anti-Zionist aspect of American Jewish identity. Second, the current pro-Israel hegemonic ideal has never been monolithic within the establishment itself. No prominent idea just springs onto the stage of history fully formed like Hobbesian men/mushrooms. Third, the current hegemonic pro-Israel idea has never been without criticism from the Jewish community as a whole. The current rise of a counterhegemonic pro-Israel idea has its deep roots in the history of Jewish life.

*Due to a tendency to think ahistorically, solidified aspects of our current identities often seem always to have been with us. American Jewish pro-Israel identity is a recent phenomenon:*

Most people, Jew and non-Jew alike, tend to forget that the notion of creating a Jewish state as a remedy for the ills of the Jewish predicament is not, and has never been, universally supported by the Jewish community. In the mid-1800s, when modern Zionism emerged onto the stage of European revolutionary history, with the writings and organizing of such men as Moses Hess and Ahad Ha'am, it was by no means broadly accepted as a solution to the "Jewish Problem." Most European Jews continued to opt for the promises of assimilation, either into the general society or into other revolutionary movements such as socialism.[35] In addition, other communal responses emerged (these can still be found today) that seemed viable alternatives to Zionism. These included Bundism and the effort to achieve Jewish national status within the Jews' European home countries.[36]

When this view of history is recognized, it will come as less of a surprise to note that the American Jewish community, today world renowned for its pro-Israel power, was once decidedly non-Zionist. The dominance of the pro-Israel focus of the community came about relatively recently as a countermove to the non-Zionist leaning of the organized community. The Reform movement, which was the dominant form of American Judaism around the turn of the century, was at that time actively anti-Zionist.[37] The American Jewish Committee, formed in 1906 to deal with the political and social problems of the community and today still a dominant organization, was non-Zionist.[38] Pro-Zionist sentiment only began to grow in the B'nai B'rith, which was founded in 1843, during the 1920s and 1930s. It was not until the 1940s that B'nai B'rith leadership even began to meet officially with Zionist leaders.[39] In addition, the American Jewish socialist institutions were Yiddishists and were actively non-Zionist.

Even when Jewish leaders began to take seriously the commitment to founding a Jewish state, their Zionism was its own American version. In its weakest sense, being a Zionist is confused with being pro-Israel, favoring support for a Jewish state. Inside the Zionist movement, however, and according to the more common usage of the term outside the United States, Zionists are Jews who purposely live in Israel or make *aliya* (Hebrew for "ascent") to Israel. If anything, the American Jewish community has been more pro-Zionist, that is, supportive of others who chose to live in Israel, than Zionist itself.[40] Thus, it is also more accurate to call most American Israel-oriented activity pro-Israel than Zionist.[41] It is interesting that despite the fact that sentiment toward Israel, and the activity of the pro-Israel lobby, have taken on almost religious proportions to the American Jewish community, the community's attachment to Israel is more in the guise of this watered-down form of pro-Israel sentiment than in the form of Zionism (I leave this book for someone else to write). In fact, actual Zionist movement has been very small in the United States, although it is the country in the world with the most Jews, and still more Jews than Israel itself. Even the creation of the state did not change this. As Tivnan writes, "The creation of the state of Israel had moved American Jews very deeply, but not to Israel" (1987, 29).[42]

*Another shortcoming of the tendency to think ahistorically is that we forget the long process of politics involved in developing any current identities. The intensity of the current pro-Israel identity took time to develop:*

Once the pro-Israel lobby was formed, it took time for its rise to the dominant level at which we find it today. The first Jewish lobby was formed in 1943 as a coalition of sixty-four Jewish groups. Previously, there had been individually influential Jewish men acting as court Jews on behalf of the Zionist cause.[43] For example, Louis Brandeis was an advisor of President Woodrow Wilson,[44] and New York Reform Rabbi Stephen Wise had ties to President Roosevelt. Real popular lobbying did not begin until 1943, however, when Cleveland Reform Rabbi Aba Hillel Silver created the American Zionist Emergency Council and organized a grassroots lobbying effort from across the country on the issue of Palestine. In 1951 I. L. Kenan switched from his diplomatic post under Israel's ambassador to the United Nations, Abba Eban, to a new lobbying position for the American Zionist Council. Kenan began the effort to make the support of Israel into a bipartisan issue, moving it out from its traditional base in the Democratic Party.[45]

In 1954 Kenan formed the American Zionist Council of Public Affairs. In 1959 the organization would be renamed the American Israel Public Affairs Committee. Despite other advocacy efforts on the part of Jewish organizations, AIPAC was the only registered Jewish lobby, and remained so until 1989, when the Jewish Peace Lobby hit the scene.[46] By 1974, however, few Jews outside of Washington had any idea of what AIPAC did.[47] In addition, Kenan's budget did not exceed $20,000, half of which went to publish AIPAC's newsletter, *Near East Report*. But Kenan was already lobbying for an unprecedented $2.2 billion to help Israel rearm after the Yom Kippur War (the full impact of this figure is felt when compared to the 1972 figure of total aid to Israel from the United States: $404 million). Morris Amitay succeeded Kenan, and the narrowing of the pro-Israel attitude went into full swing.[48]

As AIPAC gained influence in Washington, D.C., the either/or pro-Israel identity most firmly coalesced. In 1980 Thomas Dine took over leadership at AIPAC. Although personally in favor of territorial compromise, Dine perfected the art of labeling "anti-Israel" anyone who disagreed with the Israeli government, which was now Likud-run and avowedly anticompromise.[49] Jews who spoke out against the Israeli government, in a number of cases even despite long years in top positions of communal leadership, could not expect to survive long in organized Jewish life. Although AIPAC lost a number of important legislative battles during his reign, most notably that over the AWACS sale to Saudi Arabia, Dine was responsible for turning the organization into the one that is well known today.[50] He managed to increase U.S. aid to Israel to nearly four billion dollars, to turn AIPAC into a Jewish household name, to open its college campus campaign, which would assure another generation of lobby-focused Jews with the devastating either/or mentality,[51] and to align the Jewish community with the most conservative forces in American politics and social movement, including the fundamentalist Christian right.[52]

In 1954, the same year that AIPAC was formed, the American Zionist Nahum Goldman and B'nai B'rith President Philip Klutznick brought together the Conference of Presidents of Major Jewish Organizations (originally convened informally to defend Israel in the face of what was seen as the Eisenhower Administration's antipathy). More recently the Presidents' Conference also has sharpened its image and has risen to first-rank Jewish organizational status. In addition, the rise of the pro-Israel PAC did not begin until the 1970s, following the new U.S. campaign financing laws. Today there are approximately seventy-five such pro-Israel PACs, including JAC-PAC, which is an all-women's organization and is one of the wealthiest pro-Israel PACs.[53]

*When people think undialectically, they lose sight of the history of struggle involved in the formation of identity. The dominant pro-Israel identity emerged within a climate of internal communal struggle among mainstream leaders and organizations:*
It took time to develop the pro-Israel lobby into the force it is today. During that time, however, it was never without its critics from within the Jewish establishment itself. Even the creation of an appearance of unity for which the American Jewish community has been so well known—to the delight of Jewish leaders and the frustration of American politicians, grist for the mill of anti-Semites, and a source of alienation for Jews holding nondominant opinions—has on some levels only been an appearance.

The Reform movement decided to participate in the August meeting of 1943, when an unprecedented sixty-four Jewish groups came together to form the first Jewish lobby, but they did so after serious debate and harsh internal criticism.[54] The American Jewish Committee, on the other hand, actually walked out of the meeting.[55] The AJCommittee continued to be a critic of both the pro-Israel lobby and Israeli government policies. In 1950 Jacob Blaustein, head of the AJCommittee, traveled to Israel and spoke critically to Prime Minister David Ben-Gurion.[56] Originally Rabbi Silver called Israel's invasion of Egypt in 1956 "an error in judgment," but, along with the Presidents' Conference and the AJCommittee which also were troubled over the invasion, he was persuaded by Abba Eban to suppress this dissent and express solidarity.[57] Even as far into the pro-Israel hegemony as 1978, the AJCommittee published a discussion guide arguing for freedom of dissent within the community. Other organizations known to have trouble with AIPAC's domination were the American Jewish Congress, B'nai B'rith, and the Presidents' Conference, as well as local Jewish leadership.[58]

There have also been a number of well-known Jewish leaders who have tried to make their individual voices of dissent heard.[59] Nahum Goldman was the cofounder of the Presidents' Conference, organized to enable the Jewish community to speak with one voice, and the founder of the World Jewish Congress (WJC). However, as politics in Israel changed, Goldman became an independent and outspoken critic of Israeli government policy, arguing that diaspora Jewry should overcome its fear of dissent and constructive critique. In 1978 Goldman actually suggested to President Jimmy Carter that he try to "break the Jewish lobby in the United States," as it had become a destructive force for Israel.[60] Goldman was not the only Jewish leader who felt this way. Around the same time, Arthur Hertzberg began to call publicly for AIPAC to be disbanded, calling the lobby an obstacle to peace. Philip Klutznick, president of B'nai B'rith International, president emeritus of WJC, and cofounder of the Presidents' Conference, was an outspoken dissenter during the Reagan administration.[61] Other high-profile Jewish leaders were also known to be in open struggle with the developing either/or pro-Israel identity.[62]

*This problem of conceiving of groups and communities as ahistorical and monolithic entities results in the loss of knowledge of the roots of current organized alternative efforts. Organized opposition from nonmainstream Jewish groups began prior to the 1980s:*

The first organized public protests of Israel by American Jews active in pro-Israel and Zionist groups began quite early in the development of the pro-Israel attitude that shunned dissent. On the student level,[63] precursors to a contemporary student group, the Progressive Zionist Caucus, may be found as early as the 1930s with a group called Avukah.[64] Avukah was a left-wing Zionist student group supported by the World Zionist Organization. In the 1930s Avukah was calling on support for a Jewish homeland in Palestine, democratization within the American Jewish community, and peace and social justice issues generally. Avukah's educational work included discussions of Israeli democracy and of problems with the indigenous Arab population in Palestine.

Later, in connection with Israeli activists, nonstudent organizing began. In the 1950s people associated with Israel's MAPAM party (the Socialist Zionist Party) and some others created *New Outlook* magazine. Their intention was to give voice to the ideas of the early Israeli peace camp and to connect Jews with similar ideas throughout the world. The magazine was distributed in the United States and elsewhere, developing a steady following among the diaspora English-speaking Jewish world.

During the same period, movement graduates of Hashomer Hatzair and other like-minded progressive Jews formed the Progressive Zionist League (later becoming Americans for Progressive Israel) and established *Israel Horizons*. Differing from the Israeli base of *New Outlook* activities, this magazine is written primarily by American Jews. Its mission is to address American and Israeli issues of concern to progressive Jews. *Israel Horizons* and API are affiliated with the Kibbutz Artzi Federation and MAPAM, and remain dedicated to promoting socialism, Zionism, and the kinship of all peoples.[65] Those involved with the North American branch of the Labor Zionist movement were also active in the United States at this time.

Alternative student pro-Israel organizing resurfaced during the rise of more general student activism in the United States. In 1970 the Radical Zionist Alliance was formed from grassroots activities on North American college campuses.[66] RZA was led by graduates of left-wing Zionist youth movements such as Habonim-Dror (the Labor Zionist youth movement connected to the Israeli Labor Party)[67] and Hashomer Hatzair (the youth movement that formed MAPAM).[68] These students were uncomfortable with the growing anti-Israel and anti-Zionist sentiment among the general student left. They thus created their own group from which they participated in American political struggles, such as civil rights and anti–Vietnam War and poverty activities, as well as in Jewish communal struggles such as progressive Zionism and Jewish education. RZA published a journal named *Nitzot*, distributed by the Jewish Student Press Service, and was a constituent member of the Jewish Students' Network. The organization only lasted until the early 1970s, as many of its active members made *aliya* (moved to Israel). RZA's dissolution left a vacuum in the Jewish student world, and there were some attempts at reorganizing.[69] In the mid- 1970s former RZA activists, still on American college campuses, formed the Socialist Zionist Union.[70]

Outside the student world, activity began again in 1973 in the form of the organization Breira. The word *breira* is Hebrew for "choice" (or "alternative") and was a play on an Israeli Labor Party slogan *Ain breira* (There is no choice). It is important to note here that an American Jewish group formed, largely consisting of community leaders who joined Breira prior to the 1973 War in Israel (their ranks grew tremendously after the war), to assert that there was an alternative to the Labor Party's sluggishness in pursuing peace. Breira founders were highly Jewish identified, and most had spent significant time in Israel, where they learned this political perspective from the emerging Israeli peace movement (which included both Zionist parties in the Knesset, such as MAPAM, and individual Labor Knesset members, such as Arie Lova Eliav).

This handful of groups is the precursor to the flood of progressive pro-Israel groups that would emerge in the 1980s. Until this point individual groups emerged one at a time. Early in the 1980s, however, a number of groups formed at once and set the stage for a new wave of pro-Israel organizing and the articulation of different visions for democracy and discourse within the American Jewish community.

*When a dialectical—fluid and connected—vision becomes part of mass politics, identities long experienced as stable become highly contestable. New American Jewish pro-Israel groups emerged in the 1980s:*
The New Israel Fund was the first of the new groups intent on challenging concrete reality and the ideas with which Jews go about politics. In 1979–80 NIF was formed as an alternative venue for philanthropic pro-Israel sentiment.[71] American Jews were becoming more and more aware that their many United Jewish Appeal (UJA) donation dollars were also going to help build Jewish settlements in the Territories occupied by Israel. Despite the public pro-Israel/pro–Israeli government equation, settlement building in the Occupied Territories has long been viewed by the dovish Zionist and pro-Israel camp as illegal, immoral, a waste of Israel's resources, and a threat to the long-term democratic character of the Jewish state, and has long been denounced as an act of Jewish suicide. These donors wanted their money going elsewhere in Israel to help build the country in a manner more in line with the politics of their Zionism, still distinctly Labor and dove oriented.[72]

The New Israel Fund supports the type of grassroots organizations that traditionally have been excluded from the UJA budget, because knowledge of their existence destroys a mythic idea of Israel as the Promised Land. NIF, with its technical support project SHATIL, helps grassroots efforts on behalf of battered women, Arab-Jewish coexistence projects, prisoner empowerment, gays and lesbians, abused children, and the discriminated against Ethiopian and Sephardic and Mizrachic Jewish communities in Israel. As part of the development of the dominant pro-Israel idea, American Jews had been cultivated to see Israel only in terms of its myth in order to extract such large sums in philanthropic dollars.[73] Many American Jews can still relate only to an Israel besieged from without and pure from within.[74] The social realities of Israel, which sorely need attention, but suggest that Israel may be in part responsible for its problems, traditionally demanded blindness from American Jewry. Changing this situation has been one of the challenges of the dovish 1980s pro-Israel groups.

In 1981 Jewish students who had been involved in progressive Zionist education and activism on their various college campuses, set up a national office to help coordinate their activities. The effort took on the name Progressive Zionist Caucus, a caucus because it was committed to the grassroots nature of the local groups that would have to respond to the very different circumstances among their campuses (large and small schools, schools with large and small Jewish populations, and more or less right-wing Jewish student organization and anti-Zionist left-wing organizations). The left-of-center Zionist youth movements and their *bogrei tnuot* (Hebrew for "movement graduates"), such as Hashomer Hatzair (MAPAM), Young Judea (Hadassah), and particularly Habonim-Dror (Labor), provided the backbone of PZC; their previously nonaffiliated recruits provided a swelling of the ranks and new energy.[75]

It was within the environment of intense campus identity politics of the 1980s that PZC came into existence and quickly grew. Within a few years after PZC's establishment, the Reform and Conservative movements would form Zionist branches and would also work closely with PZC for their campus needs. Relations with Hillel, the largest campus organization, improved to a more symbiotic level, and PZC joined and quickly became essential to NAJSA. PZC went from relative obscurity, and demonization by mainstream pro-Israel forces to a central position in Jewish campus politics and into broader mainstream recognition as well.

In 1982 a Queens College professor, Mark Rosenblum, began spreading the word in the United States about the massive Israeli peace movement, Peace Now, started there in 1978.[76] In 1983 Rosenblum made a conscious decision to include Jews involved in the broader American Left into APN activity. As identity politics gained currency in the United States, many Jewish leftists were beginning to struggle with their Jewish identity. As such, many progressive, politically aware Jews were having a lot of trouble relating to the Israel of the 1980s. Organizations such as APN enabled many of these Jews to reestablish links to the Jewish community and to reexamine the meaning of being pro-Israel in nonhegemonic space. It was not until 1984 that the Israeli Peace Now decided that Rosenblum should be paid as a North American representative and organizer. Soon the organization changed its name from American Friends of Peace Now to Americans for Peace Now, demonstrating its additional commitment to American Jewish communal politics.

Similar to groups such as PZC, APN spent many years in the 1980s on the sidelines of American Jewry. The organization was portrayed by the organized mainstream as either unimportant or as a dangerous threat, depending on which suited the pro-Israel hegemony at the time. APN, however, had the advantage of being aligned with a legitimate Israeli movement, supported by many prominent Israeli political leaders and literary figures, lending it credibility and supporting its claim to be pro-Israel . . . only in a different version than found in AIPAC. APN did some organizational remodeling at the end of the 1980s and began attracting additional well-known American Jewish personalities to add to the grassroots base it had built up in the interim years. By the early 1990s its budget was approximately $1.5 million, it had about ten thousand members, and its ability to be heard by the community and offer Jews a positive and informed way of relating to Israel had increased dramatically.[77]

The struggle these groups entered into with the defenders of the dominant pro-Israel idea was difficult; it was also confusing in the face of the facts. Poll data reveals that American Jewish opinion, at least by the early 1980s, was decidedly anti-Likud, in direct disagreement with AIPAC, and supported both a Palestinian state and talks with the PLO.[78] However, in an effort to present a unified Jewish public image, AIPAC continued to target those who were known to hold such views, although they were the majority, and any public expression of these views consistently was stifled.[79] In a 1978 Israeli newspaper interview, Jewish fund-raiser Lawrence Tisch criticized Menachem Begin's policy of settling the West Bank. However, he refused to go on the record with these opinions in English here at home. Tisch claimed that his remarks were to remain "in house."[80] When Klutznick publicly urged the Reagan administration to pursue peace, AIPAC launched a smear campaign against him. In 1983 a group of eighteen American rabbis went to Washington and met with fifteen well-known pro-Israel legislators. Their agenda was to ask these legislators to oppose Israeli government policy on the peace issue. It was an unprecedented event, but it received no coverage in the media.[81] Later in the 1980s, Michael Berenbaum, now Project Director of the United States

Holocaust Museum, wrote an article published in the Washington, D.C., *Jewish Week* that the Israeli ambassador regarded unfavorably. Although Berenbaum was journalist for a mainstream local Jewish paper, he was removed from the list of those with access to the embassy.[82]

The situation had become so ridiculous that reports in the United States of even mainstream debate commonly found in Israel were branded here as anti-Israel. A number of Israeli Knesset Members from various center-left Zionist parties—such as Shinui, RATZ, MAPAM, and even Labor— came to the United States to talk to American Jews, until the late 1980s, they consistently were poorly received. Educational material published by the Israeli Labor Party, the dominant party from the conception of the state until 1977, that was circulated to Jewish student organizations on American college campuses was criticized as anti-Israel throughout the 1980s and into the early 1990s. Peace Now activities in the United States were branded extremist and were shunned by the organized mainstream, when its parent organization in Israel already had come to be called Israel's mainstream peace movement,[83] and its rallies in Israel would attract literally 15 percent of the country's population. Progressive Zionist Caucus activities on North American college campuses were treated as dangerous by campus Jewish organizations, although within the Zionist movement bureaucracy the organization was solidly supported.

However, with the Israeli invasion of Lebanon, and news of the massacres at Sabra and Shatilla, American Jewish politics took a decisive turn. The early 1980s marked the beginning of a new era in the communal politics of identity.[84] American Jews who were already pro-Israel began to question more seriously what kind of Israel they wanted to support. Other Jews who had felt themselves to be on the outskirts of Jewish community began to explore more democratic, and to them more palatable, ways of relating to the Jewish state. The notion of being pro-Israel began to grow away from its conception as the either/or unqualified assent to government policy. A responsible, moral, and democratic vision of being pro-Israel began to take mass form. Compared to the 1970s when Breira—an organization of committed Jewish intellectuals, rabbis, and other Jewish professionals that asserted that one could be both a Zionist and a dove on Israeli peace and security issues—was silenced, the continuing shock of Israeli politics produced levels of moral outrage among American Jews that would buffer the new attempts at alternative, non–hegemonically defined organization. Grassroots movement got under way and provided a home for Jews who had been alienated by the mainstream pro-Israel view, and increasingly for Jewish leaders who had long been disturbed by the dominance of the narrow, either/or pro-Israel relationship. Despite all the effort to present a supposedly single-minded American Jewish community, in order to bolster its power in United States interest group politics, the community never really fit this paradigm. As Jewish women had done in the 1970s with respect to feminism, by the 1980s more and more American Jews refused to accept this popular and either/or definition of their pro-Israel selves.

Although New Jewish Agenda was formed in 1980 as a multiissue progressive organization, by middecade NJA's Israel and Middle East peace work began to overshadow much of the rest of the group's activities. The organization was unique in that it brought together religious and secular, Zionist, non- and anti-Zionist Jews who were committed to *tikkun olam* and coalition solidarity work. Among its founders were people who today are Hillel directors, and the founders of the new breed of 1980s mainstream pro-Israel organizations such as the Jewish Women's Consultation and Project Nishma.[85]

In 1981 the American-Israeli Civil Liberties Coalition was formed, and in the latter part of the decade additional alternative foundations emerged such as the Abraham Fund and the Amy Adina Schulman Memorial Fund. In 1990 Amcha for Tsedakah was founded.[86] Other Jewish peace groups attending to Israel and the Middle East that were formed in the United States included the International Jewish Peace Union, the Jewish Peace Lobby, Friends of Yesh Gvul, Friends of *New Outlook*, Friends of RATZ, the Jewish Women's Committee to end the Occupation of the West Bank and Gaza (and affiliates such as the Hannah Arendt Lesbian Peace Patrol[87]), the Road to Peace, the Jewish Peace Coalition, Project Nishma, The Jewish Women's Consultation, and the Dialogue Project. These groups joined the effort of other American affiliates of Israeli organizations such as the International Center for Peace in the Middle East, Americans for a Progressive Israel (connected to MAPAM) and Friends of Labor Israel/Labor Zionist Alliance (connected to the Labor Party). The older Jewish Peace Fellowship, a Jewish pacifist organization, also began to focus largely on Israel and on Middle East peace in this period, working closely with the newer groups. *Tikkun*, a progressive intellectual Jewish magazine devoting much attention to issues of Israeli politics and to the problems of the mainstream American Jewish pro-Israel attitude, hit the stands and quickly achieved the highest circulation of any American Jewish publication. In the late 1980s *Tikkun* conferences each would attract four thousand Jews.[88] In addition, by the end of the decade and early into the 1990s, *Tikkun*, the JPL, NJA, and APN would all discover the campus and expand on the work of PZC; independent student groups also emerged on individual campuses across the country.

Clearly, through the 1980s, a significant change had taken place. In the late 1990s, AIPAC and the Presidents' Conference still dominate pro-Israel affairs, but there is actually an alternative Jewish world attracting previously alienated and unaffiliated Jews, as well as longtime communal participants and leaders.[89]

In the midst of the frenzy at the 1989 Council of Jewish Federations–General Assembly in Cincinnati, caused by the Letter of Forty-One, Ester Leah Ritz was asked by a newspaper reporter if she thought anyone agreed with her. She replied, "I don't take polls, but everyone I talk to seems to agree with me." For the 1991 CJF-GA in Baltimore, the Wilstein Institute of Jewish Policy Studies, with the help of Project Nishma, released the poll that Ritz as an individual could not have taken. The November 1991 Survey of American Jewish Philanthropic Leaders revealed that leadership was unquestionably "security-oriented doves" and was closely divided on public criticism of Israel and on public warnings to Israelis. Many of the 49 percent (48 percent did not, 3 percent were not sure)[90] who supported Jewish public dissent increasingly were putting their names on the line and joining the grassroots effort to renew a vibrant discourse in a more open Jewish communal political arena, challenging the common conception of American subcommunities as monolithic.[91]

## Jewish Groups and the Atomistic, Isolated Self

A. F. Bentley, founder of modern group theory, asserted that groups and their interests are one in the same. When we looked into Hobbesian thought, we found an understanding of interests as singular and coherent which represent atomistic units with clearly defined boundaries. The previous section provided a challenge to the notion of a group or community as singular, and its interests as static and natural. The American Jewish community and the pro-Israel lobby are among the best-known examples in American politics of unity, cohesion, and identification of group interest. The dialectical interpretation does not challenge the notion of a strong and coherent community, but it does challenge an understanding of such strength and cohesion that is ahistorical and monolithic. Such a discussion has important implications for the Hobbesian notion of the self as atomistic and isolated, as it applies to Jewish groups and group-based democratic theory.

The American Jewish community and even its strong pro-Israel identity are complex and shifting. What happens to the clearly demarcated
boundaries of the Liberal self when its definition is no longer monadic,
but dialectical? In what ways does this dialectical approach shift our understanding of the Jewish community and the role of contesting groups
within it? How are we to understand the self when we see its constitution, its sense of self/interests, as a multiplicity full of movement, contradiction, and connection? The American Jewish community, particularly in
terms of its pro-Israel self, comes alive. This self is at once itself and a product of its social relations (which includes the history of those relations). It
is a self that is whole in itself as well as being a part of something larger
than itself. The self becomes an identifiable, unique, and irreplaceable being that is simultaneously nothing—is not itself—without its connections
to other beings.

Is this self a mere fantasy of feminist philosophy,[92] or is it an empirical
reality? A study of Jewish political groups engaged in the struggle to redefine the community's pro-Israel identity provides an empirical grounding for such a theoretical positing of the dialectical self. Analysis of the
Jewish community/pro-Israel lobby demonstrates the multiple, historical,
and developed (as opposed to natural) being of the self. To demonstrate
the permeability of its boundaries and its connective constitution, I will
change the level of focus. To explore the possibility of groups in connection, rather than in isolation, I will address the particular groups engaged
in the struggle to redefine the pro-Israel identity, in this case from the
emerging sector of Jewish politics, the 1980s alternative pro-Israel groups.

Research on the newer pro-Israel groups reveals a perception of the self
as part of a community. In contrast to the vision put forth by Browne (1990,
192) that most organizations seek to avoid all circumstances that bring
them into relationship—either cooperative or competitive—with others,
these groups are firmly rooted in relation. Members of groups within this
community feel inherently bound to the emerging sector that the groups
constitute individually as well as to the Jewish community as a whole.
Members of the 1980s pro-Israel groups whom I interviewed expressed
simultaneous loyalties: on one level to their individual groups, while on
a second level to the community as a whole. An in-depth look does not
reveal a vision of groups in atomistic isolation. Instead, these individual
groups exhibit a specific sense of self tied to a collective sense that extends
beyond the particular group ego.

In light of the activities of these groups and the self-perception of
the members, the theory of atomistic selves with thick, self-defining

boundaries does not hold up.[93] As Keller (1986) writes, the identity of the separative self, inherited as part of the Liberal legacy, is either "this" or "that." More in line with Keller's web thesis, members were aware of how their groups were influenced from without, and how their groups helped to shape the destiny of other groups. Members discussed how their groups were affected by the world around them, by political events on various levels, by the media, and by the activity, success, and failure of other groups. Their responses evoke the notion of a self with permeable boundaries, constituted through interaction in the world around it.

The connective self is further demonstrated by an analysis of case study groups that challenges the assumption within traditional democratic theory that particular interests necessarily contradict general interests. By exploring the correspondence of group goals with each other and with the whole of which they are a part, the empirical presentation continues to challenge the Hobbesian sense of self. A discussion of coalitions demonstrates that a self can be both autonomous and relational. The lessons to be gleaned from a deep look at identity in a particular subcommunity are many.

## In Conclusion

Thomas Hobbes was not wrong, exactly. We do fear, and we do lust. Many live, or have lived, in the history of their communities, in a state of war and in the shadow of an all too likely possibility of violent death. Jews know this experience all too well. Hobbes was not right either, however. In fact, he was so one-sided that his concern over fear became his obsession, and so has ours today. Hobbesian philosophy, while helpful perhaps in forcing us to look in the face of violent death, is utterly inadequate. Hobbes began with the individual, a distorted shell of a man so alienated that he suffers through a living hell all of his days. The Hobbesian man has no history and no connections. He knows neither love, warmth, nor true joy. He is calculating, rather than living in process, and is forced into a state of possessive acquisitiveness to fill the empty chasm of his soul created by his inability to share.

Perhaps we all know this man. We can sympathize with his alienation and his dejection because there may be a bit of him in all of us. However, this does not describe either the whole for most of us or the whole of Jewish life. The Hobbesian man, or group, is a creature made of but one perception of our total experience. Hobbes has drawn the boundaries around our alienated self and focused in. It is, then, as if the boundaries were never drawn, and the abstraction is taken for the whole. We become, in full, alienated and distorted selves. Our being becomes so deformed and static that this state becomes our future as well. Thus, Hobbes and those who ascribe to a Hobbesian worldview not only describe alienation, but serve to create the world in its image.

Hobbes (and the Hobbesian mind-set) has been rather successful. Over three hundred years after his death, we live in a world that much more alienated. The most influential of our scholars and political actors even have forgotten that the Hobbesian separative self was originally but an abstraction. Contemporary democratic theory and the expectations of political groups reflect such a phenomenon. The Hobbesian mushroom of a man is now taken to be the reality of the group and community. Isolated and singular, with static and natural interests, the political group is a model of the Hobbesian self. However, as the Hobbesian man is but a poor abstraction of the full self—of all the selves and their possibilities that we are and see every day—the political group described in much of contemporary group-based democratic theory is a distortion of the group universe. Despite the pressure to become such a group,[94] we find many who resist. The history of American Jewish pro-Israel identity is testament to the struggle of real groups with a connected sense of self to exist and be effective in a political environment perceived as an Hobbesian alienated and brutal realm.

In the 1700s Rousseau saw his ideas as clearly differing from those of Hobbes. Although he is a controversial figure in modern feminism, much of Rousseau lives on in feminist philosophy. As contributors to an emerging multiculturalist democratic theory, Jews, feminists and Jewish feminists have updated and elaborated on Rousseau's vision of the self as developing and participating. Buber and Waskow, Daly and Keller, Plaskow and Setel, Gilligan and Benhabib, write about a self/community that is diverse, historically grounded, and connected. With their help, we have been able to see pro-Israel identity in its multiplicity, but this could not have been done without the application of some very basic techniques of Marxist dialectics.

Marxist dialectics is at once a theory, a methodology, and a plan for political action. It is based on the affirmation of life in its dynamic and relational form and is thus an attractive tool for understanding and stimulating efforts of alternative, more inclusive politics within the Jewish community and elsewhere. Engels points out in *The Dialectics of Nature* that concrete identity includes difference.[95] In the dialectical view of the law of identity, espoused by Buber and Daly as well, a thing actually is itself and its opposite at the same time.[96] This is how we can name the pro-Israel identity of the American Jewish community as simultaneously unified and contested. In *Anti-Duhring* Engels writes that such a contradiction is missed when things are considered "static and lifeless."[97] He shows that as soon "as we consider things in their motion" we are forced to confront them with their contradictions. Thus, "a living thing is at each moment itself and yet something else." Or, as Buber writes in *The Way of Response*, the "truth reality of life as one lives life" is a "unity of contraries" (1966, 111).[98]

With this in mind, it is possible to see that the Jewish community is a community, a unity, with all of its difference. The pro-Israel lobby, with the common perception of it as powerful not necessarily challenged, is a phenomenon of history. The apparently monolithic voice of Jewish leadership has always embodied dissent. The current redefinition of being pro–Israel is movement communally generated. Far from being the result of external agitation or self-hating sentiment, the new pro-Israel groups are the outgrowth of the community's internal contradictions. It is the contradiction of our recent history that the pro-Israel hegemony's rise to dominance produced pain, alienation . . . and the desire for a more informed and open communal experience.

# Chapter 2

# Diversity

As played out in the U.S. political system, the assumption that group identities are static and singular is largely an application of the Liberal notion of the atomistic self. A more helpful understanding involves seeing autonomy and identity as dialectical: multiple, fluid, and changing. Rather than referring to "Jewish interest groups" as isolated Hobbesian mushroom-men, the broad historical overview suggests that it is more reflective of actual groups to understand them as whole communities whose needs and self-conception change over time, are multiple, and are often self-contradicting. Furthermore, the fates of two groups, Breira in the 1970s and APN in the 1980s, challenge the assumption that identities which are thought to be singular and static interests are also narrow and selfish.[1]

When the newer pro-Israel groups emerged in the 1980s, they were labeled threatening to Jewish well-being. Dominant communal organizations treated the newer groups like special interest groups and therefore worked to silence them in the name of what was perceived to be the common good of the Jewish community. How do Jews committed to democracy and to their community, lifting their voices from the depths of their hearts, come to be seen at worst as, threatening, and otherwise just as additional interests selfishly fighting for power? What do interests have to do with it? Those struggling for concrete political change will find that contemporary group-based democratic theory[2] tends to understand political groups as Madison understood factions[3]: They represent "interests" that are seen as inherently parochial and antisocial.[4] We can understand better the concrete obstacles faced by the alternative Jewish groups when we realize that the problem of a politics based on the notion of self-interest is that it tends to squelch diversity behind a mask of the "common good" supposed to transcend our "particulars"—or differences—resulting in a closed political space.[5]

## Diversity and the Constitution of Interests

Pro-Israel groups working in the Jewish community are situated within a larger political system defined by bourgeois categories and concerns. Liberal democratic theory, the theory of this system, commodifies the needs, visions, and aspirations of individuals and groups, transforming them into interests,[6] "something transcendent."[7] In the process, the content of politics is translated from the concrete conditions of people's lives into an abstraction. This is problematic, because once our needs and yearnings are translated into these bourgeois abstractions, they can be traded like other commodities.[8] The bourgeois process of abstraction, in its commodification of everything, serves to negate the inviolability of human needs and dignity. It is precisely at this moment, through the abstraction, that the point of social organization ceases to be the meeting of people's concrete needs or hearing the call of groups in pain. In the bargaining among abstractions, the goal of politics becomes obscured and people's needs and genuine concerns can go unattended to.

This does not necessarily explain the inegalitarian bias inherent in the notion of interests, however. Why did so many Jews who were working for change, particularly in nondominant organizations, feel stifled? The alternative pro-Israel groups claimed that, in the name of the common good, the way the Jewish community had been doing politics was conservative, that it inhibited change and protected the dominance of certain hegemonic organizations. We can clarify the challenge faced by the originally marginal pro-Israel groups by unmasking this notion of a "common good"—that can be set apart from and opposed to private interests or the differing understandings of subgroups such as the newer pro-Israel organizations—as a mythic construction of the particular interests of some, called upon to justify the stifling of others. Long before James Madison designed the United States political system, which ignored and subsumed diversity under the pretense of protecting the general interest,[9] Liberal philosophers posited that individual interests are narrow and selfish.[10] From the notion, as Locke quotes from Hooker, "that the interest of everyman is toward himself . . . and therefore that strife and troubles would be endless" (1980, 48), Liberal philosophy has claimed the "narrowness of party" (ibid., 26) and its threat to the commonwealth. This idea stems from the role of fear in the Liberal mind-set[11] and in particular the fear of diversity. American Jewish politics currently takes place in the context of Liberalism:[12] an example of a world view in which difference is seen not as benign, or exciting,[13] but as mutation, something threatening. The world is divided into Us and Them. It is this foreign Them that the Liberal man fears; he then seeks to exclude Them, and sets up his commonwealth to protect himself against Them. Thus, one who cannot "accommodate himself to the rest," according to Hobbes, "is to be left out, or cast out of Society, as cumbersome thereunto" (1983, 209).

Who will come to be considered the threatening Them? Is it merely chance that the 1980s groups were labeled as threatening outsiders? Or, within the broader political system in the United States, was this inevitable? Historically, various nondominant groups have been set up to serve the role of the outsider, who must be left out of society if the "worthy" are to come out of the state of nature, that awful state of war, and enter into the more commodious life with a government in civil society. Rousseau reminds us that the state of uncertainty, which Hobbes posits plagued the precivil society, was mostly the predicament of the wealthy.[14] Locke tells us explicitly that the aim of forming the social contract is the preservation of private property; as in Locke's version there is already an inequality of property by the time people form civil society, the real aim of the contract is to protect that unequal distribution of property.[15]

The property holders whom our political system was designed to protect seemed to share other identity characteristics: They were also male, light-skinned, Christian, middle-aged, and able. So, although we are all asked to surrender our rights and freedoms to the sovereign in order to bring us out of the state of war and into the protection and stability of civil society, we must remember that the sovereign is constituted by and mostly designed to protect a certain class of people. We find that in society everyone has relinquished their powers mostly for the benefit of a particular class. Under the guise of what is accepted as the common good we end up with a system that precludes most people from entering the public sphere to struggle to meet their needs and that thus is able both to establish and to guarantee enormous inequality.

Subgroups espousing alternative ideological visions for their communities often suffer the same obstacles as do the nondominant identity groups such as women, the propertyless, those deemed disabled and people of color/Jews in the broader society.[16] This is the dynamic on which we must focus if we are to understand how the mainstream Jewish groups could get away with silencing the different visions put forward by the nondominant pro-Israel groups. When a universal common interest is seen as somehow above or transcending the particular, that particular is seen as opposed to the universal. Those who insist on pursuing their particular perspectives are labeled as threatening, and the sovereign is justified in squelching their attempts—as dominant organizations within communities justify silencing oppositional groups in the name of their communal good—in effect justifying discrimination, barriers to participation in the public discourse, against those not able to accommodate themselves to the status quo.

Through a set of arguments concerning the Liberal abstraction of needs into interests, contemporary group-based democratic thinkers have updated the notion of a public sphere that virtually denies the possibility of open conversation and real struggle.[17] Given pluralist theory's reliance on self-interest, it continues to distance itself from a discussion of concrete needs, aspirations, and dignity. Political groups organized by American subcommunities seeking to have their needs met, aspirations fulfilled, and dignity cared for, are perceived instead, in the early Liberal view, as individual men defending their narrow selfish interests at the expense of common good. Thus, Ackelsberg writes that "as generations of critics have noted, the 'rules of the game' of [l]iberal democracy—the emphasis on isolated individuals with independently constructed interest profiles—benefit those already in power and prevent others from recognizing their differing needs, let alone articulate and struggle for them in the political arena (1991, 178).[18]

The Jewish activists' experience teaches us that for a politics of needs to be more egalitarian than one based in ideologically constructed interests, it must also be rooted in diversity, striving to overcome the fears of difference we have learned under our present system. The respect for and fostering of diversity are essential because within our present context even needs-talk can result in further inequality if we are not conscious of who is naming and interpreting the needs, in what sort of power structure, and to what ends.[19] If, as Marx wrote, "the ideas of the ruling class are in every epoch the ruling ideas,"[20] then we must remember that in politics interpretations developed by nondominant groups must be brought up in counterhegemonic fashion into the political process. Through that process these interpretations will likely develop and change as the previously marginal groups rediscover their histories and find their own voices in contemporary context. Thus, for a transformation to a politics that is affirmingly attentive to people's needs to achieve broader inclusiveness—equality in a more open public sphere—this transformation must be accompanied by a corresponding change from a process rooted in sameness to one open to difference. We must move from our current understanding of the common good to a particularly constituted discourse whose intent is to foster groups' access to their own and to broader social resources, collective memory, and deliberative space in the process of politics.

Is this possible? The story of Breira unfortunately demonstrates that the American Jewish community of the 1970s, in terms of its relationship to Israel, was plagued by efforts to keep the public discourse of the community closed through a politics of silencing. In this case, difference was perceived by those in power as a direct threat to the overall identity and interests of the community. The resultant manner of politics was extraordinarily painful for the many committed Jewish activists and ran counter to the fostering of a healthy vibrant polity.

By the 1990s there was a clear shift in the way the community engaged in politics. Although much work remains to be done, the case of APN's involvement in the 1992 Democratic Party platform indicates a shift in the direction of a more open public space with various—and very different—groups struggling to figure out how to keep the dialogue going and the politics responsive to multiple visions of the community's needs and aspirations. This second example offers a glimpse of intense and high-pressure politics that works with diversity. The history of APN shows that movement stimulated by the silencing of Breira confirms the benefit of, as Cornel West names it, an "audacious hope," in this case, that a closed political space indeed can be transformed.

## Breira:  A Tragedy of a Closed Public Space

The Israeli Labor Party was in power from the Yishuv (the pre state settlement period) until 1977. Throughout this time, the main alternatives to Labor's power did not, as recent politics might have one believe, come from the right represented by such parties as Herut/Likud. Actually, the party to achieve the second largest representation in the first Israeli Knesset was MAPAM, the Socialist Zionist Party. Beginning with the earliest Zionist thinkers in the 1800s, there was intense internal debate and criticism of the Jewish community in Palestine, especially concerning its relationship to and responsibility for the indigenous Arab population. After the Yishuv period, there were Zionist policy challenges to Labor's policies, especially concerning Arab representation in the Histadrut (Labor Federation) and elsewhere.

By the 1950s, intellectuals, coming primarily from the MAPAM camp, had begun publication of the English-language dovish Zionist magazine *New Outlook*, intended to inform and connect Zionists in the peace camp worldwide. By the early 1970s, given the dangerous potential of the new

Israeli occupation, a distinct peace camp had emerged within Israeli Zionist circles. It included the support of MAPAM, independent Labor Knesset Members, and others. Those who eventually were to form Breira in the United States were among the many American Jews who spent much time, or lived temporarily, in Israel as part of their Zionist ideology, learning about and participating in the local politics.[21] Especially at this time (the early 1970s), many of these people were drawn to the indigenous emergent peace, environmental, civil rights, and burgeoning women's movements. It was from among this ideological branch of Zionists, who had extensive experience in and connection to Israel, that Breira was brought to life.

In March of 1973 progressive Jews held a meeting by invitation only at the Hillel at Rutgers University in New Jersey. The agenda of their dialogue was twofold: between committed Jews who were Zionists and those who were non-Zionists, and on the question of new *halacha* (Jewish religious law). Out of the dialogue on Zionism emerged something that the participants named A Call to Discussion. This forum was aimed at generating honest and open conversation within the community on some very difficult communal questions such as Zionism, Palestinian nationalism, and self-determination.

The group held a few meetings throughout the summer of 1973. In response to the shock of the Yom Kippur War in October of that year, the group took a more solid shape. The Yom Kippur War showed ever more clearly that the situation in the Occupied Territories was untenable and could not last. The organizers felt that if Israel did not begin to make swifter, more concrete moves in the direction of a peace process, the future would be likely to see more such wars and other horrors.

In November of 1973 A Call to Discussion changed its name to Breira: A Project of Concern in Diaspora-Israel Relations, formed a steering committee, and began more serious organizing within the American Jewish community. In 1974 an Advisory Council was created that grew to more than two hundred and fifty members, including nearly one hundred Reform and Conservative rabbis.[22] The choice of using a Hebrew name, and specifically a play on the Labor Party slogan *Ain breira* (There is no choice),[23] was a deliberate act to show the group's commitment to Israel and reflected the members' high level of connection to and involvement with Israeli politics.

Breira's goal was "to build creative links between independent minded Diaspora and Israeli Jews based on shared values and traditions, as well as a shared responsibility and commitment to solving the problems which confront the Jewish people as a whole." In terms of Middle East politics, Breira sought to focus on a variety of political and socioeconomic concerns that Israel was facing, such as "the development of a socio-economic gap between a largely Ashkenazic [Eastern European] middle class and the Sephardic [Eastern] poor; by the schism between religious and non-religious which is fostered by the politicization of religious life; and by the erosion of the civil liberties, particularly, though not exclusively, of its Arab citizens." Breira asserted the legitimacy of diaspora communal life and believed "that some important policies of the Israeli government, developed under intense pressure of foreign hostility and domestic distress, have been unwise and ineffective."[24]

One of the most interesting aspects of Breira is that, although many of the early participants were connected to the new Havurah movement and the organization was decidedly disestablishmentarian, it was not really a countercultural group. Breira began, and largely remained, an organization of Jewish intellectuals, rabbinical students, and Jewish professionals from such establishment organizations as the American Jewish Committee and B'nai Brith and the editors of Jewish and Zionist magazines such as *Haddassah Magazine*, *Sh'ma*, and the *Jewish Spectator*. It never held any demonstrations, organized sit-ins at AIPAC, or broke windows at the Israeli embassy.[25] Instead it sent out letters and information to its membership, put out a small magazine called *interChange* with articles by leading American and Israeli Jewish figures (and, due to its intellectual character, with many contributions from non-Breira members) on various topics of Jewish concern, and published translations of articles from the Israeli press and pamphlets containing speeches by Jewish leaders and Israeli Knesset members. It also sent Israeli Knesset members and army generals—such as former Labor Party Secretary General Arie Lova Eliav and retired Major General Matti Peled—around the United States to speak to Jewish groups.

Breira received a lot of positive attention early in its organizational life both within the Jewish community and in broader American political circles. The organization was favorably quoted in a *New York Times* editorial (11 May 1976) and in articles in the *Washington Post*, the *New York Times*,[26] and the *New York Post* (28 April 1976). In 1976 its executive director, Bob Loeb, testified before Congress on alternative American Jewish and Israeli views concerning Israeli peace with Palestinians. Its message spread quickly and within a couple of years, twelve chapters formed in cities around the country. In terms of budget and membership size, the organization was at its height within a few years with up to fifteen hundred members and a budget of almost $200,000. On 20–22 February 1977, Breira held its first national conference, drawing approximately three hundred participants, but this first conference was also its last. By the time the conference was held, Breira was already under enormous attack. As early organizer and Working Committee member Gerry Serotta remembered, the organization "just bled to death over the course of the next year [following the conference]."[27]

Breira had been calling on the Jewish community to accept and work with difference. Thus, at the center of the controversy the group elicited was fear of the kind of deep challenge it posed to the perception of communal unity. The problem with including the above-mentioned issues on the agenda of American Jewish organization meant that adherents, even if Zionist or claiming to be pro-Israel, would then be expressing public dissent from Israeli government policy. The attack on Breira was an extreme example of a communal politics that sought to silence dissent in a broader political climate unpracticed in a politics of difference; it was evidence that the community could not yet tolerate the public space of "open discussion and debate," for which Breira was calling. Zionist Organization of America President Sternstein was quoted as demanding that Breira "be scoured from the community."[28] Despite the credentials of its membership, and despite the service and leadership its members had long performed within the community, these attacks sought to delegitimize Breira by painting a picture of the organization as comprised of Jew/self–hating,[29] anti-Zionist Fatah supporters. People who at any time had been associated with the organization came under attack and found themselves the subject of organizational memos and of speculation in the Jewish press. The positions of those members who held jobs as Jewish professionals were in danger, and Max Ticktin, a high level B'nai B'rith professional, was pressured to retire from his post.[30]

The attack on Breira was so intense and organized that many felt it had to have been orchestrated.[31] There is some evidence that Breira had come to the attention of the Israeli Labor government by the middle of 1976, just prior to the most intense round of attacks.[32] Tivnan reports that Rabin was "in a panic" over this group of American Jewish dissenters. Foer cites an AIPAC file that suggests that the Israeli government became directly involved. It states that Israeli Ambassador Simcha Dinitz "sent out word to consulates that Breira is poison" (1983, 22). By the end of that year an ultra-right-wing Zionist group called Americans for a Safe Israel (AFSI) published a scathing and largely spurious report condemning Breira members as dangerous PLO supporters.[33] The rest of the attack, largely fired by irresponsible journalism, was basically a restatement of the contents of this pamphlet.

In this pre-1977 period, AFSI was an unknown group. It was then a new organization, formed in a split from Meir Kahane's Jewish Defense League, and the pamphlet on Breira was one of the first projects it undertook. As a group of far-right-wing activists, it opposed such Labor policies as returning the Sinai to Egypt. Given the Labor-dominated environment, a pamphlet produced by such a new and radical right-wing group probably would have gone unnoticed (as did many of its later pamphlets). However, AIPAC and several other national Jewish organizations that were (and continue to be) members of the National Jewish Community Relations Advisory Council (NJCRAC) actually began to distribute the pamphlet, as if it were an authoritative document, to Jewish organizations and editors around the country.[34]

Pluralism has trouble with diversity, translating a "diversity of needs" into a notion of "conflicting interests at odds with the public good."[35] It is, therefore, telling that the front page attacks on Breira that began in the Jewish press, by such "eminent and well-known" journalists as AYSHET ITON,[36] were published in direct response to the *New York Times* article (30 December 1976) discussing a diversity of opinion among Jewish leadership on talks with the PLO and Breira's role in fostering such a discussion. The *Times* piece reporting diversity was interpreted as casting the Jewish community as in the midst of a "civil war." On this issue, diversity and discussion became "a split." Different voices were seen as factions, what Madison called the dangerous vice threatening a well-constructed union. The national media was accused of exploiting this split to weaken the Jewish communities of the United States and Israel, and those leaders held an unrepentently dovish Breira directly responsible for the demise of the Jewish people.[37]

Following the distribution of the AFSI pamphlet, organizational studies and reports,[38] as well as a flood of pieces in the Jewish Press (many written under the pseudonym AYSHET ITON) were published.[39] In January 1977 a resolution that condemned Breira's existence was passed by the Washington Jewish Community Council and distributed to the Washington Jewish community.[40] Two high-level executives at the Anti-Defamation League and the Jewish Defense League are reported as having said of Breira, "We did them in, we had to."[41] A few individuals did come out publicly in Breira's defense. However, the smear tactics originating from the right were given credibility when others who had been known for their more progressive politics also began publicly criticizing the organization.

History teaches us the dangers of a silencing politics: Later these same leaders would themselves come under attack as "anti-Israel" due to the same kind of closed political environment they helped solidify in the silencing of Breira. The attack was vicious, and even at the time some leaders associated with the forces launching the attack felt that it was hysterical.[42] Other leaders who condemned Breira at the time later said that they had been wrong to do so.[43]

In its response to the case of Breira, the American Jewish community drew upon an aspect of its own political tradition often resorted to, and at the same time it responded to pressure from the expectations of Liberal democratic politics in the United States. Jewish leadership in the diaspora has often relied on the strength of a united community, especially when interacting with forces outside the community and in the face of adversity coming from those forces. In this case, however, key centers of mainstream pro-Israel power responded to the challenge presented by Breira's "alternative" with a smear campaign designed to delegitimize the organization. This politics of silencing was disguised as a plea for "unity" behind the "common good." Even though in this case those silenced were not always members of nondominant subsections of the communal polity, the content of their opinion was decidedly nondominant.

It is also important to note that a politics of unity that actually masks a politics of silencing is not only the result of an internally generated pathological reflex. The fact that American Jewish pro-Israel groups are trying to make their way in a broader political environment cast predominantly in the Liberal mode has a very real effect on their creation of an inclusive political process within the community. The American Jewish community historically has come under intense pressure to conform to the Liberal democratic model of interest politics, where, as Ackelsberg writes, "in treating people as mere bearers of interests, liberal democratic individualism masks structures of power and, in particular, relations of domination and subordination that affect people (and structure their 'interests') as members of subnational collectivities" (1991, 180).

In the form of common interest politics, some American politicians have been quite explicit in their attempts at "exploiting splits among the Jewish leadership," or pressuring Jewish leaders to speak with one voice while claiming this to be in the "Jewish interest." Many pro-Israel leaders have talked about the pressure on them to present only one Jewish view, voicing the pressure they feel under expectations that, as Truman (1951) wrote, the actuality or at least the appearance of unity is essential in group politics. The community can only hope to be recognized if it puts forward a singular "concrete demand." Thus the community has also been pressured by expectations of a Liberal polity to play the exclusionary game of unity, or a mythic common interest politics that must subsume difference.

It is essential to acknowledge that a community with differences, despite Liberal opinion, is not necessarily a divided community. Diversity is an element essential to a thriving community and to an open communal politics.[44] This was the point argued by those in positions of leadership within Zionist and American Jewish organizations who did not agree with Breira's politics or method exactly, but defended their call to the community to revitalize discussion and to listen to itself carefully.[45] However, the community traditionally has not paid sufficient attention to the longer-term internal costs of succumbing to such expectations in the pursuit of communal goals in the larger political arena.

The American Jewish community has often fallen into the trap of equating diversity with weakness. As it does for Liberal democratic theorists, fear plays an essential role here. The Jewish community has often sought to minimize difference, even to the point of silencing, particularly in the face of fear from an external threat. When the community fears, or is insecure in its position in the broader political environment, it understandably wants to respond in strength. Unfortunately, fear and the perception of constant crisis can become an ongoing motivation for political action. When strength is equated with putting up a united front, and there is the perception out of fear that we must always stand strong, the community falls into the habit of a politics of silencing.

Given anti-Semitism, Jews often find themselves in, or fearing, crisis. Hobbesian philosophy fundamentally responds to such a state and concludes that in these circumstances a divided community is easily defeated. This conclusion, however, also can be fatal for a community. Perhaps the most important time for open honest dialogue within a community is during a time of crisis. It is at these crucial points when the community is faced with choices—especially limited choices and dilemmas—that may fundamentally affect it, that the community most needs to hear of the fears and alternative creative assessments and solutions generated in all corners of its universe.[46] Particularly under these circumstances, when outside pressures are demanding a unified voice, we must take extra care not to assimilate this pressure into our deliberative space by silencing internal debate or even the activity of some who still feel compelled to pursue their alternative avenue. The more the dialogue continues and various—even radical—groups are made to feel welcome within the public space and are kept connected, not only are we less likely to have harmful renegades, but it is also less likely that some legitimate voices that could not come under the communal umbrella at a certain point in politics will end up being harmful or permanently alienated.[47]

Of course, many people may agree that there may be times when a group must put aside its differences, or seek especially to work on the level of common ground. However, such a path ought not to be taken lightly, nor can this be a basis for ongoing communal politics. It is a politics that may demand blindness to difference, one that does not practice and experiment with its diversity. It often leads to having a closed public space, where dialogue and authentic struggle are squelched, as a political norm. The community suffers tremendously from such a politics; it inflicts much pain on itself by stifling discussion and alienating its members. Such was the case with the silencing of Breira.

As Plaskow suggests, dialogic process is essential to a politics that strives to affirm the call of individuals and groups with dignity, and not necessarily (as Mill uses it, as a justification for a free marketplace of ideas) because it will produce truth. However, the case of Breira is all the more poignant when we realize the particular way in which the silencing of Breira was a tremendous loss to our community and to the movement toward deep struggle with a peace process in the Israeli-Arab and Israeli-Palestinian conflicts. Twenty years later, Breira's calls for a reevaluation of American Jewish self-conception and priorities, a revitalization of American Jewish culture and communal life, and its responsibility in world Jewish community are still the cries from a community in crisis.

In the early 1970s Breira, in connection with the Israeli peace movement and in particular an organization named the Israel Council for Israeli-Palestinian Peace,[48] advocated negotiations with the PLO, staged withdrawals from the Occupied Territories, demilitarized zones, mutual inspection, and "real peace" based on a full range of diplomatic and economic relations—not merely an end to belligerency. History and the current peace process[49] have shown that Breira's platform is the most plausible and secure guideline for Middle East peace. The rest of its Middle East platform, including discussion of a Palestinian state and a unified Jerusalem, are issues that are beginning to surface as additional positions to consider. Unfortunately, with the silencing of Breira, the community was deprived of a leading voice in that process for twenty years; in that time thousands have died, have been physically injured, and have been emotionally scarred by fear and hatred. The silencing of a movement that develops before its time, while people suffer waiting for the world to catch up means a tragic period for politics, when politics does have an "alternative."

# The Potential for Community in the 1990s: Americans for Peace Now

The story of APN shows that movement toward dialogic politics is possible even within a system in which silencing is constitutive of the primary political philosophy.[50] Breira as an organization was killed, but Breira as a call did more than survive; history has shown that as a call to the community, Breira actually has flourished. The silencing of Breira scared many people, to the point that the stifled voice of alternatives still often stumbles in fear today, a generation later. However, people also learned from Breira's experience and immediately moved on to form other organizations.

Immediately after the fall of Breira, progressive Jews in North America, committed to working on opening the deliberative space within the community, organized another forum, which came to be called New Jewish Agenda (NJA). Although NJA did not face quite the same resistance in 1980 that had been faced by Breira earlier, it also was not accepted into the community. Soon after the formation of NJA, the Israeli war in Lebanon had so mobilized the Israeli public that a solid mainstream peace movement had emerged in the form of Shalom Achshav (Peace Now). Peace Now organizing in the United States, intended to help educate the American Jewish community concerning questions of responsibility, war, and peace in Israel, began locally in 1981 and nationally in the following year. In the early years, even though APN was organized as a legitimate support group for an indigenous Israeli organization—which was itself mobilized by Labor Party generals and high-ranking army reserve officers—it too was castigated and utterly marginalized by the organized American Jewish community.

The practice of silencing politics, common in the broader pluralist system in the United States, was by now well rooted in American Jewish communal process. The Israeli Labor Party had so influenced American Jewish pro-Israel organization as to discourage any dissent from the Israeli government line from surfacing; once Labor became the opposition party in the Israeli Knesset, supporters of its policies no longer had a voice. Thus, APN, despite the overwhelming public support its parent organization was receiving in Israel, was kept out of American Jewish communal affairs.

The period ten years after Peace Now began organizing within the American Jewish community, in the late spring of 1992, followed a decade that witnessed an explosion of new dovish pro-Israel groups organizing within the community, due to the inroads made by APN and by some other groups with similar goals. The Soviet bloc had fallen, and American military might had changed the stakes involved in world politics. The Gulf War was over, and various hard-line Middle East leaders had been forced to come to the negotiating table. Middle East peace talks were under way, and, despite the electoral loss of the British Labour Party in early 1992, conservative governments were being challenged around the globe in a manner to which they had been immune for more than a decade. Such were the circumstances in which the American and Israeli peoples entered into their respective election seasons.

The final language of the Middle East plank of the Democratic Party platform for the national election of 1992 is an embryonic example of the hegemonic pro-Israel idea giving way to a counterhegemonic notion.[51] The stories of Briera and 1990s APN together present a stark comparison. Obviously a Democratic Party platform is hardly a revolutionary site of struggle, and influence therein is not inherently indicative of a fundamental political transformation. The 1990s did begin, however, as a decade in which the American Jewish community was less likely to accept an either/ or conception of what it means to be pro-Israel. Those disagreeing with the Israeli government line are slowly being allowed participation in the communal debate over what kind of Israel the community is "pro" and what role this opinion ought to play in its relationship with the community in the Jewish state. APN is one organization that increasingly has been raising its voice, calling on the community to listen and to allow it a place in the public space. In part due to changing power centers in Israel and the United States and to the use of new political strategies, APN has begun to be heard outside the community. The mainstream centers of pro-Israel power, such as the Presidents' Conference and AIPAC, have began to take notice, and to listen, too.

In an unprecedented step, AIPAC and APN worked together on drafting language to present to the platform committee of the Democratic Party (and the Republican Party as well, although that activity is not analyzed here) on behalf of the Jewish community in the United States. Obviously no one, nor even a coalition of organizations, can speak for a whole community. However, on 18 May 1992, Linda Kamm, a Washington, D.C., attorney who served as general counsel to the Department of Transportation in the Carter Administration, testified before the Democratic National Platform Committee in Cleveland in her capacity as a member of the Board of Directors of APN and as the cochair of the Center for Israeli Peace and Security, APN's office in Washington, D.C. She spoke of the peace movement and of pro-peace public opinion in Israel. Kamm described the recent surveys of American Jewry that "found that a majority of American Jewish leaders favor active U.S. involvement in the peace process and territorial compromise between Israel and its Arab neighbors,"[52] and an overwhelming majority of 88 percent of grassroots American Jews agreed that "Israel should offer the Arabs territorial compromise in the West Bank and Gaza Strip in return for credible guarantees of peace."[53] Kamm thus claimed credibility by placing her recommendation within the majority of American Jewish public opinion as revealed in direct survey data, not in the empty rhetoric of assumed Jewish unity. Until recently, even such overwhelming domestic public opinion was disregarded because it did not coincide with the Israeli government line.[54] AIPAC, the main pro-Israel organization claiming to speak for the American Jewish community, did not endorse these positions, thus alienating a majority of American Jews.

It may sound surprising, then, that the 1992 Democratic Party platform supports the Middle East peace process based on the Camp David Accords, reiterates all the traditional AIPAC language of the "special relationship" between Israel and the United States, and affirms Jerusalem as the capital of the state of Israel and as an undivided city. At first glance the 1992 platform may not sound too different from previous platforms with which only AIPAC was involved as a contributor to the deliberations. In fact, in an op-ed piece in the *Washington Post* (2 July 1992), James Zogby, president of the Arab American Institute, wrote that "this platform sends the wrong message to Israel, to the Arabs and to the American people. By failing to distance himself from the hard-line pro-Israel lobby, the Democratic nominee has aligned himself with Israel's fading right wing and ignored an increasing number of people in this country and in Israel who want a fair and lasting peace in the region."

The development of such language was, however, far from an example of the process of politics as usual in the American pluralist system. This was actually the first time that a group solidly identified with the peace camp, in opposition especially after fifteen years of Likud rule, was a part of the platform negotiations. Americans for Peace Now was actually an equal partner with AIPAC in proposing the language. Leaders of APN and AIPAC met in advance and negotiated the language that the groups eventually proposed to the party. In contrast to what democrats have grown to expect from a pluralist interest group politics, two groups with historically very different visions—one decidedly hegemonic and the other long playing the role of a counterhegemonic force—came together to work out language that each felt could sufficiently represent their differing pro-Israel aspirations. The development of the actual language shows that such cooperation made an enormous difference in what came to be understood as the community's common goal.

APN's primary goal for this platform was to secure a commitment to the peace process. In the afterglow of AIPAC dominance, this was to be no easy task. When AIPAC took on President George Bush over the issue of the American loan guarantees to Israel, and lost, the American Jewish community found itself at a crossroads. The anti-Semitic tone of the loan guarantee battle set many Jews on edge, placing the community back into the all too familiar crisis mode. AIPAC was able to use the fear generated to paint a picture of the president as the ultimate enemy of the Jewish people. Despite the fact that polls showed a majority of American Jews favoring a curb on settlements and an active role for the American administration toward that end, there were forces in AIPAC hoping instead to use the loan guarantee fiasco to push the agenda in their chosen direction: Right-wing Jewish players inside the Democratic Party were hoping to influence the Clinton campaign to demonstrate his difference from President Bush by staking out a position even further to the right.

In this political environment, the fact that the opening line of the Middle East section reads "support for the peace process now under way in the Middle East, rooted in the tradition of the Camp David accords . . . with no imposed solutions" is a significant shift suggesting the successful incorporation of a long marginalized dovish pro-Israel aspiration. APN was able to hold back right-wing pressure intent on undoing the accomplishments already achieved in the peace process. Moreover, it was able not only to elicit a firm commitment to continuing the talks, but also to continuing them in the spirit envisioned by those new voices being heard in the community that have asserted that the ends of the talks can only be determined by the parties themselves through political negotiations.

Furthermore, APN, which disagreed with AIPAC's position on the loan guarantees, was able to keep the issue of the loan guarantees out of the platform altogether. This demonstrates another instance in which involving a counterhegemonic group helped reshape communal priorities. The Democrats were already indicating that they might position themselves against the Republicans by denying any association between the loan guarantees and the settlements, effectively upholding the Likud/AIPAC position.

Zogby's criticism of the platform mentioned "a provocative section calling 'undivided' Jerusalem the capital of Israel, in effect predetermining the outcome of the most sensitive issue to be negotiated in the peace talks." Although he had a point, the issue was a bit more complicated than he indicated. One of AIPAC's primary goals for this platform was to get "Jerusalem back in," after its absence from the 1988 Democratic Party platform. Given this situation, APN's presence was still essential to the outcome. APN was able to keep out a statement on moving the embassy to Jerusalem, which is the concrete political commitment that AIPAC still demands as part of discussions of the fate of Jerusalem.

A joint letter to the *Washington Post* (25 July 1992) by Peter Edelman and Stuart Eizenstat responding to the Zogby piece points out that the platform "simply repeats what has been U.S. policy under every president since the 1967 War, mainly that Jerusalem should not be divided again, as it was between 1948 and 1967. . . . The U.S. government has been able to maintain this position without offending Arab nations by leaving the issue of sovereignty over the undivided city to the final negotiations between the parties." As Bill Clinton and Al Gore personally favored moving the embassy from Tel Aviv to Jerusalem,[55] keeping the issue out of the platform so that it could be introduced "when it would not detract from the peace process" was the result of a new mode of politics: AIPAC's having to come to terms with another pro-Israel vision from within the American Jewish community.

The *Washington Post* response represented this unprecedented AIPAC-APN alliance. For publication, Edelman and Eizenstat gave their non-Jewish credentials as, respectively, a professor of law at Georgetown University, and a member of the Democratic Platform Drafting Committee and former chief domestic policy advisor to President Carter. Edelman and Eizenstat also wore other hats as APN and AIPAC representatives, respectively. Their joint response struck the balance between an AIPAC tone also concerned with appeasing the ideological hawks within its organization, and APN considerations that claimed to represent the actual majority of Jewish public opinion as well as evenhandedness to the Arab and Palestinian players in the peace process. With the two writing together, the community's leadership avoided what it had feared in the past: the public presentation of a divided community. Instead, by working with dissenters, AIPAC was able both to present a more inclusive pro-Israel policy position and at the same time to avoid the appearance of a split that it so much feared.

It is important to note that as historic as was this first attempt at inclusion and working with dissent, it was certainly not a perfect model of authentic dialogue in a genuinely open communal public space. Many involved in the newer dovish pro-Israel groups were aware that AIPAC's relative acceptance of APN may have had more to do with fears of personal job security in the face of a significant Labor electoral challenge (this process began before the 1992 Israeli election) than with a sudden commitment to more open politics.[56] In addition, given the concrete conditions under which the two groups were working, there were breaks in the broader communication. Zogby's response represented one critical voice from outside the community, though very different from previous policy deliberations, in terms of the past nature of pro-Israel politics.

Some activists on the Jewish left also have been critical of APN's involvement in the platform and of its recent move into mainstream organizational life. Some progressive Zionists, pro-Israel doves, and other Jewish leftists feel that progressive Jewish organizations should remain as opposition groups, and go down fighting over issues such as a commitment to the creation of a Palestinian state in the West Bank and the Gaza Strip. Some voices on the left say that any compromise is too great, and an unacceptable price to pay for access to the halls of power: In seeking a major transformation of communal politics, compromise over specific policy is seen at times as deflecting the "real" issues. There were also a number of Jewish activists who, like Zogby, originally criticized the outcome of the proposed language feeling that if APN was agreeing with AIPAC, the group must be selling out. When APN responded to these concerns within its own organization, it was able to make the case that its participation in the process made a concrete contribution to a new pro-Israel direction within the community.

Finally, there were complaints from further right within the Jewish community. There was some evidence of the older type of pro-Israel process, common in pluralist interest group politics, that relied on delegitimizing others with different perspectives. Morris Amitay, past director of AIPAC and president of Washington PAC, was reported to have said of the APN affiliated people in the Clinton campaign that "many of these people never did a thing for Israel." Again, despite APN's credentials and long years of involvement with pro-Israel politics, Amitay said that some "had no history of involvement in the Jewish community," thus casting APN activists as the Them to be feared and ignored. Leaders such as Amitay have not given up their use of a politics of silencing through delegitimizing committed and responsible pro-Israel advocates who take dovish positions.[57]

In the interest of building a more open and democratic communal politics, these various voices of dissatisfaction deserve attention. However, despite its embryonic nature, it is clear that APN's role in developing the 1992 Democratic Party platform on the Middle East marked a turning point in pro-Israel politics. It stands as a tremendous acknowledgment of a decade of work by APN and its supporters, **and a** significant accomplishment of the activity and values of many progressive Zionists, pro-Israel doves, and Middle East peace activists toward opening the public space within American Jewish pro-Israel identity politics. Much has changed in pro-Israel politics since the days when Breira silenced. Most of Breira's and APN's policy proposals concerning Israel are identical, and well-known and respected American Jewish leaders were involved in both groups. Although there were other pressures on AIPAC working with APN besides a sudden commitment to dialogic politics, this more recent collaboration must be seen in the context of a decade of intense, concerted activity by a spectrum of dovish Jewish groups that had begun to be heard by the late 1980s. When understood in this historical context, the difference between the fates of Breira and APN involves more than a simple policy shift. The difference is directly related to the developing ability of the community to open its ears, to tolerate and work with dissent. The case of APN suggests that the changes sought by such groups involve more than their simple entry into the existent power structure, where they would be allowed to battle it out with the dominant interest groups. The American Jewish community has not yet figured out an appropriate mode of communal politics that can actually hear all of our voices and encourage diversity, but, if a comparison of the two cases can be a proper demonstration, it has made enormous strides in this direction.

## In Conclusion

In contemporary group-based democratic theory, selfish interests become the very "stuff" of politics. Since Bentley (1908), communities acting politically, then, have been seen as special interest groups. From this base, the "process" of politics becomes a limited one of mediating between the conflicting demands of these special interest groups.[58] In contrast to this understanding of the stuff and process of politics, the work of the pro-Israel groups of the 1980s suggests a critical approach rooted in an alternative understanding of politics as an arena where communities engage in the activity of collective memory, ever reinterpreting/experiencing their historical mission.[59] Here the political process is one in which communities,[60] comprised of members[61] and in the presence of other communities,[62] reevaluate and seek to meet their communal calling. In other words, attention to the call and activity of American Jewish pro-Israel groups teaches us that politics is about "figuring it out."

When the "process" (the "figuring") of politics is understood as (re)interpretation and—in the Buberian sense—meeting, the "stuff" (the "it" that is figured out) of politics becomes the needs of people, in terms of their concrete material needs as well as their aspirations and dignity, as they are ever changing and/or being reinterpreted.[63] The interplay of the ideologically diverse pro-Israel groups suggests that if there is a common good for groups and communities, it is a changing and imperfect understanding—composed of the actual needs and aspirations of individuals and of their intersecting groups—produced in this process of "figuring it out."[64]

# Chapter 3

# Relationships

The preceding chapters dealt with questions of identity in terms of unity and difference. In the first section I discussed how a new reading of the history of the pro-Israel identity of the American Jewish community challenges the Hobbesian understanding of autonomy which is understood in contemporary democratic theory in terms of the naturalness of interests, or group identities, and their indivisibility. The analysis in Chapter 2 showed that when needs come to be seen as narrow self-interests at odds with the public good, the result is a politics that squelches diversity, as was demonstrated by Breira's situation. An analysis of APN's more recent work suggests that group ideals need not be treated as such. An understanding of the cluster of groups involved in the creation and re-creation of pro-Israel identity in relation to one another is vital. There were so many groups working on basically the same issue. Was this necessary? How can we explain their interaction? Did it help develop communal political process in a more democratic, supportive, and interactive manner? Did the fact of so many closely related groups present obstacles? Were there pressures to interact in certain ways as the groups struggled within the larger American political system?

When we listen to those within the groups speak for themselves, we hear that much of their relations were characterized by cooperation and, to a great extent, mutual aid. However, the groups constantly wrestled with the expectations that they should be in competition. In a pluralist system, groups and individuals are expected to compete to satisfy their selfish interests. This "conflict theory"[1] is based on the assumption of a hostile environment in which only the fittest survive the struggle for existence.[2] To lose the struggle is to die, for the means of survival are a peculiar sort of power: a scarce commodity one has over others.

## Group Relations and the Constitution of Power

Political groups active within the American Jewish community are affected by norms of the larger American political system, which is decidedly bourgeois. In the mid-1600s, Thomas Hobbes wrote to both promote and justify this new order, which had its roots in private property. In this scheme, power comes to be seen as a commodity that one owns.[3] Although many societies have had some notion of private property, of the ability to possess things, this becomes a fundamental characteristic of the emerging bourgeois society. Not only does property become something one can possess, but justice (in the form of modern Liberal rights) and power (the basic ability to satisfy one's needs) come to be understood as possessions as well. Thus, the new Jewish groups are struggling within a larger political system in which political relations are predominantly viewed as market relations.[4]

The interpretation of politics in free market terms colors the rules by which groups are expected to struggle for power because what gets possessed, in a politically Liberal understanding of power, is an ability one has over and above that of another. For example, on the first day of a basic Introduction to American Politics class, students across the country will learn contemporary democratic theorist Robert Dahl's definition of power: A's ability to make B do what A wants, whether or not B wants to.[5] Legitimate power is then defined as A doing that without the use of physical force. These recent definitions come from early Liberal formulations such as Hobbes's "Men naturally love dominion over others." To Hobbes, power is "power-over," rather than a power within or between. Macpherson highlights how, since Hobbes, Liberals take power from a relatively neutral state, to this power-over construct (1962, 35). Such a move is possible because Liberals do not discuss man's natural power in terms of his natural abilities, but in the "eminence" of man's ability. Power is always a comparative quantity, and is only that which one has above the powers of others.[6] Macpherson writes that "a new postulate is implied in this redefinition of power, namely that the capacity of everyman to get what he wants is opposed by the capacity of every other man" (1962, 36). Regardless of the understanding of power those in alternative groups have, such as those in the new pro-Israel groups, all political actors must interact with many Liberal-minded actors who only think in these comparative, power-over terms.

In *The Leviathan*, Hobbes writes that man "cannot assure the power and means to live well, which he hath at present without the acquisition of more." The only way to explain this is to add the concepts of the zero-sum nature and scarcity to the discussion of power. Political activists must engage with those who think that, because power is possessed in a zero-sum way, it cannot be shared.[7] Therefore, in this view, if I need some power in order to live, I cannot acquire it without depriving the next person of some. What I have, the next person cannot have, and vice versa, as implied by Macpherson's interpretation.[8] However, if abundance were assumed, that next person would presumably not care that some of his power had been taken away. If a man had plenty of power and was not in danger of having too little in order to live, he would not have to worry about acquiring more power, even if someone took some. This is not the situation many Liberal actors think they are in, nor is it what Hobbes describes.[9] Instead, Hobbes says that man, just to assure his current status, will always need to acquire more. This is because when I took power from that person, he was then left in need. If he possessed an excess of power then he would not be in the situation that Hobbes describes, of needing to acquire more.[10]

Thus, in this Liberal view, what we have is the situation in which every time a man[11] turns his back, someone will be making use of that opportunity to take his power away from him for the other's own purposes. Because of the zero-sum/finite nature of power in this conception, his gain is registered as a loss to the first. Due to scarcity, this loss will leave the original man in need. He is thus forced to take power from someone else. As a human condition, we then have the situation in which everyone is constantly taking other people's power. Man may not be inherently greedy, but this situation of zero-sum, scarce power-over, has created the social necessity of greed: the social condition of man's "perpetual and restless desire of Power after power, that ceaseth onely in death."

Thus, Hobbes wrote that "men are continually in competition." To Darwin this continual state of competition meant the competitive "struggle for existence" in the animal world. To Madison, "the latent causes of faction are sown in the nature of man," causing us always to "vex and oppress" each other. Thus, for Bentley and contemporary group-based democratic thinkers, the competitive "struggle for existence" is found in the political world, where groups are seen as "fighting" it out. Competition tends to be so thoroughly assumed that pluralists see it as the nature of the political process itself,[12] and it defines the political environment in which the 1980s pro-Israel groups were engaged. This leads to the inability of many to recognize real instances of sharing. For example, these zero-sum assumptions color the way group scholars see coalitions. Theoretically, coalitions are potentially noncompetitive examples of group interaction, and empirically, coalitions are common.[13] Thus, the extensive employment of such a strategy of cooperation potentially could challenge the assumption of the norm of competition. However, coalitions are usually assumed to be merely a means of expedience: temporary ventures to achieve particular goals.[14] Commonly, coalitions are not seen outside the zero-sum paradigm as an example of mutual aid, or genuine cooperation. The overall assumption of competition remains unchallenged.

However, such is not the reality of all groups. The cluster of new pro-Israel groups work in and out of coalition as part of an ongoing network. This is because not all groups view their power as power over others, their powers/resources as zero-sum or finite, or their power/resources as scarce. Such assumptions do have influence on these groups, and they are not beyond responding to such expectations of their perceptions and behavior. However, if we listen closely to the newer pro-Israel groups, we can hear a very different understanding of power at work.

## The 1980s: Cooperation through Coalition Politics

Some group scholars have suggested that conflict among organizations will increase the more the organizations share certain attributes.[15] Such an expectation that intimacy promotes conflict reflects James Madison's thinking. Madison promoted distance, as exemplified territorially in his argument for a large republic, as a solution to the negative effects of the natural conflict of men living together in society (*Federalist* 51).[16] The story of the 1980s groups presented here directly contradicts such assumptions. These groups share much, but their level of competition is decidedly lower than even that which is presumed among less intimate groups. These groups have a fluid relationship, and they are in close contact and move in and out of coalition at various times, in an overall semicooperative style. In contrast to the way many scholars understand coalitions as temporary and merely expedient, without the recognition of a more basic commitment of the groups to each other, these groups tend to work in ongoing community coalitions as a way of life.[17]

Perhaps the most concentrated period of coalition work between these newer counterhegemonic groups began in the late 1980s.[18] In 1988 an unprecedented coalition effort of over nineteen groups came together in the form of the Passover Peace Coalition.[19] Previously, different groups that were closely related ideologically did work together. This was the first time, however, that Jewish Zionist and non-Zionist peace groups worked together on a project. The main objective of the Passover Peace Coalition was to organize an afternoon demonstration and rally to protest the Israeli occupation of the West Bank and the Gaza Strip. Although all the groups assembled agreed on this specific policy goal, they were otherwise ideologically and strategically diverse. Despite the difficulty of working across their political differences, the event was deemed a success. It was estimated that up to 4,500 people came to the rally in 1988,[20] and the following year the coalition regrouped. The 1989 Passover Peace Rally was, however, less successful than the first. This was for two major reasons: First, it rained on the day of the rally, and second, coalition energies had been deflected toward another project that year.

During 1988 there had been developments in the international political scene, and in March 1989 *New Outlook* and *Al-Fajr*, one an Israeli Jewish publication and the other a Palestinian publication, organized a conference at Columbia University in New York under the name Road to Peace. Whereas the previous year marked a breakthrough in cooperation among Jewish dovish groups, this was the first joint conference between Israelis and Palestinians. The Road to Peace conference was cosponsored by American Jewish and Arab groups such as Friends of Peace Now and the American Council for Palestine Affairs. The effort and dialogue were intended to support negotiations between the Israeli government and the PLO, an end to the occupation, and a move toward peaceful coexistence in the Middle East based on mutual recognition and the right to self-determination for all peoples. Palestinians from the Occupied Territories and North America as well as PLO representatives met under the auspices of the Road to Peace with Israeli Members of Knesset from a variety of Zionist political parties and with other Israeli political personalities.[21] Although the conference space could only accommodate five hundred observers and participants, it sparked such interest that there were six thousand requests for admission.

The Road to Peace brought together Israeli and North American Jewish groups as well as Palestinian groups, stimulating the formation of other coalitions to sponsor additional events. One example of a supporting event, which in turn created a vehicle for further coalition work, was the Women and Peace Program.[22] This event was held on March 13 at the Upper West Side's B'nai Jeshurun Synagogue and was organized by Israeli and Palestinian women who had come together for the larger peace conference. In this program the participants reported on the main conference and on the role of women in the Middle East peace process. The women's event provided concerned activists from a variety of different ideological groups with an opportunity to work together as it was cosponsored by the vastly different organizations: *New Outlook*, *Al-Fajr*, Friends of Peace Now, the American Council for Palestinian Affairs, and the Jewish Women's Committee to End the Occupation.

In contrast to Liberal expectations of competition, the cluster of closely related groups continued to work together, building and recrafting their coalitions as the political situation developed. From the coalition of Jewish groups brought together under the auspices of the Road to Peace, another significant level of coalition work began. Following the actual conference, Road to Peace as an organizational structure remained in place for a while, serving as a resource center and sponsoring other educational events and gatherings. Organizers of the Road to Peace then built on the new level of cooperation among Jewish counterhegemonic pro-Israel groups—ranging from Zionist to non-Zionist and not specifically Zionist—and invited groups to join in an ongoing coalition that came to be called the Jewish Peace Coalition. This coalition's goal was to include as many groups as possible, pooling the strengths of a spectrum of groups on the left that individually reached different populations and utilized differing organizational strategies. Thus, again, the vastly different Americans for Peace Now, International Center for Peace in the Middle East, Friends of RATZ, Americans for a Progressive Israel, the Progressive Zionist Caucus, the Labor Zionist Alliance, IJPU, Road to Peace, NJA, the American-Israeli Civil Liberties Coalition, JPF, Friends of *New Outlook*, and the JWCEO came together and met regularly until the middle of the Gulf War in 1991.

The war in the Gulf caused a tremendous strain on the Jewish Peace Conference coalition, as it was causing tremendous strain within most of the organizations themselves.[23] Due to Israel's position in the conflict, the mainstream Jewish communal position was to back the involvement of the governments of the United States and Israel against Iraq. The memberships of most of the more Zionist-affiliated groups of the peace coalition, however, were split over support of the war, stimulating intense dialogue and struggle toward developing organizational responses. The explicitly non-Zionist groups such as IJPU and the pacifist JPF were able to come out, as groups, condemning the war and even sponsoring the antiwar coalition marches on Washington, D.C., in January 1991.[24] Groups with mixed memberships (including Zionists, non-Zionists and anti-Zionists), such as NJA, were situated in the middle and publicly called for a cease-fire. Although NJA, particularly with the help of JWCEO, was able to organize over four hundred activists to participate in the January 26 march on Washington, it could not endorse the march officially, as the larger antiwar coalition was at that time calling for unilateral withdrawal of U.S. forces.[25]

At this time, in early 1991, the Jewish Peace Conference coalition began to dissolve. As relations between the United States and Iraq deteriorated, the Jewish Peace Network, formed by those groups more comfortable with public opposition to the Gulf War, emerged. The Jewish Peace Network consisted of IJPU, JPF, JWCEO, NJA, and Road to Peace. Although no longer formally together in broad coalition, this set of groups often still acted in collaboration with the other groups from the earlier Jewish Peace Conference, specifically A-ICLC, Friends of New Outlook, and PZC, on specific projects, as well as with the Jewish Peace Lobby and the Jewish Committee for Israel-Palestine Peace. On many specific points these independent groups were able to join in the work of the Jewish Peace Network as it sought to support and foster ongoing communication with American Jewish, Israeli, and Palestinian antiwar activists; organized an American Jewish appeal to help purchase food and medical supplies for the Palestinian community in dire straits under the Israeli wartime curfew in the Occupied Territories; and responded to the arrests and campaign against Palestinian peace activists Sari Nusseibeh and Faisal Husseini. Thus, despite the breakup of the Jewish Peace Conference, these groups within the Jewish Peace Network remained in close contact with the other groups from the earlier, larger coalition.

The story of cooperation among the newer groups does not end here. Despite the difficulties of organizing across difference during the frenzied period of the war in the Gulf, these organizations continued to wrestle with the issues together. The Jewish Peace Network groups, independent Jews, and individual members from other Jewish peace groups (who could not come out publicly to oppose the war), formed into local coalitions such as Jews Against the War in New York. Other local Jewish antiwar groups sprung up around the country as well, such as a Georgia effort named Atlanta Jews Against the War and another similar coalition in Berkeley, California. Various other organizations with differing stands on the war in general, and on practical policies in particular, also worked together beyond their local centers, giving Jews across an ideological spectrum an opportunity to raise their voices. National Jewish coalitions, such as the Emergency Jewish Peace Coalition, emerged. This coalition was sponsored by the Shalom Center, *Tikkun*, NJA, JPL, and JPF. It organized actions such as the public mourning, with rituals performed on the steps of the Capitol building in Washington, D.C., and a public fast toward seeking peace, at the end of January and the beginning of February 1991.[26] Some organizations provided activists to lobby select members of Congress at the time. These groups all also participated in the Shalom Center's public conference held over January 6–7 of that year at New York's Columbia University.

Thus, the period of the late 1980s into the early part of the current decade was a time of intense connection and coalition work between the groups. Political differences, surfacing again particularly at the height of the Gulf War, caused shifts in the alliances between the many groups.[27] However, these groups of the pro-Israel counterhegemony still worked closely, in varying relationships. More recently, APN, for example, continues to work with other newer groups such as the Jewish Women's Consultation, Project Nishma, *Tikkun*, and others. Conflict, struggle, and serious differences remain among the groups. However, overall, despite Liberal expectations, coalition and mutual support, rather than competition, are the relational norms between these political groups. Certainly, some coalitions last longer than others, but the tendency of groups to work together over time is the reality of these dovish groups.

One might suggest that these groups, as a whole, can cooperate and do not assume competition because they are not involved in the "hard" world of politics in Washington, D.C. One might argue that these groups can act in a relatively nondominant (non-Liberal) manner because the American Jewish community as a whole has groups such as AIPAC to take on the burden of such a role; these newer groups are protected in that they are still part of the counterhegemony and cannot yet work within the more Liberal, government-oriented political arena. However, Liberal political actors and group-based democratic thinkers tend to assume competition in the whole world of political groups. This norm would thus be found outside of Washington, D.C., as well. But the groups whose primary focus is not legislative do not confirm the expectation of competition. These groups, based in Washington, D.C., are at least trying to effect change directly in the same sphere as groups such as AIPAC.

The activity and perspectives of those involved during the 1980s in the pluralist political system of groups primarily focused on the legislative arena also do not reflect the high level of competition that one might expect after having read the academic groups literature. There is some discussion in the congressional literature that provides a base for the new empirical findings. Hinckley, for example, suggests a lobbying atmosphere that looks rather noncompetitive from the perspective of legislative, rather than interest group, studies (1978, 51–54).[28] This literature suggests that groups engage more in an exchange (it was popular even to call it "friendly") than in competition.[29] Such a conception is much more descriptive of the perceptions of the 1980s pro-Israel groups than those found in traditional group-based literature. People from organizations involved in lobbying with whom I spoke described such exchange, reinforcement, and activation when discussing their legislative-directed activity. They did not present the relationship between themselves and other similar lobby groups, or between themselves and the legislators, in the wholly competitive terms found in the interest group literature.

For example, Jerry Segal, president of the newer Jewish Peace Lobby, discussed his organization and its relationship to the older and more established "Jewish lobby" group, the American-Israel Public Affairs Committee (AIPAC) in noncompetitive terms.[30] Traditional studies would lead to skepticism about JPL's claim that they are not "anti-AIPAC." Utilizing zero-sum thinking, it is impossible to see two groups with different opinions on issues as not in direct competition.[31] However among the variety of people involved with the different lobby-style groups, neither staff, board members, nor rank and file activists used this zero-sum language. In fact, a number of Jewish activists clearly expressed their opinion that it is precisely this noncompetitive approach that has contributed to the success of the newer pro-Israel groups.[32] Let us now explore more carefully the visions of those in the newer groups so that we may understand why their relational norm is so highly cooperative.

## Pro-Israel Identity Politics as a Power Struggle

The 1980s pro-Israel groups contend that the large mainstream organizations have developed a conception of what it means to be pro-Israel that has become hegemonic. The multiplicity of voices in the community has been stifled, and there is no real dialogue through which the community engages in a grand process of valuation. This is harsh criticism rooted in the pain experienced by people who are deeply Jewish identified, but who feel alienated from the community. They criticize certain parts of the organized community for having sought power over the ideas and modes of expression of the rest of the community. The unfortunate and painful politics involved in silencing these groups rests on the established mainstream organizations' understanding of power as power-over that directly leads to a politics of domination.[33]

What of the understanding of power within the newer groups? What kind of change were these groups seeking? Did they perceive themselves as a simple counterhegemony striving to overpower the hegemonic ideas? In other words, did they see the goal of their political process as the substitution of one dominant paradigm over another? Or did they see their goal in different ways? If so, what other modes of power were they working from that stimulated such intense coalition work?

Contemporary critical theorists have devoted much attention to the power-over model and its consequences. They suggest alternative understandings of power that tend to be more liberating, either because by doing so they help us to locate sources of domination, or because they provide us with a transformative discourse to understand our own power. For example, Foucaultian theory highlights the Hobbesian understanding of power as a thing to be possessed. Instead, Foucault saw power as a relation.[34] Feminist theorists such as Starhawk make a similar critique of common conceptions of power. Differing from Foucault, however, they see power as action or as potential ability.[35] Although the story is complex, these critical theories of power are far more expressive of the activists' guiding visions than is the view that they confront in the larger Liberal political arena.

## Power-Over/Power-Within Relations

It was easy for people in the cluster of newer pro-Israel groups to use the language of power-over in discussing the nature of the change they sought. For example, sometimes people expressed their goal in terms of "making everyone think the way that they do," or "becoming mainstream." In one way, such language suggests the acceptance of a power-over model of power and political change. A "changing of the guards," in a system based on domination, does not challenge the power-over construct. This conception of politics seeks merely a shift in the allocation of concrete goods/ powers, rather than a more fundamental shift in terms of the very "stuff" and "process" of politics.

In other ways, however, the desire to become mainstream suggests alternative aspirations. People from these groups also discussed their ideological goals in terms broader than their concrete positions on such policies as the "land for peace" equation of Israeli foreign policy. As important as these policy issues are in politics, group activists also talked much of diversity within the community. These groups sought to be accepted into the communal discussion; their members discussed the need for the community to be more inclusive, welcoming, tolerant, affirming, and encouraging of difference. Activists explained the need to create an environment in which a real exchange of opinion would be safe and respected. They also discussed the necessity of acknowledging the particularity of one's views, and of ending the pretense that any one view represents the whole of the Jewish community.

These people certainly want their particular political positions adopted. In only a half-joking manner, a number of activists talked of wanting their positions to be "the" positions of the Jewish community, perpetuating the problematic notion that there can be any single voice of the community: a continuation of a closed political space that is deaf to diversity. Yet, they also meant something different by becoming "mainstream" that explodes the power-over construct itself. In talking about a community that has as its "mainstream" ideology the respect and fostering of difference, respondents were utilizing the power-within conception of power.

For the most part the activists suggested, in contrast to Liberal definitions, an understanding of power that is affirming and not dominating. There is, of course, always the danger of which Marshall Berman reminds us. In *All That Is Solid Melts Into Air*, Berman writes that "a more typical bourgeois pattern is to praise freedom when in opposition and to repress it when in power" (1982, 113). The challenge that these groups face if they are truly interested in exploding this pattern, then, is that of continuously recommitting to their ideology of diversity not only as a means by which they will establish power, but also as the process by which they will exercise it as they succeed in displacing the current hegemony. It is thus important to note that the affirmation of such a notion of power was a guiding vision of the future that they worked to bring about, and it was also their guiding vision for the means to such an end. Although it can be difficult to employ in all the particulars of day-to-day organizing, activists talked much of the need to relate means and ends as the only way to transform the current political climate, which relies on silencing as a strategy. As such, the predominance of this power-within concept among the newer pro-Israel groups led them to strategies of cooperation and mutual aid, rather than solely of competition.

## Win-Lose/Win-Win Relations

Rather than operating out of a zero-sum understanding of the political process, those involved with these groups perceived resources and success in more mutual terms, seeing their success in tandem with the success of other similar groups. This view is essential to intense coalition work, even when the particular coalitions shift and develop over time. Occasionally members of one of the more successful groups used dismissive language in answering questions concerning the mutuality of many groups' success. They were, at times, less willing to acknowledge the way that the smaller groups also helped to create a supportive political climate. However, even those members neither viewed their own group's relations with others as necessarily competitive, nor success among the groups as zero-sum. In fact, even outside of formal coalitions, the 1980s groups cooperated often on specific projects, both short-term and long-term. Activists reported that sometimes they felt hesitant sharing certain resources, wanting to be protective of the little they had. All the groups, however, actually did combine many of their resources in terms of both information and material supplies. Despite the tendency to hoard and compete that we learn as actors in the broader political system, in practice, these groups found it more beneficial to share.

Another good example of the way these groups do not succumb to zero-sum thinking concerns the issue of overlapping memberships. Most people involved in the 1980s groups believed that high percentages of their members held additional memberships in other similar organizations. This is not a zero-sum reality, in which the addition of each new member means that there is one less member for another group. In addition, most activists did not see such overlapping membership as problematic. There were some concerns about the amount of energy and other resources that members would be able to devote if they maintained allegiances to a number of similar groups. Due to the relatedness of group goals, however, overlapping membership was seen by most activists as understandable if not expected.

Most of these groups did not act competitively with one another because, even when in coalition, members perceived the groups to have different strengths and characters.[36] They saw themselves as fulfilling certain needs of the community, and not others. Other groups were perceived as filling gaps in the community that their own group could not fill, or did not intend to fill. Acknowledging that these needs might be felt by different types of Jews, they also realized that individual Jews would themselves have more than one set of organizational needs.[37]

There are many examples of this overlap/differentiation among the new pro-Israel groups. The Progressive Zionist Caucus and Americans for Peace Now take similar stands on many issues, and attract people with similar backgrounds. However, they cater to two distinct subpopulations within the Jewish community, students and nonstudents respectively. Although the groups are often found helping each other, each simply cannot offer what the other can. The groups thus retain their separate spheres, and do not end up competing with one another, but they cannot be described at all as disconnected.

Following an ideological continuum, APN and PZC are very much in contact, for example, with groups such as Project Nishma and the Jewish Women's Consultation. It is clear that PZC has a separate, though related, constituency, but so do the others. There is certainly overlap between the members of the various groups, but both leaders and participants continuously asserted that each distinct group is needed in order to fulfill the various needs of different people in the community. In contrast to the pressures in mainstream visions of politics, and also to the picture painted in groups literature, participants and leaders of these groups spoke at length about the effectiveness of such a web of distinct, yet connected, groups working together for both particular and overall communal goals.

When asked why people would join their particular group rather than, or in addition to, another similarly oriented group, most activists pointed to the particular goals and character of their organization. In contrast to the assumption that this differentiation is an attempt to avoid competition through separation, the members very clearly described the groups as functioning/thriving as part of an organizational web. Respondents saw each group as having its own strengths and character but participating as part of a larger effort within the Jewish community, and as part of the whole community outside the American Jewish world. The basic norm expressed by respondents was that of organizations with fluid boundaries working collectively. Whereas examples of tension do exist, that tension was an undulating part of an ongoing dynamic—not necessarily competitive—collective effort.

It is thus interesting to compare the reality of the phenomenon of overlapping, found concretely in the world of the Jewish groups, to the discussion of the issue found in the group literature. There is an assumption, generated from early pluralist writings, that overlap encourages democracy.[38] The idea is that members will belong to more than one group and that the connections developed will help to limit the excess of conflict and promote better representation. However, it was decided that overlapping memberships will not be sufficient to temper the virulence of conflict.[39] This was argued because there will not be enough overlap in society to affect the harshness of the reality of social conflict.[40] Hayes finds that there is significant overlap among similar issue groups. He continues to affirm the conflict model, however, because he asserts that these members will not have meaningful ways to meet and create the feeling that would provide the theoretically anticipated buffer.[41] This attempt in the literature to find an alternative to conflict was too short sighted. It looked at a possible factor—membership overlap—in isolation from other factors that might contribute to cooperation. It thus refuted the possibility of this theoretical suggestion and reconfirmed its overall assumption of the inevitability of competition.

This is not to say that membership overlap itself reduces conflict; this is not the only logical possibility. Cooperation is so obvious among the cluster of the Israel-oriented Jewish groups that sprung up in the 1980s, that the inadequacy of this factor as suggested in the literature has no real descriptive power. Instead, the view from the groups suggests that membership overlap is an aspect of a broader-based relationship between groups themselves, despite the level of staff (rather than membership) activity. These groups acted more cooperatively than the group literature expects them to act because they did not assume competition as the relational basis of the political process itself. They perceived themselves as connected to other similar issue groups, working together for overall goals; this includes the fact that each was an independent organization with its own strategies to achieve these goals.

Activists explained that membership overlap did contribute to cooperation, in the face of expectations of competition, but that it did so as part of a more complex set of relational aspects. This more in-depth understanding of relationship between groups suggests that conflict and competition are not wholly characteristic of group interaction, but rather that cooperation and mutual aid are essential characteristics of the actual political process in which these groups are engaged.

## In the Face of Scarcity

Finally, the question of whether these groups function under the assumption of scarcity also needs to be addressed.[42] While these groups did not assume scarcity in a general way, those involved did talk of financial and other resource concerns. Although they are realistic about resources, they were not consumed by fears of scarcity. Many involved in the groups discussed proceeding consciously in the face of such expectations of scarcity, or future scarcity, consciously operating with the idea that they must assume that their needs will be met, somehow, and refuse to be limited and forced into total competition due to "doomsday" predictions of the "well drying up." They relied on their belief that their other resources and creative management would help them meet any such situation if and when it occured (and such crises often did). One may call such a strategy foolhardy. Perhaps it is, but those involved pointed to the many concrete crises of scarcity that they had faced in the past and to their ability to overcome each situation as it presented itself. Under these circumstances they often found ways to stretch their resources much further than they would otherwise have thought possible. Thus, even an objective assessment of scarcity was challenged in their day-to-day activity as they relied on cooperation and mutual support to achieve goals that a competitive environment would have made more costly.

Activists also discussed their awareness of the expectation of scarcity, especially where money was directly concerned. However, even here many of the most high-level respondents reported that they did not exactly find scarcity to be the reality. As Clark and Wilson (1961) suggest, we might expect to find a high degree of competition among groups that relied on shared members, markets, and resources applied toward shared issue goals. This makes intuitive sense: If similar issue groups are relying on the same people and sources for resources, one would assume that they must compete for these limited resources. A look at the intimate world of the 1980s groups, however, suggests a different reality. As suggested by the discussion in chapter 1, finiteness is associated with Hobbesian boundaried autonomy. Once boundaries are seen more fluidly, the concept of finiteness loses some of its meaning.

This was expressed concretely in the perspective held by some of those involved in fund-raising for the groups, that "people who give, give." Non-Liberal feminist theorists, for example, posit that when boundaries are seen more fluidly, the amount one can give is potentially endless. People involved in these groups found, in contrast to capitalist expectations, that even material resources are not exactly finite. They found that the availability of material resources is often more a state of mind, or a moral experience, than an objective one. Such views are increasingly being expressed in the alternative funding sector.

In the midst of the recession of the early 1990s many nonprofit groups reported that they were suffering from a "tight" economy. Relatively successful enterprises such as *Tikkun* magazine and the national level of New Jewish Agenda[43] faced serious challenges as many of their supporters expressed concern over economic scarcity (and in the case of *Tikkun* it was often the fear of "future" scarcity in a presently troubled economy).[44] Other progressive enterprises, such as the Jewish Women's Committee to End the Occupation, closed down. Surely if a group such as JWCEO had more resources, its committee members might not have felt so overburdened, and perhaps they could have kept the central organization functioning.[45] However, in this context scarcity is not an objective fact, and members of the committee attribute the decision to disband to changing organizational needs based on the advent of the 1990s Middle East peace talks.

By the 1990s, much talk in the organized Jewish mainstream concerned the economic future of central fund-raising agencies and other large-scale organizations, raising the specter of scarcity. A number of dovish pro-Israel foundations and organizations, such as the Abraham Fund, are actually enjoying economic success, however. The coming of age of the relatively well-off "baby-boom" generation, as well as a spirit of "sharing" have resulted in a "rise of new donors" and a growth in new forms of "charitable giving."[46] Even in the midst of the recession, NIF sustained itself in 1991. NIF's 1992 struggle to meet its fund-raising goal also has been attributed more to the changing political environment than to a scarcity of funds.[47] These trends show concretely that scarcity is more a perception with political consequences than an objective reality.

Social theory based on scarcity, such as Hobbesian and pluralist group-based democratic thought, concludes that the world is a place of domination and submission in which winners win and losers lose. The way to act in such a world is to compete for a piece of the finite pie. Social theory that does not necessarily assume scarcity can describe a world where, despite some "nasty and brutish" behavior, people and groups can and do work together to create the most fulfilling conditions. The way to act in such a world, then, is to care for oneself, to work with others in a mutually beneficial way, and to watch the possibilities unfold.

## In Conclusion

In the 1800s, Peter Kropotkin conducted fieldwork to test Darwin's scientific findings. Kropotkin noted many examples of competition among animals in the natural world. He also noted many examples of mutual aid and concluded that those species practicing mutual support fared much better than those he observed practicing competition. Although the individualist creed is fashionable, he wrote, we also must attend to our inclinations toward mutual aid.

Despite dominant views of power-over, and the expectation that groups engaged in politics will necessarily be in conflict, the alternative Jewish groups formed in the 1980s present a very different understanding of group relations. Struggling in a highly competitive political arena where the very language used to describe engagement is based on war metaphors, these groups sought a world of peace and cooperation. In their day-to-day organizing, in their wrestling within dominant paradigms, the groups were creating a politics based on mutually reinforced support. In some ways the groups were very similar to one another; in other ways they were quite distinct. Each pursued its visions in its own way, devising unique strategies, while they came together to connect, share resources, gain strength, and add to the vibrancy of their political worlds. Thus, in the words of one group director, "the network of related but different Jewish groups working together is the most effective organizing arrangement I have seen."

The following chapter begins to explore whether these groups have been successful in their strategy of mutuality. It will examine the criteria for success as found in the group-based literature and the roots of such criteria in Hobbesian thought. As we continue to listen to those within the groups speak for themselves, we hear a different vision. The guidelines for success that the 1980s groups have used to assess themselves and others stand as a critique of Liberal democratic theory and suggest an alternative.

*Chapter 4*

# Success

Although it received much early acclaim, Breira was short lived. One of the first activities undertaken by the new right-wing group Americans for a Safe Israel was to publish a booklet designed to delegitimize Breira. Despite AFSI's relative obscurity as an organization, its booklet was given unofficial communal support and distributed throughout the country as if it were policy. Breira and its members came under virulent attack, and the organization folded shortly thereafter.

In 1990 AFSI published another of its infamous booklets, this time on an alternative fund-raising organization, the New Israel Fund.[1] AFSI's NIF exposé, however, met with a very different fate than that of its anti-Breira work. In this case, not only did NIF survive, but the controversy sparked a tremendous response within the community criticizing AFSI's tactics as dirty communal politics. The mainstream Jewish press, which at the time was not very sympathetic to the political goals of an organization such as NIF, published numerous articles denouncing this attempt by one organization to—in Hobbesian terms—kill another. In the interest of more honest politics within the community, even representatives of the mainstream pro-Israel structure came to the defense of this alternative group's engagement in communal politics.[2]

The NIF case plainly is different from that of Breira. The anecdote suggests that something significant shifted in American Jewish communal politics over the course of the 1980s. But political scientists and democratic theorists tend to have a very difficult time telling if groups engaged in the political process actually have any effect in their worlds of political experience.[3] This is the question I re-visit in this final chapter: How will we be able to tell if our lives are fundamentally shifting?

The attempts made by political scientists and Liberal democratic theorists to answer this question exemplify what progressive activists and transformational theorists are calling a thin theory of change. Refined assessments are rare, and often success is measured in more superficial quantitative, rather than qualitative, terms. A philosophical examination shows that it is not possible to learn from pluralists how to measure group effectiveness, in the process of social transformation involved in serious identity politics, because these scholars are working from a theory of democracy that has no room for deep change. The standards and measurements most often used to evaluate whether groups are successful in their attempts to affect the world are rooted explicitly in the traditional Liberal theory from which they are generated. However, groups seeking transformation themselves define measurements for success differently. Listening to the 1980s pro-Israel groups articulate their own guidelines can give activists and new democratic theorists a much deeper, qualitative measurement. Such an approach is useful in discussing the effectiveness of the groups involved in transforming American Jewish pro-Israel identity.

## Identity Transformation and the Constitution of Success

Scholars often measure the effectiveness of groups in terms of legislative victories. This is because in much American democratic theory the political process is reduced to the arena of government.[4] Much of the real life of politics gets lost in the reduction and leaves no room for a serious exploration of the concept of transformation. The tendency to reduce the political universe to the governmental has roots in the philosophical separation of the public and the private into the realms of rationality, law, and economics on the one hand, and the realms of emotion, custom, and family on the other.[5] Hobbes, for example, evaluates the causes of society's war of each against all in both public and private terms; his solution, however, is decidedly a public one. Emotions such as fear and insecurity are for Hobbes major contributors to the social angst. However, Hobbes proposes only a legal remedy: Men will enter into a social contract and erect a sovereign.

Benhabib discusses the problem of offering a legal, public solution that does not transform society, but rather only encages, contains, and institutionalizes social problems. She describes how this kind of political philosophy has been the saga of the autonomous male ego who suffers "loss in his confrontation with the other, and the gradual recovery from his original narcissistic wound through the sobering experience of war, fear, domination, anxiety and death" (1987, 84). Benhabib writes that "the last installment in this drama is the social contract: the establishment of the law to govern all." This is crucial to the project of classical political philosophy; "the establishment of private rights and duties does not overcome the inner wounds of the self: it only forces them to become less destructive."

This may not be the fault of social contract theory itself. Rousseau posits that man is changeable and that his natural predicament is moldable. He thus envisions a social contract that will facilitate man's development from egoist to citizen.[6] In Rousseau's scheme, civil society will be distinctively different from the state of nature. In contrast, the Hobbesian paradigm still posits a brutish civic realm. The difference for Hobbes is not in working through our actual troubles, but that within this contracted realm we can exist a bit longer than in the state of nature. Benhabib writes,

> The original narcissism is not transformed: only now ego boundaries are clearly defined. The law reduces insecurity, the fear of being engulfed by the other, by defining mine and thine. Jealousy is not eliminated but tamed; as long as each can keep what is his and attain more by fair rules of the game, he is entitled to it. Competition is domesticated and channeled towards acquisition. The law contains anxiety by defining rigidly the boundaries between self and other, but the law does not cure anxiety. . . . The law teaches how to repress anxiety and to sober narcissism, but the constitution of the self is not altered. (1987, 85)

From Madison,[7] through Bentley,[8] to later pluralists,[9] modern democratic thinkers generally accept this formula of basing inquiry in human nature while exploring alternatives merely in varying forms of government. Thus, most contemporary works that purport to study political groups, in their attempts to understand social relations and stresses, focus their study on groups whose arena of activity is government.[10] By defining politics in this narrow way, much of American democratic theory actually leaves no room for fundamental social transformation in politics as it is part of the very fabric of our lives. A closer look at a number of contradictions in Hobbes's thesis further explains this lack in contemporary democratic theory.

For Hobbes, life in the state of nature is "solitary, poor, nasty, brutish and short." The central problem of man in his natural state with other men is, however, that he is in "continuall feare, and danger of violent death." Benhabib's insight is that under the social contract, Hobbes has not promised that life will no longer be so brutish, and so on. Hobbes merely suggests that men who lay down their rights to the sovereign will be free from that facet of their situation that is most unbearable—this fear of violent death.[11] His aspiration toward a commodious life offers only that it will no longer be quite as short. As he does not really address the qualitative issues of life in civil society, the Hobbesian standard becomes primarily quantitative: the pursuit of a merely longer life.

Like the Hobbesian sovereign and Madisonian republican government which play no favorites among subjects, the role of government in pluralism is supposed to be that of a relatively passive and neutral broker,[12] or a disinterested umpire.[13] To avoid a situation in which, due to the competitive struggle, one group may overpower another, the government is in place to assure that groups struggle by the rules.[14] Robert Dahl's defense of his perception of the American political system is that eventually everyone's interests will be met. A group may lose a political battle from time to time, but they will not lose the war: the war of each group against all groups. This is the guarantee of American democratic equality.[15]

## A Short and Brutish Life and a Violent Death

There is a problem, however, with the promise that groups will be guaranteed longevity. Not a few scholars have pointed out the fallacies of group-based democratic theory that assumes that groups will be guaranteed life. The first main criticism claimed that pluralism ignored the inequality that is a fact of American political life. This critique showed that not all groups will succeed at even this basic level of survival.[16] When pluralism is understood in its Hobbesian context, such an inadequacy can be expected.

To Hobbes, man's fundamental concern is the continuation of his own life. It is in response to the constant risk to man's life in the State of Nature that Hobbes suggests a social contract. He suggests that men agree to give their individual rights up to a sovereign.[17] Under these conditions, the sovereign then becomes the sole possessor of killing capacity.[18] Granted, under the Hobbesian social contract, men have the right to defend their lives if they find themselves threatened by the sovereign.[19] However, sovereigns have the right to try to overpower citizens. Given the enormous power of a sovereign invested with the resources of a whole society, it is obvious who will win.[20]

The contradiction here is clear. Men enter the social contract to solve the problem of the fear generated from the knowledge that at any moment they may be killed, yet under the social contract they confront the same situation. The difference is that the threat will not come from everyone in society, but only from the sovereign and the sovereign's representatives. This is hardly a consolation, especially given the sovereign's arbitrary nature. To men who fear death, there is not much practical difference between death at the hands of a peer and death at the hands of a superior.[21]

And yet, this contradiction—that we agree to certain rules of politics for protection but might not enjoy such protection in reality—remains unreconciled in modern group-based democratic theory. Dahl's pathbreaking work ignored this reality (1961). Moreover, despite Lindbloom's renunciation of the original version of pluralism, Manley (1983) points out that even later versions of pluralism still cannot reconcile the privileged place of business, for example, with their idea of balance among groups. Despite the numerous criticisms that focus directly on this point, many scholars since Dahl have refused to let go of this paradigm[22] and continue to believe in the pluralist notion that group life is guaranteed.[23]

## The More Excellent Sex . . . ?

The Hobbesian guarantee of basic existence that we find constantly replayed in contemporary pluralism is an empty promise. Despite the rhetoric, man is not guaranteed life in Hobbesian civil society. The problem actually goes deeper. Schattschneider wrote, "Probably 90 percent of the people cannot get into the pressure system" (1975, 35). This situation in pluralism, in which some groups will not even be allowed entry into the political arena where they might play the game and struggle for power, has its roots in another Hobbesian contradiction brought to light through his treatment of gender equality.

In *The Leviathan* people are supposed to be equal. We are often told that when writers such as Hobbes say "men," they really mean "people."[24] What, then, are we to make of his discussion of sovereignty in the family? On the one hand, Hobbes does say explicitly that mothers and fathers are equal.[25] However, sovereignty to Hobbes is singular, and men can only have one sovereign at a time. Thus he writes that the mother and the father cannot both be the heads of the family, it "is impossible; for no man can obey two Masters." Because Hobbes can only accept a singular sovereign, he is forced to choose between the mother and the father: He chooses the father. Why? Hobbes claims that men will be sovereign in the family not because men and women are inherently unequal. Instead, the reason he offers for domestic patriarchy is that men rule society; he says that fathers, not mothers, erect commonwealths. Thus, although he makes a claim of an equality, Hobbes provides a justification for actual inequality in that there is already such systematic inequality.

Again, the contradiction is clear. We are encouraged to enter into a social contract that will guarantee our right to participate in a moderated war. We are promised that we will be able to fight it out like everyone else, pursuing our interests under the protective shadow of the sovereign. What we find, instead, is a gap. We are not really all invited to match power with power. When Hobbes denies women access to power in the family, he denies them access to power in general: Some are barred from positions of power simply because they are not the ones already in power.

Works such as Schattschneider's are essentially accusing pluralist theorists of the same lie that Hobbes tells through the example of women and sovereignty in the family. Such critiques show that despite a pretense to equality in society, Liberal democratic theory also accepts the fundamental inequality of some members of society. Despite the promise of access, these lesser equals are denied entry into the political arena.[26] As so many activists know, the reality is that they either have a much harder time organizing, or will never be able to organize at all. Those already disadvantaged will not be able to compose themselves in such a way as to give voice to their experience; due to the inequalities already in place, they will be barred from forming groups that can then fight it out in the competitive political arena. As we now see, contemporary scholars studying group success are grounded in supposedly democratic theory that does not incorporate the possibility of transformation as it glosses over the silencing of less powerful groups that may pose a fundamental challenge to the system.

## Groups Redefining Political Success

Most political scientists who attempt to study the success of groups seeking affect in the political world will suffer a tremendous handicap. They will not be able to tell us anything about transformation, as they operate within a larger theoretical paradigm that can barely envision change. Despite the contradictions in Hobbes's theory, Hobbesian philosophy can at best promise a merely quantitatively longer life in a civil society that retains the existential fears we feel in the brutish state of nature. Such a base translates into three major criteria for the success of political groups in contemporary research. They are all quantitative measures: longevity, budget size, and membership numbers.

This approach can only go so far toward assessing the actual strength and success of political groups when politics is understood not in this limited Liberal sense, but in the broader sense of politics as "figuring it out." Here, as we learn from the 1980s Jewish groups, politics is understood as the struggle for dignity and fulfillment through intersecting communal reinterpretation, meeting, and ongoing valuation. When our understanding of politics remains connected to the loss, anxiety, celebration, and concrete needs of our very lives, counting roll call votes in Congress is a minute, and often misleading, measure of success. Thus we find voluminous scholarly research, based on such standards of success, amounting to what Schattschneider called "a mountain of data surrounding a vacuum" (1979, 8).

## Longevity

Like Hobbesian men who seek to avoid death at all costs, groups are expected absolutely to seek to avoid disbanding so that longevity is an unquestioned organizational goal.[27] Thus, a primary standard of success remains a group's staying power. In our Liberally created common sense, the folding of a group is considered a failure. In its expectation of survival as a measure of group success, the literature assumes that groups are not interested in engaging in the political process in any meaningful way or where they see a real need. Or, perhaps, even if they honestly began with such an intent, they, like individual men, are subject to Hobbesian laws of nature. Groups, despite their intentions, will succumb to the iron law of self-perpetuation. Like Hobbesian men who must keep moving—like sharks—lest they die, it is assumed that groups will seek to exist and to expand at all costs.

Is this the reality of all groups? My research has shown some evidence that corroborates this assumption. However, this is by no means a total picture. An interesting case is that of Americans for Peace Now. APN was formed in the early 1980s as an attempt to support Peace Now (Shalom Achshav) the massive mainstream peace movement in Israel. On the one hand, APN has always claimed that its goal is to "go out of business." When Israel has achieved peace with her neighbors, the organization will shut its doors. Granted, this just may be public relations rhetoric and it would not be easy for an organization to disband. What is interesting, however, is that APN is not the only dovish organization that has risen to power describing its goal in direct contrast to the expectation of longevity. Another example is a group called Project Nishma.

Formed later in the 1980s, Project Nishma (Hebrew for "Let us listen") works within the establishment of the American Jewish community, combining unequivocal support for the peace process with a strong concern for Israel's security needs. Although Project Nishma has an organizational infrastructure that has developed as the organization has gained recognition and has taken on more complicated projects, its founders used the term "project" intentionally, to indicate the organization's semi–ad hoc nature. Even after the first few years of its existence, its leaders remained consciously committed to its temporary nature.

I do not wish to suggest here that groups will not become entrenched. My research suggests that groups feel keenly pressured by this expectation of success. However, there is a substantial level of group commitment to the cause. When group members were asked to evaluate other groups, the responses affirmed respect for other groups' commitment to ideological goals rather than self-perpetuation. Furthermore, nowhere did members of these organizations offer longevity as an example, or self-measure, of their own success. A deeper look uncovers the criteria that groups use for their own assessments.

## Numbers

Such a pursuit is not that simple. Groups feel additionally pressured to succeed in other quantitative ways, assumed by legislators and political scientists, which do not necessarily express their own standards of success. For example, many scholars assume that membership size connotes success.[28] The general exception to this standard is seen when a group purposely seeks to remain small. J. Q. Wilson suggests cases in which a group would not want to expand: if there are limited economic incentives that a larger membership would dilute, a radical group that wants to stay ideologically pure, or a group that has exhausted its entire potential membership (1973, 262). Aside from these cases, groups would seek to expand their numbers, thus making size a measure of success.

In general, as the reasons for exclusivity suggested by Wilson do not apply to the 1980s groups, one might expect that these groups would see size itself, as a gross measurement, as a standard of their success. When asked what they would consider success for their group, some activists did answer in terms of membership size. One or two people even made it plain that numbers, in a narrowly quantitative sense, is an important measure. They said that congresspeople want to hear that an organization has many members. Numbers often impress funding sources, the press, and other centers of power. As these groups exist in this kind of political world, numbers are definitely a consideration.

However, it would be absolutely incorrect to say that such quantitative measures are the standards by which these organizations gauge their own strength. Actually, there is much evidence showing that growing numbers are often a cause for concern, and not only for the reasons Wilson suggests. There was a perception in some groups that smaller numbers would increase effectiveness (not because they sought more exclusive memberships to build prestige). Several reasons were suggested by those involved in the groups: increased ability to communicate across geographical boundaries, increased intimacy among members, greater benefits enabling activists to do more solid work in the local organizations, and a facilitated consensus method that allowed for a stronger decision-making process.[29]

Not everyone wants a small group. Activists definitely feel the pressure to prove their strength in terms of their numbers, and a large membership could indicate a broad base of ideological support. When a group's goal has more to do with deeper conceptions of politics, however, the issue of membership size becomes a topic of strategic and ideological discussion, rather than just being accepted as a simple measurement of success. One interesting point is that many of these groups were much smaller some years ago, and activists then said similar things. Size and the perception of optimal group size are thus relative measures in themselves.

Second, there are some contradictory perceptions about the benefits of membership size. Group members suggested that smaller numbers enabled the group to make clearer policy statements. On the other hand, there was an indication that more emphasis on outreach would force the group to clarify its positions. The difficulty in having fewer members was also addressed. For example, one woman noted that in her local group, despite the benefits of having a small cohesive group, smaller numbers could also be limiting. Not only did active members burn out from having to take on much responsibility; the situation also put off potential members. Her experience was that some people interested in joining the group were excited by the activity, but decided that it would be too much work. Obviously, with more members each individual would have less work, but the perception remained a deterrent.

The experience of the cluster of 1980s pro-Israel groups indicates other evidence, however, suggesting that mere numbers were not a standard by which those involved in these groups measured their success. For example, members did not perceive that their groups were more concerned with expanding the number of members when compared to consciousness-raising and developing relationships between the members. The basic feeling was that by developing a stronger membership, the organizations would be made more solid. Even when asked about involvement in the presumed Hobbesian world of pressuring U.S. political actors, members expressed their own standards of strength in other than numerical terms.

With respect to the goal of expansion, activists said that developing the character of the organization and its members was necessary for expanding in what they characterized as a more important way. While expanding the number of members was a goal, there was also concern with the qualitative aspects of membership. They were interested in expanding in ways that promoted the quality of the organization (including building infrastructure and developing membership skills). This view was reiterated in some of the more exclusive organizations, such as Project Nishma and the Jewish Women's Consultation, as well. This decision to expand with care, which was expressed by activists across the board, demonstrates that quantity ranked well below quality in the groups' own perception of success.

## Money

Another example of gross measurements is found in the commonly held expectation that money is power.[30] The newer pro-Israel groups felt the pressure of this standard of success keenly as well. It was not that these groups were not concerned with money, and did not seek larger budgets. In a capitalist world money often is power. However, I have been arguing that capitalist expectations have not been fully absorbed by society as a whole. Relatively unalienated islands exist in this alienated sea. Not only did the groups' difference from the perceived norm affect their internal life, but it affected the way that they interacted in the hegemonic sphere as well. The issue of money as power, when probed, demonstrates that there are groups struggling to find alternative ways to interact with the dominant paradigm itself.

The Progressive Zionist Caucus provides an interesting example. PZC is a grassroots organization working with a minuscule budget. It constantly faces debt and the threat of dissolution based on financial problems. However, not one of the respondents in PZC mentioned money when asked how they measured their own success, nor did they suggest monetary considerations when questioned about their standards of success for other similar groups. It is interesting that all of the respondents had financial responsibilities and pressures, and dealt with the financial requirements of their part of the organization on a constant basis. Although money seemed to be a fact of life that they had to contend with, budget size itself was not a standard of success.

For the most part, PZC members did comment on the benefits that a larger budget could have for the organization, though this was expressed directly in qualitative terms. Despite the desperate need for funds, the organization has committed not to fund-raise at the expense of solid programming, a qualitative measure. Such a decision has been upheld numerous times in the face of intense pressure to fund-raise. In addition, some respondents noted that there were years when the organization ran on larger budgets and was less effective than it had been in other years with smaller budgets. It is also helpful to remember that the relatively large budget Breira managed to achieve did not help avert its rapid demise. Thus, research shows that despite intense concern over funds, members still did not consider budget size to be a dominant measure of success.

The case of APN is more complicated. In direct APN responses, more references were made to quantitative measures of success than were made in some of the other organizations. When questioned on this issue, one APN woman said that she "does not really care about the members, [she] just wants their bodies." Another woman said, "If I believed that there were a way to make governments move without members, I would dispense with the membership. But, it is a democratic tendency . . . " to rely on numbers. "We are not trying to develop our membership for the sake of the members, but for political reasons. We are trying to develop clout."

It is clear from some of the APN responses, therefore, that dominant expectations definitely affected the organization. However the voices of those involved in these organizations reveal significant evidence of qualitative, nonalienated thinking as well. On this issue, APN is an excellent example of a group struggling between the vision that many members joined with and that the organization proposes to pursue, and a largely alienated legislative arena in which only quantitative evidence of success tends to be taken into account. In this case, it is possible that more APN members used Liberal language because they were more influenced, due to their closer involvement, by that part of the political universe than were some other groups' members. However, this is not a sufficient explanation for the different levels of alienation.

First these same respondents used qualitative language when discussing the same issues, but in different contexts. One who said, when asked directly, that success should be measured in terms of money and numbers, talked of moral imperatives elsewhere on this issue. In his response to a different question, he talked of the role of the organization in terms of teaching and mobilizing people. The person who "just wants their bodies" also talked about the need for creative involvement, and the need for more emphasis in the Jewish community on education than on fundraising. She talked about members' needs to become "broader, deeper, smarter and wiser." The respondent who would "dispense with the membership" if she could said that she found in her concrete, daily political activity the way for activists to change and to create environments where people would be able to develop. She stressed the importance of day-to-day work with the people involved in the organization about issues that were both political and emotional in effecting real political change. Another who also used much quantitative impatient language when responding to certain direct questions talked of the need for the younger generation of Jews to reconnect with the community. She said that the most important thing APN could do as an American Jewish organization is to provide a home for these people. The research design allowed the respondents room for a fuller reflection on these issues. In each case, in the more detailed responses, these visions of a "deeper, broader, smarter, and wiser" community emerged. Connections between the roles of quantitative and qualitative factors demonstrated a wider range of ways to understand group success.

Second, other groups whose focus is legislative influence did not use the same degree of quantitative language as did those in APN. Leaders of these organizations discussed success in much more qualitative terms. They talked of mobilizing, encouraging, and empowering members. They also mentioned the need to feel in touch with the community, to listen and to engage. Some of the alienated language used by APN members was related to their suggestion that a membership organization was the only legitimate pathway to power in Washington, D.C., and that they thus felt pressured to build membership size. However, as Hayes has noted (1983, 120), a group does not need to be a membership organization to have influence. An important contrast to such number-based expectations is, therefore, the alternative path chosen by Project Nishma, which also works in Washington, D.C., and also has achieved quite a measure of success without operating on the principle of a large membership organization. The Jewish Peace Lobby is another example. Although the organization seeks to expand its membership, district representation and activist commitment and resources are essential. Thus, the standards by which these groups measure themselves, and the language they use, demonstrate that lobbying does not necessitate wholly acquiescing to alienated expectations of success standards.

These groups also have been able to function in their relatively non-alienated way within the current political expectations of groups through their use of coalitions and mutual support. In their reliance on cooperation rather than more on competition, groups have been able to work, and further seek, to work, with the size and wealth with which they feel comfortable, and that will not force them to abandon their longer-term goals. Small groups staying more responsible to their organizational aspirations can still act effectively in an alienated political environment through pooling resources. For example, during the Gulf War, a coalition of small groups was able to lobby in Congress claiming strength in the groups' joint numbers. The groups did not have to abandon the particular characteristics and platforms that made them unique, but bolstered their effectiveness by joining forces when appropriate.

## Redefining the Political Sphere

It is possible that examining only groups that are primarily lobby groups will generate a certain perception of success. The standards assumed in the groups-based literature may be applicable, but only to a subset of political groups. Yet, the fact that most traditional studies look at lobby groups cannot entirely explain why they have such narrow expectations of group behavior and success. Particularly in light of the tendency to reduce politics to government, it is important to remember that the world of government is but a slice of the political universe. Among the groups that focus on legislative influence in Washington, D.C., however, such narrow expectations do not adequately reflect even the standards they apply to themselves.

Like the interest groups usually studied by group scholars, the pro-Israel groups also want to have an impact on government policy. However, the groups tend to perceive the political world with which they are engaged as also consisting of broader concerns than their relationship with governments. Their political world is also the world of the community. To these groups, politics also involves consciousness and identity, reinterpretations of history, and reenvisioning the future. Politics is a process of empowerment of individual members and of the collective. What we see is that the way a group defines its political world and the political process affects its standards of success.

The groups organized in Washington, D.C., are aware of, concerned with, and motivated by their relationship to their community. They are concerned with their standing among other Jews. They are also concerned with foundational questions of identity and the need for a more affirming political process. Some group members discussed their role as listening to the community, responding to its needs, and helping shape its future. Thus, even among lobby and advocacy groups these considerations of what politics is ultimately about suggest that measures of success must be based on standards that go far beyond traditional group theory's base in legislative victories.

Those groups not primarily focused in the legislative arena definitely see their relationship to the community as essential to their raison d'être. They define success in terms of the community's being able to hear their voice and recognize them.[31] They talk about promoting dialogue and more open relationships within the community. These people have refused to be marginal, and they care deeply about the content of Jewish life in the United States (and certainly globally).

Activists across the spectrum of counterhegemonic groups talked about success in terms broader than their influence in government or counting legislative victories. In response to questions concerning their measurement of the success of their organizations, they frequently spoke in terms of their relationships with individuals and with other groups within the community. Group members discussed the quality of their programming, and whether they were being heard by the organized mainstream and by nonaffiliated Jews. They talked about educating and empowering people, and about reinvigorating the community as a whole. The responses from those involved in these political groups suggest that scholars who measure group success must take into account the groups' relationships with society as a whole, and not just with government. Thus, we learn from these organizations that success for political groups involves making progress in the more basic effort to create a public sphere in which conversation and empowering struggle are possible.

## Success in Pro-Israel Politics

We must now ask finally whether these new Jewish groups have been successful in their attempts to redefine pro-Israel identity politics in the community. By the early 1990s, most of the groups reported being better funded and increasingly influential with the United States government, as well as attracting new members. But our assessment must look further than these measures. We must ask if and how the newer groups of the pro-Israel counterhegemony are succeeding in transforming communal politics, responding to the painful cries of Jews alienated in the years of silencing politics, and redefining the relationship between the community of Jews in the United States and that in Israel. It is thus necessary to recall the historical dialectic out of which these groups were generated, and within which they came to participate.

Many American Jews and organizations were not quick to embrace the

Zionist alternative to the Jewish predicament. In the aftermath of the Holocaust of European Jewry, however, more and more Jews came to accept, if not to champion, the notion that within current global politics, statehood can be an important vehicle for collective security. The political construct of the modern nation-state came to be seen as a step toward ending group oppression and enhancing a people's ability to live together and, grounded in its own history, to explore and create its future.[32] For many Jews, Zionism—organic movement toward the liberation of the Jewish people through statehood—came to be seen as a particular historical experiment that is part of a larger process toward ending a global politics based on exclusion and domination, and reconstituting that politics based on empowerment.[33] Many American Jews yearned for the creation of the state of Israel, celebrated its formation, and—although they did not choose to move there themselves—wanted to support and encourage its enterprise.

Unfortunately, given various pressures, the form of support for Israel that emerged from American Jewry became stifling for communal politics. Out of diaspora Jewish fear,[34] Zionist hubris,[35] and the expectations of a Liberal mode of American group politics, the pro-Israel identity of the American Jewish community was reduced to a simplistic equation: The world was split into those who were pro- or anti-Israel. Support for Israeli government policy constituted a pro-Israel position; whereas questioning, challenging, or even listening to such questioning and challenging constituted an anti-Israel position. Those not labeled "pro-Israel" were tainted with the label "anti-Israel," were called enemies of the Jewish people, and were turned upon by the organized mainstream of the community. Jews across an ideological spectrum from Zionist to anti-Zionist were subject to the same standard of support for Israeli government policy, let alone that questioning the very mandate of Zionism itself would have been unthinkable. Such a politics caused much pain to many Jews, many of whom had demonstrated their commitment to the Jewish people through long years of involvement in Jewish communal life, and others more peripherally connected, confused by this simplistic presentation of Jewish identity.

Like any functioning modern democracy, Israel has often fallen short of its mandate. The Israeli Declaration of Independence reads:

> The State of Israel will be open for Jewish immigration and for the ingathering of the exiles; it will foster the development of the country for the benefit of all its inhabitants; it will be based on freedom, justice and peace as envisioned by

the prophets of Israel; it will ensure complete equality of social and political rights to all its inhabitants irrespective of religion, race or sex; it will guarantee freedom of religion, conscience, language, education and culture; it will safeguard the holy places of all religions.

As a complex modern society, however, coping with internal contradictions, regional hostility, and global power-over politics, Israel has many problems. Within its society many Israelis, grounded in prophecy and Zionist ideology, have always worked hard to transcend those problems. Many concerned Jews, supporters of Israel, and Zionists outside of Israel have sought to support those efforts within Israel working toward peaceful and just solutions to its social problems, and to help Israel live up to the general responsibilities of a modern nation-state and particularly to its own aspirations, as envisioned, for example, in its Declaration of Independence.

However, given the development in the United States of the dominant either/or pro-Israel politics, committed diaspora Jews who sought to support those in Israel in their struggle toward fuller democracy found themselves limited. Social protest, work toward enhancing justice in the world, invariably challenges the powers that be: governments, dominant paradigms, and so on. Committed Jews, pro-Israel activists, and Zionists within the American Jewish community who were concerned with the character of the state of Israel and the nature of Israeli society (rather than only with Israel's basic existence) thus ran into trouble with the American Jewish establishment.

In the hegemonic pro-Israel political sphere within which these groups engage, they were subject to many efforts to silence their emergent voice. Despite this rather hostile and painful environment, these newer counterhegemonic groups continued their efforts and gradually began to shift the pro-Israel paradigm. By the end of the decade, drastic changes became visible. In 1988, AJCongress, AJCommittee, and the Reform movement cosponsored an event in Chicago, called Israel's Dilemma and Ours, at the North Shore's largest synagogue. The more than two thousand participants gave a standing ovation to the speaker who called on American Jews to end their era of silence.[36] The Passover Peace Coalition and the Road to Peace Conference demonstrated the power of mutual aid and coalition politics in 1988 and 1989. Suggesting to the pro-Israel hegemony that diversity and strength are not contradictions, Project Nishma released its Letter of Forty-One, and Americans for Peace Now began to be wooed by the Conference of Presidents, on the road to a more honest and dialogic communal politics. By 1989 *Newsweek* would headline an article on religion and society "A Family Quarrel: Once American Jews loved Israel blindly. Now they're learning to ask hard questions."[37]

This development has been anything but linear, however; these last years have been a time of tremendous struggle for many concerned Jews, pro-Israel activists, and progressive Zionists. In 1988, a Philadelphia-area Reconstructionist synagogue actually split over pro-Israel politics.[38] Sixty percent of Congregation Beth Israel voted not to continue the synagogue's programs addressing issues of Israeli politics and the Middle East conflict. In June of that year, Rabbi Brian Walt and part of the congregation split from Beth Israel to form Congregation Mishkan Shalom in Havertown. In their new synagogue the members committed themselves as a congregation not only to exploring the issues, but to actively supporting "those groups and individuals within Israel who are working for a just end to the [Israeli-Palestinian] conflict and a long-term solution based on mutual recognition."[39]

In 1991 a progressive Jewish student group brought a local Palestinian woman to campus to perform a one-woman play about her own experience.[40] The group asked the campus Hillel to cosponsor the event and requested space in the Hillel building. They were turned down by the Hillel board in both instances. The sponsoring group also asked the Hillel director, who they knew was sympathetic to their politics, to introduce the event as an individual, not even as a Hillel representative. The director's friends and Hillel colleagues recommended that she turn down the offer because the issue was "too hot." She did turn it down. The local Israeli consulate, however, believing that Hillel did cosponsor the event and that the director was to introduce the actress (because they never contacted Hillel directly), circulated a letter to Federation and other Jewish communal leaders stating that the Hillel was anti-Israel and that the director was not fit to hold her job. Only a flurry of letters by the local JCRC, the Hillel council, and the local Hillel board, coming to the director's defense, saved her job. This response was quite different from the treatment of critical Hillel directors in the 1970s. The consulate, however, never retracted the accusations concerning her qualifications.

Fear within the remnants of a silencing politics still haunts American Jews. In the spring of 1992, Jewish students at a Midwestern university were told that they could not print news of New Jewish Agenda in their campus Jewish newspaper. The students, upset by such political silencing, requested a grant from the North American Jewish Students Appeal to publish their own newspaper, in which students could feel more free to discuss their issues of concern. The students received the grant. When I phoned the student publisher to inquire about the incident, he claimed he did not know what I was talking about. I was rather confused; I had heard the story from a highly responsible Jewish professional. Later I was told confidentially by that professional that she had received a call from the student following my conversation with him: He was furious that she had told me the background to their grant proposal. He was too afraid to have the problem known within the community.[41]

Despite this recent history, however, these newer groups have succeeded tremendously in redefining the pro-Israel identity politics of the community. These alternative groups have been listening to those who felt alienated from the community and have been demanding that the mainstream listen as well. Over time, their cries are increasingly being heard. The more obvious example of the counterhegemony's success was the election of a Labor government in Israel and great strides in the peace process. But I want to argue that these groups' success must be seen in more grassroots ways to be fully understood. Recently groups such as APN and Project Nishma have been brought into the center of the communal pro-Israel discourse. For example, some of the pro-Israel people President Clinton has named to his administration are APN members, and APN has joined the Conference of Presidents of Major Jewish Organizations. In addition, in December 1992 Project Nishma organized an unprecedented joint statement by American Jews and Arabs asking then President-elect Clinton to give top priority to continuing the Middle East peace negotiations. The statement was signed by the executive directors of both the American Jewish Congress and the National Association of Arab Americans.

At that time, Project Nishma also arranged a meeting to demonstrate that there is a growing constituency in the United States that supports the American-led talks, despite their recent lull. This session was attended by fifteen Arab-American organizations and more than twelve American Jewish organizations.[42] The language of the meeting, drawing heavily on the lessons of the Women's Dialogue Project, was dialogue and cooperation. Jewish activist and briefing organizer Jonathan Kessler was quoted in the Besser pieces (1992 a–d) in the Anglo-Jewish press as saying, "Clearly, the American Jewish Congress and the National Association for Arab Americans have gone out on a limb to push a new vision of dialogue between the two communities. . . . And Project Nishma has moved into the forefront in helping to reposition the American Jewish community." One participant was often quoted as saying, "Only one out of ten questions contained any of the language of conflict. . . . All the others were questions that used the language of conflict resolution."

Thus, the emerging pro-Israel politics that these newer groups are succeeding in creating aims at inclusion, which is simultaneously respectful of difference. Within the American Jewish community joint efforts and broad-based coalitions of different types of groups on issues relating to Israel are increasingly common. The models suggested by the Jewish Women's Consultation and the Dialogue Project, models of dialogue and building relationships to overcome politics based on fear and silencing, are being taken up by previously hegemonic pro-Israel forces. The talks in Norway that enabled the current peace process were modeled on the experience of many prominent Jews and Palestinians in the work of the women's Dialogue Project.

At this confusing point in the historical transition, many questions remain that challenge the assertion that these newer groups are successfully transforming American Jewish pro-Israel politics. For example, some have asked, in the aftermath of the 1992 Israeli Labor Party victory and the start of the formation of a Palestinian state, whether the recent changes are simply corresponding to the new Israeli government lines, and are not indicative of a more fundamental change in the very nature of Israel-diaspora relations and American Jewish politics. This may be possible in part. However, counterhegemonic activity began long before the more recent Labor victory, and group success has been noted as beginning long before the victory could have been but a glimmer in even a Labor Zionist's eye.

Dovish pro-Israel activists are now celebrating with caution. Many are asking whether the Labor-led Israeli government, now in coalition with leaders of the peace movement, might demand the same level of unequivocal support from the American Jewish community as did the pre-1977 Labor Party, or as the recent Likud-led government demanded. Certainly; just because in their years of opposition Labor leaders called on American Jews to break their silence does not mean that they will continue to take such a position now that they are back in power. Even with the tremendous advances in the peace process during the 1990s, it is important to remember that it was Yitzhak Rabin, as prime minister in 1977, who called together the private meeting with American-Israeli professors in a panic over the "dissenting" Breira. It was Yitzhak Rabin, as defense minister in 1988, who had the "orthopedic problem": calling for breaking bones to be the Israeli policy in response to the Intifada. It was Yitzhak Rabin, as new prime minister again in 1992, who deported four hundred Palestinian leaders of the Hamas movement, with peace movement leaders from the Meretz Party in the Cabinet supporting the action.

The community does well to ask whether the Labor Party has really changed since its early years. As soon as he came to power, Rabin called for the resignations of the opposition/Likud– supporting pro-Israel leaders of the American Jewish community. Will this Israeli leader, who immediately appointed himself foreign minister as well as prime minister, be any more willing to accept dissent from American Jews than he was in 1977? Time will tell. In addition, it is impossible to predict the effects a Likud victory in the next election might have on American Jewish politics. In the meantime, other ruling coalition Knesset Members, such as Deputy Foreign Minister Yossi Beilin, Shulamit Aloni, and Benny Tempkin, have been visiting the United States since the 1992 Labor/Meretz victory and have called on the American Jewish community to stay active, honest, and critical of the Israeli government. This is a good sign for the development of a more open pro-Israel politics.

What of the future role of pro-Israel hawks in the new environment? Actually there have been three types of pro-Israel hawks leading the pro-Israel establishment since the 1977 Likud victory: Some have been private doves who believed the dominant pro-Israel line that support of Israel necessitated support of the Israeli government; they thus appeared hawkish from their public statements. If the Labor Party continues in power, their public statements—as they become more free to express their actual views—will become increasingly dovish. Some American Jews have apparently been in earnest in their claim that a pro-Israel stance is one that supports the Israeli government, whatever the policy of that government. Thus, there are pro-Israel activists who until June 1992 advocated Likud positions, are currently advocating Labor positions, and will continue to change with the tides. Their situation is rather precarious. Finally, there are the ideological pro-Israel hawks. These people do not seem to have had much difficulty dissenting in the past; they have thus resumed their position of opposition now that a more dovish government is in power.

How will these people be treated in the new, more dovish environment? Many pro-Israel activists are wondering whether American Jewish Labor supporters and those in solidarity with the Israeli peace movement might abandon their call for a more honest and open dialogue with Israel and their claim for the legitimacy of dissent.[43] It is possible. Groups such as APN are now playing in a new league of Jewish mainstream and Washington politics in which the pressure to conform to Liberal standards is tremendous, as it was on AIPAC. There is reason to believe, however, that these groups will continue to struggle against the dominant expectations and to pursue an alternative model of politics. For example, Ted Mann, active with Project Nishma, wrote an op-ed piece for the Philadelphia Jewish *Exponent* warning the newly powerful dovish pro-Israel groups not to silence dissent from the right, as pro-Israel hawks had traditionally done with respect to the left. In addition, APN disagreed with key actions of the Israeli Labor government (such as deportation of Hamas leaders) and has remained loyal to its commitment to the legitimacy of public dissent.[44] Finally, the new level of violence from the extreme right, demonstrating its members' dissent, has helped leaders and other Jews of good will to denounce at least ultrasilencing politics.[45]

Finally, will the courtesy of inclusion be extended to committed Jews further to the left of these more mainstream dovish groups—such as APN, Project Nishma, PZC, and the Jewish Women's Consultation—that are rapidly moving into centers of the old hegemony? If these groups are to remain committed to their broader political goals of moving toward a more authentic communal politics, such a commitment demands that they remember that until recently (and still at times currently) they were lumped together with the spectrum of Jewish peace groups including pacifist, non-Zionist, and anti-Zionist groups. The pro-Israel politics that refused to hear dissent and that ignored calls for democracy and dialogue within the community was a politics that silenced the Zionist left along with further marginalized Jewish activism. According to the vision of open dialogue that guided these groups in their rise to power, continued marginalization of these other groups is too great a price to pay for access to mainstream power centers and would constitute a betrayal of the broad-based efforts and ethical call to which the more mainstream groups owe their recent success.

Benhabib is giving us a practical recommendation of Plaskow's non-Millian conception that we can use in American Jewish communal politics concerning Israel. Those trying to transcend a dominant paradigm (previously including progressive Zionists and pro-Israel doves, and in the current shift, more exclusively non- and even anti-Zionists), are required—and not merely in the lesser Liberal order of being "free"—to state their case. Although the current communal conversation is framed by Zionist and pro-Israel considerations, committed Jews— especially given the historical dialogue within which Zionism was merely one strain of argument—who are non- or anti-Zionist must be permitted a role in the communal conversation. On the other hand, from the purview of communicative ethics, it becomes incumbent on those with dominant views to invite the others in and only after listening to and struggling with their challenge to recommit—or not—to the status quo vein of the conversation. This scenario avoids painful silencing, exclusion, and alienation. It keeps the community grounded as it allows growth and change, avoiding both relativism and essentialism. It allows the communal conversation to keep going, which is the most empowering guarantor of Jewish continuity offered thus far.

In sum, many ask how we can be certain that dovish pro-Israel groups will not utilize their new abilities to silence others with whom they do not agree. We cannot. Marshall Berman (1982) correctly maintains that it is a lot easier to call for basic change when in opposition than to realize that vision when in power. As a practical recommendation, Rousseau suggests that those who disobey the general will shall be "forced to be free." Is it possible that this haunting Rousseauian image, in which freedom can be forced upon us by the collective, actually transcends the Hobbesian politics of force? It is a tricky point. On the other hand, how can a politics committed to fostering an open public space[46] not disintegrate from an inability to distinguish among values, aspirations, and concrete claims? Again, there are no guarantees.[47] Process-oriented, open politics is dangerous politics; it threatens the status quo, but will not guarantee an outcome. It is possible, however, to defend this sort of dangerous politics.

First, our dominant Liberal politics, which relies on a closed public space, causes much pain and is increasingly untenable. Such a politics is rooted in inequality and power-over and thus directly results in a politics of domination and silencing. We can know that we do not want to continue in our current mode of politics. We can know that we need to try something different. Second, in contrast to the closed model, an open politics that is committed to diversity-based egalitarian empowerment is not only less likely to eventuate in a new version of the Hobbesian paradigm, it is highly unlikely that it will do so: Its potential for equality and freedom of expression and affirmation is rooted in its foundation. Thus, perhaps providing a less frightening recommendation than Rousseau's, many have noted that it is not a contradiction in the development of a more open politics, but a necessity, to state the parameters of such a politics.[48] What of the practical side of such theorizing? At this point we can only note the embryonic aspects of the new politics as offered in this work on a changing Jewish identity, continue to demand an honest exchange and, as Benhabib suggests, work to keep the moral conversation going.[49]

## In Conclusion

Pluralists tend to reduce the political world to the governmental arena. They follow a common paradigm, utilized by Hobbes and Madison before them, that seeks solutions to societal problems, identified as based in a common angst, only in the public legal realm. Hobbes envisioned a solution to the problem in the state of nature only in that our solitary, poor, nasty, and brutish lives may last a bit longer. With this focus, much of the qualitative nature of our political aspirations and particular group goals is lost. Group scholars discuss success in distinctly nonqualitative terms such as longevity, membership numbers, and budget size. Despite the criticisms made of pluralist theory, such standards share their roots in Hobbesian assumptions of the quest for mere survival (in Mary Daly's fashion).

The Jewish groups, on the other hand, demonstrate that the world of politics is much broader and reaches deep into the very consciousness of community life. In addition to delineating their goals of affecting policy, activists talked about qualitative engagement with a living, diverse community even more so than they did about influence in government. They discussed success in terms of being sensitive to the various needs of the community, and they discussed vitality more than numbers. Also, more than gross budget size, they talked of the need to be creative and effective. Those involved in these groups, on the whole, seek a politics of true dialogue, stimulating and empowering people, and promoting qualitative connection to Jewish life. The groups feel tremendously pressured to prove their success in certain superficial, quantitative ways: government policy, larger budgets, increased memberships. Despite these external expectations, however, the groups measure themselves and other groups by a web of more qualitative standards. Their visions point to a theory of democratic politics defined by such process-oriented engagement. For those working to build a new democratic theory that includes a commitment to social transformation, such standards will be more fully expressive of our success or failure to bring about such transformation.

On these standards, then, we have been able to identify a shift in the pro-Israel identity politics found today within the American Jewish community. Examples reflected in communal relations, not only in governmental influence, show these newer groups of the pro-Israel counterhegemony as successful on their own terms. Drawing on their successes of the past decade, and given the new so-called window of opportunity provided by the 1992 elections of more dovish administrations in both Israel and the

United States as well as the great strides in the peace talks, these new groups are now presented with their most serious challenge thus far. Now more than ever, in their recent rise to power, these groups are struggling to remain committed to politics as a process of "figuring it out": to the pursuit of a more diverse, open public space where individuals and groups are encouraged to engage in authentic conversation and struggle to identify and meet their needs.

# Conclusion

The Jewish community in the United States is in a period of significant transition. The world let out a cry of joy when Palestinian Liberation Organization Chairman Yasir Arafat shook the hand of Israeli Prime Minister Yitzhak Rabin in the fall of 1993. For most American Jews, however, the celebratory tears expressed caution and fear, as well as hope. This moment on the White House lawn was many years in the making, not only for world politics but also in terms of an existential transformation for the American Jewish community.

The politics of identity formation and transition as that occurring within the Jewish community in the United States has been understood by many political actors and theorists in particularly pluralist terms. Liberal democratic theorists have tended to conceive of the political sphere as a realm in which selfish interests compete for concrete divisible benefits. Political groups and communities have been equated with these interests and are seen as the bearers of the very "stuff" of politics. Groups are understood in the same light as individual men of classic Liberal theory: They are atomistic, selfish, and competitive, ever fighting for their lives and for the meager concrete goods necessary to sustain them in a brutish world. Traditional democratic theory hallows our political system for its ability to keep the fight cleaner than it might otherwise be, setting the parameters and watching that the groups play by the rules. Such theory encages groups and identity struggles in this brutish political arena, thereby limiting the possibility of alternative modes of self-understanding and action. Rather than seeking to transform the very bases of the social angst, Madisonian Liberal democracy seeks merely "to control the effect." Our system demands that if a group wants to enter into the political conversation, it must play by these rules; its success or failure rests on its ability to conform to the expectations of a "solitary, poor, nasty, and brutish" political realm.

Traditional group-based democratic theory must, however, be understood not as a description of the whole world of politics and the role of groups within that world. It must be understood, instead, as an expression of the expectations and aspirations of the dominant Liberal paradigm. Liberalism, as the hegemonic mode of discourse, seeks to have its understanding of the world accepted as truth. To further its hold on our lives, its proponents claim that this is the way of the world; we are then presented with certain options for maneuvering within such a world.

The American Jewish community, like other communities and individuals, has been offered primarily these Liberal options. Despite the particularity of its history and the richness of its own political tradition, in many respects the American Jewish community accepted these options and played according to the accompanying rules. As Israel contributes a central component of the identity of the American Jewish community as a whole, the community's pro-Israel politics has been particularly subject to the expectations of this paradigm.

When AIPAC and the Presidents' Conference wanted to support Israel, they often played the limited game of Washington politics. They scrambled for the support of the administration and for congressional votes on U.S. aid to Israel; they thus also accepted the rule regarding the necessity of presenting a unified front. The UJA felt that in order to be successful, in order to raise funds desperately needed to support Israel and American Jewish institutions and social welfare programs, it had to play by the dominant rules. It thus chose to capitalize on fear, a fear generated in the equation of difference with "other," with "threat." The UJA campaign highlighted anti-Semitism and the need for a safe place for Jews in the world. It painted a glossy picture of that place, Israel, but included threatening strokes of darkness around its edges. It treated the American Jewish community as simplistic and superficial, unable to relate to its Jewishness with any depth, unable to confront itself and its needs, hopes, and desires in any meaningful way. It assumed the community could only relate to its Hobbesian gut fears of threat, and only support a mythic place which could stand up to that threat.

These dominant American Jewish organizations relied on the Hobbesian idea that life is a war of each against all in which we are forced to watch out for ourselves and ourselves only. They reified the notion "Don't trust anyone," so that we would act according to Hillel's maxim, paraphrased:

If we are not for ourselves, who will be for us? In a Hobbesian world, this line makes a good fund-raising pitch. These groups fell into the Hobbesian trap of a socially constructed greed that proclaims: In a world full of back-stabbing thieves, take what you can, when you can.

The pro-Israel identity politics of the American Jewish community has been plagued by its acceptance of these assumptions, and its political process thus plummeted into silencing politics. American Jews have in many ways become a people afraid to treat themselves honestly, to explore their world with courage, to reach out to each other and to non-Jews stepping forward with complex memory and pride into their future. American Jewish politics has taken on a tragic either/or coloration. When this occurs, a part of the Jewish spirit dies; people become afraid, alienated, apathetic, or hostile, and polarized. In short, the traditional pro-Israel identity politics of the American Jewish community became dominant and supported itself at grave expense to the life of the community, both for individual Jews and for our common identity.

Hillel's first line, noted above, is powerful. It grows out of the trials of historical Jewish experience and is important for contemporary American Jewry. Anti-Semitism is a reality and again is an increasing concern of most American Jews. The Middle East *is* plagued by war, violence, and fear, and Israel has suffered greatly within this environment. But, as has been argued in these pages, Hobbesian fear is but an abstraction of the spectrum of human emotion; isolation is but one element of the human condition, and greed is but one motivator of social action. Democratic theory that accepts the abstraction for the whole has suggested a misleading picture of political groups and communities acting politically, and only sees a limited role for them in their pursuit of solutions to social problems. Similarly, the line so often quoted from Hillel is only the first of three in his famous saying.

Hillel wrote, "If I am not for myself, who will be for me?" But he continued: "If I am only for myself, what am I? If not now, when?"[1] Incredibly enough, Adrienne Rich has added a fourth line, "If not with others, how?"[2] According to new, multiculturalist democratic theory, it is not necessarily that people and groups do not fear, feel isolated, act competitively, and seek quantifiable benefits. Even within a world populated by such people and groups, many also have experienced the world differently, or with additional characteristics such as love, mutuality, and cooperation. Many see politics not in its Liberal limited role of encaging conflict, but in terms of its possibilities: its potential for transforming the very roots of social conflict, our basic social relations.

For the most part, the 1980s Jewish pro-Israel groups have stepped forward into the public space and have engaged others in the political system toward these transformative ends. In doing so, these alternative pro-Israel groups have had to work within an arena understood by many in Hobbesian terms. They must work with other groups who do act atomistically, competitively, and according to their narrow selfish interests for their piece of the perceived finite pie. The dovish pro-Israel groups themselves have had to respond to the pressure to act thus, and have at times succumbed to these expectations. Social transformation based in concrete conditions is truly a struggle, for as Berman reminds us, "The politics of inauthenticity is an integral and indispensable part of the politics of authenticity" (1970, 320). But these groups also have striven toward self-understanding, political visioning, and strategies that go far beyond such Liberal expectations.

The mainstream understanding of American Jewish pro-Israel identity, which these groups hope to transform, has for the most part relied on an abstraction of Hillel's imperative, thus skewing communal politics. The larger story of the American Jewish pro-Israel attitude, however, is the tale of a historical dialectic. Within that dialectic the other aspects of Hillel's imperative have come into focus. The newer dovish groups are successful to the extent that they are actually changing the very level of abstraction of pro-Israel politics in the United States.

The pro-Israel politics that demanded unequivocal support for the Israeli government and sought to cap dissent made for a closed communal political space. Exploring the trials of the Zionist experiment, coming together as a community to evaluate how Israel was faring on its road to being a democratic Jewish state, was branded by the pro-Israel hegemony as dangerous to the security of Israel. Educating ourselves, reaching into communal memory to formulate aspirations that can then serve us as guidelines for the kind of Israel we want to support, and acting on these new visions are all dangerous to an either/or, unity/interest politics.

Authentic politics is "dangerous." There is no doubt about it. But in a threatening world, seeking life is dangerous. In a politics of silence, the quest for genuine dialogue is dangerous.

In Liberal democracy, as Hobbes wrote, groups who cannot "accommodate" themselves to the dominant paradigm are "left out, or cast out of Society, as cumbersome thereunto." Within the pro-Israel hegemony, groups that cannot acquiesce to the dominant line are shunned and marginalized as troublemakers. If there is a dialectic in history, it has shown us that out of our contradictions, counterhegemonies will arise.

Although there always have been attempts to speak out and to organize support for the moral imperatives of the Zionist mandate, the 1980s was a decade of unparalleled activity of this kind. The policies of the Likud-led, post-1977 Israeli government grew harder to justify. The war in Lebanon, the massacres at Sabra and Shatilla—and later the Intifada—led many to say clearly that the traditional pro-Israel identity had become untenable. In the early 1980s, as Israeli citizens by the hundreds of thousands began to take to the streets to protest the policies of their own government, the American Jewish community had to grapple with an important political lesson. Majoritarian rule has a limited capacity for representation and responsiveness; supporting even a democratically elected government's platform is not always the same as supporting its people and its people's historical mission. Within their own community, American Jews increasingly affirmed that a vibrant and thriving community committed to democracy must have an open public space where members can engage collectively in recommitting to their ever transforming identity.

With Israel in dire straits, and in the absence of dialogic communal politics, the American Jewish community reached a breaking point. The 1980s saw an explosion of new Jewish pro-Israel groups committed to recreating communal public space. These groups sought a new politics in which American Jews could explore ways to reconstitute the Israeli-American diaspora relationship and reevaluate how to be pro-Israel. At this point in the 1990s, the more Zionist-oriented among them have entered solidly into mainstream American Jewish dialogue; all of the newer groups together, however, have enabled many American Jews, whether previously alienated or active, to reconnect in newly defined ways to their Jewish and pro-Israel identities. These groups are reformulating communal pro-Israel politics by reclaiming it as a collective multilayered process of figuring out how best to support the people and mission of Israel.

The focus on the interplay of groups affecting Jewish identity politics is one step in the midst of the broader multicultural move toward diversity. Democratic theory must acknowledge the complexity, the contradictions, and the dialectics of groups and their role in the political process. Adrienne Rich wrote, "*Politics*, you'd say, *is an unworthy name for what we're after. What we're after* is not that clear to me, if politics is an unworthy name."[3] In an attempt to clarify what we're after that we are naming "politics," new democratic theory offers a vision of a process in which individuals and multilayered groups struggle to understand themselves and their social relations, where they come from and where they want to go. The work of these Jewish pro-Israel groups shows us that we must remember that politics is about "figuring it out"—in these very broad and deep senses.

# Organizational Mission Statements

## The Abraham Fund

The Abraham Fund, a not-for-profit public foundation, was formed in 1989 with the exclusive mission of furthering coexistence and equality between the Jewish and Arab citizens of Israel.

It is the only institution focusing exclusively, singularly and broadly on the enhancement of the quality and quantity of Jewish-Arab coexistence in Israel.

It was formed specifically for the purpose of developing, furthering, and otherwise encouraging and enabling the myriad of institutions, programs and projects in Israel which are focused on enhancing coexistence and equality between Jew and Arab in Israel. The goal of The Abraham Fund is to enable those institutions to better develop both existing and new programs and projects which specifically involve both Jew and Arab.

The fulfillment of its purpose necessitates developing The Abraham Fund's capacities:

1. To be knowledgeable about the separate and collective needs of both Jewish and Arab communities, determining how these needs can best be met.
2. To support, reward, and publicize individuals and institutions involved in enhancing coexistence and reconciliation between Israel's Jews and Arabs.
3. Educating others of the importance of adequately financing these needs, and successfully fundraising.

The Abraham Fund is efficiently developing, planning, coordinating and networking functions, drawing upon the separate and collective existing resources, strengths and capacities of the Jewish and Arab communities, filling gaps where they may exist.

## American-Israeli Civil Liberties Coalition

The American-Israeli Civil Liberties Coalition was created in the United States and Israel, respectively, by concerned civil libertarians and political activists.

The Coalition's purpose is to work to publicize and expand the knowledge of Israeli Jews and Arabs about the nature, meaning, and importance of civil liberties and civil rights; to disseminate information otherwise unavailable in the U.S. about the state of civil liberties in Israel; and to act as a catalyst for groups concerned with a meaningful American-Israeli dialogue about the dignity of individuals and the creation of civic forces necessary to the protection of that dignity. The American-Israeli Civil Liberties Coalition takes as a starting point the Israeli Declaration of Independence.

In addition, Israel does not have a Constitution nor a Bill of Rights. It does, however, have a strong tradition of civil liberties which is evident particularly in its protection of free speech and assembly. Its understandable preoccupation with security matters combined with the lack of a Bill of Rights, a deemphasis of public discussion and education about the nature of democratic society, and the important role played in public affairs by organized religion, has led to problems in such areas as religious liberty, freedom of the press and of information, sexual equality, academic freedom, and minority rights.

Two overriding problems that must be resolved by Israel are the role of religion in a modern Jewish state and the relationship between Jews and non-Jews—the latter referring to the status of Israeli Arabs, the crisis of the West Bank and the Palestinian right to self-determination, and the relationship of Israel with other nation-states. Much of world Jewry, living in western democracies that secure for them the kind of religious, ethnic, sexual, and political equality unavailable in large measure to secular Israeli Jews and to Israeli Arabs, blindly support Israeli institutions and policies which are violative of individual rights and against which Diaspora Jews would fight were such infringements attempted by their own governments.

The Coalition hopes to help bring about the vision most Diaspora Jews have of Israel. We bring together groups and individuals looking for the means by which to combine their energies to realize the norms of a modern state in Israel.

Our main goal is to stress education. The American-Israeli Civil Liberties Coalition looks forward to continuing to help in exposing and eliminating ignorance in the crucial area of civil liberties, human rights, and the democratic process, while providing individual and group experience in the exercise of those rights and the necessity of their inclusion and protection in any democratic society.

## Americans for Peace Now

Americans for Peace Now is the only national, not-for-profit organization in the United States that works in partnership with Israel's Peace Now movement.

Since 1981, U.S. friends of Peace Now have mobilized financial and grassroots support for Israel's largest peace organization. Americans for Peace Now (APN) conducts informational programming, policy analysis, and political advocacy to educate Americans about the peace process. As more Americans come to understand the realities of the Mideast conflict and the importance of security through peace, their support enhances Peace Now's credibility with both Israeli's and U.S. leaders.

In addition to marshalling support among the American public, APN promotes an active, substantive, and sensitive U.S. role in the peace process. Historically, American involvement has always been critical. Indeed, every Arab-Israeli agreement since 1948 has been brokered by Americans. Only days after the momentous June 1992 elections, APN sent its leaders to Israel—the first American Jewish organization to do so. In meetings with Knesset members (many of whom are now Cabinet members), policy analysts, Palestinian leaders, and Peace Now's Israeli activists, APN began to chart the course for U.S. involvement in the pivotal months and years to come.

In March 1990, APN established the Center for Israeli Peace and Security (CIPS) in Washington, D.C., to coordinate its U.S. advocacy efforts. Through briefing sessions, Congressional testimony, meetings between Israeli policy experts and U.S. lawmakers, and other efforts, CIPS enhances APN's grassroots activities and builds crucial support for the peace process among American decision-makers.

## Americans for Progressive Israel

A socialist Zionist organization that calls for a just and durable peace between Israel and all its Arab neighbors, including Palestinian people; works for the liberation of all Jews; seeks the democratization of Jewish communal and organizational life; promotes dignity of labor, social justice, and a deeper understanding of Jewish culture and heritage.

API was founded in 1947 as an organization of Zionists and non-

Zionists "on the left" to support Israel in close cooperation with the Progressive Zionist League, a political organization formed a bit earlier by adults who had been leading members of the North American branch of Hashomer Hatzair, the Socialist Zionist youth movement formed in Eastern and Central Europe 80 years [prior]. Among the activities of the PZL was the publication of a magazine, *Israel Horizons*, beginning in 1952. Sometime in the mid-1960s, PZL "folded" into API, which exists today as the left Zionist presence within a number of domestic and international Jewish and Zionist frameworks. In the mid-1970s, the Canadian branches of API "seceded" and formed an independent organization, Friends of Pioneering Israel (FPI).

From its inception, API has been the American voice of the Israeli peace camp and the democratic left within the Zionist movement and the State of Israel. For much of our existence, this has focused on representing the actions, ideas and ideals of the Israeli party MAPAM, the Kibbutz Artzi Federation of Hashomer Hatzair, and many of their affiliated bodies.

PZL and API developed contacts with the broader Jewish and general community. To cite one early example, we were instrumental in getting Henry Wallace and the Progressive Party to change their Middle East plank of the party's platform from support for a binational approach to support for Jewish and Palestinian aspirations within a framework which we would today call a "two-state solution." More recently, in the late 1970s, API paved the way for the early incarnations of "American Friends of" Peace Now . . . and in the 1980s, API worked with the New Jewish Agenda, Jewish Peace Fellowship, and other groups in the formation of the Passover Peace Coalition, which demonstrated its support for the Israeli peace camp in the streets of New York City.

## Avukah
## The Program (1938)

*We must fight anti-Semitism* by bringing out into the open the violations of the rights of Jews as citizens, and the difficulties of their position. *We must take part in the wider fight in defense of civil liberties,* for many of the effects of anti-Semitism are infringements of these liberties and must be met as such. Above all, *Jews and Jewish groups must participate in anti-fascist action, and in democratic and progressive movements* which ward off fascism and which give promise of a fairer social order. Jewish organizations must be ready to do this, or new ones must be formed in their place.

*We must liberalize and modernize the Jewish environment* along the lines which we have seen. We must oppose those institutions which evade or falsify the Jewish situation, and steer clear of those which are artificial to our needs. We must create institutions and organizations and schools based on the needs of the new generation of American Jews; these will be secular in character, and will deal with the situation of Jews here, and with their relation to world Jewish problems and to Palestine.

*We must organize for maximum assistance in the migration of Jews to Palestine*, and in the development there of a progressive Jewish center, free from the Jewish minority position, and united with the democratic and progressive areas of the world.

These are three aspects of one attitude, three fronts of one action—the action of American Jews to improve their group situation, doing their part in the world-wide action for improvement and progress.


## Breira
## A Project of Concern in Diaspora-Israel Relations

. . . Particularly as Jews, it is incumbent upon us to raise our voices in support of Israel's apparent willingness to make territorial concessions in hopes of achieving a lasting peace. We hope that Israel will be willing to take those risks for peace which may be necessary in order to negotiate meaningfully with all of the parties. In this context, is it not time to recognize the legitimacy of the national aspirations of the Palestinians, and to seek some way (possibly an independent demilitarized West Bank) to resolve this aspect of the conflict? . . . Now more than ever, we must turn our attention both to issues and problems connected with the State of Israel itself, and its relationship with the Diaspora. We do this in light of the idealism and thought of many early Zionists with whom we identify.

Specifically, we have been troubled by the development of a socio-economic gap between a largely Ashkenazic middle class and the Sephardic poor; by the schism between religious and non-religious which is fostered by the politicization of religious life; and by the erosion of the civil liberties, particularly, though not exclusively, of its Arab citizens.

As American Jews, we are saddened by the extent to which American Jewish life has come to consist almost exclusively of vicarious participation in the life of the State of Israel. Support of Israel has so captured the energies of American Jews that many have abandoned hopes for the development of vigorous and creative Jewish communities in the Diaspora.

Specifically, we are uneasy because Israel relates to Diaspora communities primarily as reservoirs of financial aid and immigration and particularly because American Jewish organizations have acquiesced to this trend; we are troubled by the increasing alienation of the Israeli Jew from his fellow in the Diaspora; *finally—and this is the reason we join together now—we deplore those pressures in American Jewish life which make open discussion of these and other vital issues virtually synonymous with heresy.*

Nothing is more important for the continued vitality of Jewish life than extensive discussion and debate within the Jewish community about the State, its problems, its policies, its relationship with us, and our hopes for it. We are firmly convinced that the cost of silence would be greater than the potential hazards of open discussion. We believe that ultimately such debate and exploration of alternative approaches can only enrich and strengthen Jewish life—here and in Israel.

## Education Fund for Israeli Civil Rights and Peace

Although Israel is often referred to as the only democracy in the Middle East, the country has no constitution or bill of rights to guarantee basic freedoms. It does not provide for separation of religion and state and, consequently, the religious minority exercises tremendous control over the entire population, many of whom are not observant Jews. Most Israelis are denied the freedom to practice their religion or not as they choose, without interference.

The rights of women and ethnic and racial minorities in Israel are often ignored or abused. Members of these groups are subject to economic and social discrimination.

Israel is in dire need of both reform within its own political system, and a negotiated peace agreement with the Palestinians and its Arab neighbors. The Israeli economy is burdened by the constant threat of war and the continued occupation of the West Bank and Gaza Strip. The tremendous influx of new immigrants has placed an even greater financial strain on the country.

It is time to cease aggravating conflict, to work toward a secure peace, and to concentrate on the momentous task of building Israel as the Jewish homeland envisioned by its founders, one which is able to absorb immigrants and guarantees freedom and equality for all of its inhabitants.

The Education fund for Israeli Civil Rights and Peace was formed in 1991 to provide American Jews with a framework to address these crucial issues. It is allied with the CRM (RATZ in Hebrew). . . . In cooperation with other groups, it is working to educate the public about topics of

civil rights and peace in Israel, issues which have such impact on the survival and character of the state.
Goals:

- To educate the public about topics and issues of civil rights and peace in Israel, particularly those related to the values enshrined in Israel's Declaration of Independence: democracy, human and civil rights, religious pluralism, and equality for women and ethnic minorities.
- To promote, through education, an active Israeli policy to resolve Israel's conflict with the Palestinians on the basis of mutual recognition, self-determination and peaceful coexistence, and to work toward peace with its Arab neighbors.
- To initiate a more frank, open and informative exchange between American Jews and Israelis on all of the above issues, which will determine the fate and future character of the Jewish state.

## Friends of Yesh Gvul
## There is a Limit

The destinies of Israelis and Palestinians are interlocked and bound to remain so. The Iraqi aggression against Kuwait—an ominous threat to the integrity and well being of all peoples and states in the Middle East—has made it even more apparent that the occupation of the West Bank and Gaza carries with it devastating consequences for Israelis as well as Palestinians. Israel's ongoing oppression of the Palestinian population inevitably breeds the kind of daily violence that has not only resulted in the destruction of many lives, but also leads to the current impasse of the peace process.

Because recent events in the Middle East have forced the countries of the region to reconsider their own positions and alliances, this will be the opportune time for Israel to change its role from occupier to peacemaker.

Confronted with the dilemma of being patriots and occupiers, a sizeable group of Israeli soldiers and reservists have drawn a clear line between their willingness to defend their country against any outside aggressor and their refusal to take part in military activities against Palestinians in the occupied territories. These soldiers form the backbone of the Israeli organization YESH GVUL ("there is a limit/border").

We, Friends of YESH GVUL, inspired by their conviction and moral courage, call upon those who care about the future of Israel and the future of the Middle East to work together towards a just and lasting peace in the region by focusing on the urgent need to end the Israeli occupation of the territories.

Friends of YESH GVUL is a group of Israelis and Americans—Jews and non-Jews—who work for peace in the Middle East contributing support to the families of jailed soldiers and educational purposes in Israel and the United States.

## International Jewish Peace Union

Since the Middle East Conflict has linked together the lives of Jews and Arabs throughout the world, Jews everywhere have an obligation to address themselves to a resolution of the Middle East conflict, both for the sake of peoples in the Middle East, and for the sake of Jewish individuals and communities worldwide.

Concerned for the safety, integrity and future of the State of Israel, we believe that the conflict between the Israeli and Palestinian nations can only be resolved by ending the domination of one people by another, and by implementing the right to national self-determination of the Palestinian and Israeli peoples. Withdrawal from the territories occupied since 1967 is a necessary step for the implementation of this self-determination.

Therefore, we call for the opening of negotiations between the Israeli Government and the PLO Executive to achieve mutual recognition.

We express our support for the Israeli peace camp: all those in Israel working for the above principles.

## Jewish Peace Fellowship

Members of the Jewish Peace Fellowship are a diverse group of people, religious and secular Jews from all our traditions and all branches of Judaism. All believe deeply that Jewish ideals and experience provide inspiration for a nonviolent way of life.

We see Jewish tradition as a continual calling toward peace, justice and compassion, a tradition whose goal is to bring all people to the consciousness that peace and not war is where we should direct our vision, energy and lives.

We feel the rising tensions in the world today which can lead to the nuclear destruction of the planet. We are distressed by the increasing military presence and spending—and the decreasing commitment to nonviolent social activism and Jewish teachings, we are concerned with the problems facing the Jewish people and, indeed, all people.

- We WORK to abolish war and to create a community of concern transcending national boundaries and selfish interests.
- We REFRAIN from participation in war or military service.
- We RESPECT the common humanity in each person, male or female, affirming differences in religion, ethnic background, national loyalties . . . all these are transcended by belief in the sanctity of life.
- We SEEK to avoid bitterness and contention in dealing with controversy and to maintain the spirit of goodwill while trying to achieve nonviolent solutions.
- We STRIVE to build a social order that will utilize the resources of human ingenuity for the benefit of all, in which our concern for the future will be shown by respect for the precious resource of the earth.

We have worked against the draft, for ending capital punishment, for prison reform, opposed all use of nuclear power, fought the encroachment of the military into our lives, and supported religious, political and social equality for women. We have worked to help end the Vietnam War, for the freedom of Jews in the Soviet Union, in Syria, Argentina and Iraq, for the rights of Falashas and conscientious objectors in Israel, for a political solution and peaceful reconciliation in the Middle East. We work for peace in a threatened world.

## Jewish Peace Lobby

The Jewish Peace Lobby is an American Jewish organization which seeks to promote a just and lasting resolution to the Israeli-Palestinian conflict. Our roots are in the American Jewish community, but participation in our efforts is open to all.

Our central focus is U.S. foreign policy. We seek policies which will promote the long-term security of Israel as well as promote a humane Israel in which democratic values and human rights are protected. We seek policies which will promote the rights and well-being of the Palestinian people. To these ends we will regularly engage U.S. policy makers. In addition, we will engage Israeli and Palestinian policy makers.

Up to now, a single lobbying organization has presented itself as speaking for the Jewish community. Their view of what it is to be "pro-Israel" is to give largely uncritical support for any actions for any Israeli government. We have a different conception.

We believe the Israeli-Palestinian conflict is a conflict between two nationalisms which have sought their fulfillment within the same piece of territory. We believe that a lasting resolution of this conflict can only be achieved if each party to the conflict acknowledges the other as having the same rights that it claims for itself.

Thus, The Jewish Peace Lobby on the one hand supports Israel and on the other hand affirms the equal right of the Palestinian people to self-determination, including the right to establish a state in the West Bank and Gaza, which would live at peace with Israel.

The Jewish Peace Lobby does not seek to specify the exact forms through which self-determination is to be expressed. A variety of alternatives are consistent with our principles, provided that they are freely chosen. These include: the State of Israel and the State of Palestine living side by side, having resolved the issues of mutual security and demilitarization; a confederation of the two states of Israel and Palestine, or of Jordan and Palestine; or a confederation of the three states—Israel, Palestine and Jordan.

The Jewish Peace Lobby is a strong supporter of Israel's right to live at peace within secure and well-defined boundaries. However, we believe that they key to Israel's long term security lies in achieving a political settlement with the Palestinian people as well as with the Arab nations. This will require not only progress on the diplomatic front, but respect for the civil liberties and human rights of Palestinians during the period of occupation.

## Jewish Women's Committee to End the Occupation of the West Bank and Gaza
## (JWCEO)
### [from a November 1991 statement]

We, Jewish women of diverse backgrounds, formed JWCEO in April, 1988.

Some of us are American born, some survivors of the Holocaust, some children of survivors, and some of us are Israeli. We are all deeply connected to Israel.

We stand vigil in solidarity with Israeli women's peace groups such as Women in Black, SHANI (Israeli Women's Alliance to End the Occupation), and Women's Organization for Women Political Prisoners. Together with them we recognize that the struggle for social, political and economic equality for women and for Israeli-Palestinian peace are inextricably linked.

We support the efforts of the Israeli women's peace movement to dialogue and work with Palestinian women. We believe that only through continued dialogue and interaction can Israelis and Palestinians begin to build the structures to live in peace and begin to bridge the violent divisions created by war and military occupation.

Since the start of the Intifada (Palestinian uprising), the Israeli peace movement has been vigorously pursuing dialogue with Palestinians and the PLO. The Gulf War unsettled this ongoing peace work, yet our Israeli sisters continued to stand vigil during the crisis despite constant harassment and threats from the right wing. Many Israeli activists are still determined to continue working toward a settlement with the Palestinians and ending the occupation.

This is the 24th year of the Israeli occupation of the West Bank and Gaza. The Intifada is now in its 4th year; its toll on both communities has been tremendous. With Israeli activists, we believe that it is in Israel's self-interest to end its conflict with the Palestinians.

We stand vigil in Jewish communities to encourage American Jews to work toward a resolution of the Israel-Palestinian conflict and to further the dialogue that has been opened within the Jewish community.

JWCEO works in solidarity with other local Jewish women's Peace Groups in such areas as: Tucson, Berkeley, Los Angeles, Palo Alto, San Francisco, Santa Cruz, Chicago, Boston, Ann Arbor, Minneapolis, Syracuse, Philadelphia, Montpelier, Seattle and Washington, D.C.

## Jewish Women's Consultation

Peace in the Middle East, a lasting and abiding peace that guarantees security for Israel, is the most fervent wish and passionate hope of every Jew. We believe that this vision can be realized. American Jewish women desire to participate in this search for peace between Israel, the Palestinians and the Arab States. We can add another voice, an additional source of insight and energy to this extremely complex struggle.

The time is right. There have been changes in the international scene, new moves from the Palestinian leadership, an increased desire on the part of Israelis to change the status quo, and growing numbers of groups that have set aside layers and generations of hostility to come together in dialogue. An historic opportunity exists to resolve the Israeli-Palestinian conflict in a way that reconciles Israel's security needs with Palestinian aspirations. The peace process can move forward, but it needs encouragement from all parties who have a relationship to the region, including the American Jewish community and the United States government.

We wish to contribute to this climate of peace initiatives. Our agenda is multi-leveled:

A. To forge a discussion within Jewish women's organizations about the history and politics of the region and about the options facing Israelis and Palestinians.
B. To explore ways that we as Jewish women can be of most help to Israel in moving the peace process forward.
C. To engage in dialogue and activities involving American Jews of divergent political opinions, as well as American Jewish and Palestinian women.

## Mishkan Shalom
## [From the Mishkan Shalom Statement of Principles]

Mishkan Shalom is an activist, spiritual community of Jews committed to the integration of the three primary areas of Jewish life: "Avodah" (Prayer), "Torah" (Study), and "G'milut Hasadim/Tikkun Olam" (Acts of Caring and Repair of the World). Through prayer we seek to infuse our lives with the Divine Presence and with "K'dushah" (holiness). Through study we seek to enhance our understanding of our tradition and the ways in which its teachings and insights may inspire our ethical and spiritual growth. Through acts of caring and repair we seek to transform our world so that it reflects the divine values of justice and compassion.

Israel: Zion Shall be redeemed in justice (Isaiah 1:27). The state of Israel is filled with symbols and hopes for Jews everywhere: it is a link with the covenantal relationship between God and the people, a vibrant center of Jewish culture, and a haven from persecution for Jews from many countries. We are dedicated to the survival of Israel as an independent Jewish state in which Jews can live in dignity, continue and revive their traditions, and shape their own future. Our need to see a secure Israel, however, must not blind us to the suffering of the Palestinians, who also have ties to the land. The perpetuation of this suffering violates the Jewish commitments to Justice and compassion. Jews and Palestinians must recognize and support one another's rights to national self-determination in the land they share and revere. Without this, there can be no peace and no security for either people. We therefore support those groups and individuals within Israel who are working for a just end to the conflict and a long-term solution based upon mutual recognition.

This Statement of Principles articulates the fundamental beliefs that motivate and govern our existence as a synagogue. While it is written as an enduring vision an ongoing commentary by congregants will, we hope, ensure that it continues to reflect and guide the values of a vital Jewish community.

## New Israel Fund

The New Israel Fund is a joint effort by Israelis, North Americans and Europeans to strengthen democracy in Israel. Since its founding in 1979, it has provided funding and technical assistance to over 170 Israeli non-profit organizations working to protect human rights, to improve the status of women, to bridge social gaps, to further Jewish-Arab coexistence, and to foster pluralism and tolerance.

In addition to innovative grantmaking, the Fund established and operates three programs of its own: SHATIL, which provides technical assistance and organizational consultation to Israel's nonprofit sector; the Leadership Fellows Program, which seeks to identify and cultivate Israel's leaders of tomorrow; and the Israel—U.S. Civil Liberties Law Program, which has created a civil liberties/public interest bar in Israel. It also provides an extensive program of public education in North America.

In its first full year of operation (1980), 80 donors contributed a total of $80,000. A decade later, NIF had 10,000 supporters and revenues of $6.4 million.

## New Jewish Agenda

New Jewish Agenda is a national organization committed to Jewish peoplehood and to promoting the traditional Jewish values of peace and social justice.

Agenda is dedicated to fostering a progressive voice within the Jewish community, and a progressive Jewish voice within society at large.

Since its founding in 1980, Agenda has grown to forty chapters offering independent political thought and advocacy throughout the United States. Thousands of Jews, many of whom felt unrepresented by other organizations, have found a home in Agenda and are helping to build supportive, vital, progressive Jewish communities.

Five areas are of special importance to Agenda:

- Israeli and Palestinian Peace
- Worldwide Nuclear Disarmament
- Economic and Social Justice
- Peace in Central America
- Jewish Feminism

Agenda is a leading Jewish American voice of critical support for the State of Israel. Out of its strong commitment to Israel's survival and well-being, Agenda joins with hundreds of thousands of Israelis who oppose their government's occupation of the West Bank and Gaza. Agenda is a vital U.S. link with the Israeli peace movement.

Because of the Jewish experience in the Holocaust, Agenda believes Jews have a unique role to play in the movement to end the threat of nuclear annihilation. Agenda is a leading voice opposing the arms race and advocating shifts in the U.S. budget to meet human, rather than military, needs. Similar concerns, plus the long Jewish tradition of working for social good, motivate Agenda to work strenuously for economic and social justice.

Agenda has a vigorous program to help promote peace in Central America—another flashpoint, with the Middle East, for international conflict. Because Jews, as a people, know the importance of sanctuary, Agenda has worked hard to promote Jewish involvement in the sanctuary movement for Central American refugees.

Agenda wants to help empower Jewish women and to help enable them to play a prominent public role in the Jewish community. Agenda seeks to broaden the conventional definition of the Jewish family to include lesbians, gay men and others who are often excluded from Jewish life.

## Passover Peace Coalition
## Rally for Peace
## Sunday April 24th [1988]

Abba Eban

"American Jews should reaffirm their right to be heard and should boldly reject the attempt . . . to convert them into 'Jews of silence'". We are a major voice in the Jewish community.

Join us in supporting:

— A secure Israel and the forces for peace in Israel
— A mutual end to violence and a renouncement of terror
— Negotiations—based on mutual recognition*—for peace, security and an end to the occupation
— Active U.S. involvement toward peace

* The 1989 Passover Peace Coalition updated this plank to read as follows: Negotiations between the Israeli Government and the chosen representatives of the Palestinians—today undoubtedly the PLO—based on the principles of mutual recognition and self-determination for peace, security and an end to the occupation.

Sponsored by: American Friends of Peace Now, Americans for Progressive Israel (API), American-Israeli Civil Liberties Coalition (A-ICLC), America-Israel Council for Israeli-Palestinian Peace (AICIPP-NY), American Support for the Advancement of Civil Liberties in Israel (AACLI Inc.), Committee of Artists and Writers for Israeli-Palestinian Peace, Dialogue–Israeli Students for Peace, Friends of Labor Israel, Friends of New Outlook, Garin Gal Chadash, The Generation After, Holocaust Survivors Association USA, International Center for Peace in the Middle East (ICPME), International Jewish Peace Union (IJPU), Israeli Friends of Peace Now in America, Jewish Peace Fellowship (JPF), Labor Zionist Alliance (LZA), New Jewish Agenda (NJA), Progressive Zionist Caucus (PZC), and Others.

## Progressive Zionist Caucus

— Advocating responsible political and social reform.
— United by a common commitment to the state of Israel, its future, and the nature of its society.
— Working as a community toward a progressive political agenda.

PZC believes that realizing our goals of peace and social justice demands personal involvement. We encourage each of our members to consider aliyah as a means to that involvement.

Education is the essence of Judaism, and through education and activism we are working to restore visions, dreams, energy to the Zionist Movement.

In our commitment to a positive and responsible Zionism, the following are issues of concern:

- Strengthening the connection of North American youth to Israel through exposure to aliyah.
- An end to the occupation of the West Bank and Gaza Strip based on a political solution reflecting the principles of mutual recognition, security and peace for both Jews and Palestinians.
- The preservation of the Jewish and democratic nature of Israel.
- Civil rights and social/economic justice for all Israelis regardless of race, sex, religion, sexual orientation, or age.
- Respect for, and legal recognition of, the various types of Jewish religious expression in Israel.
- Peaceful coexistence between Jewish and Arab Israelis by combatting stereotypes which present obstacles to communication between Arabs and Jews in Israel.

- Commitment to the humane integration of immigrants to Israel, emphasizing cultural respect and democratic education for all.
- Support of lesbian and gay issues.

The Progressive Zionist Caucus is a network of Zionist activists on North American college campuses supported by Hashomer Hatzair, Habonim Dror, The United Kibbutz Movement, and is a constituent group of the North American Jewish Students Appeal.

## Project Nishma
### "Let Us Listen"

Project Nishma is an independent educational project on Israeli security in the context of the peace process.

Over 100 nationally recognized Jewish leaders from across the country sponsor the project.

Project Nishma

- arranges briefings for Jewish leaders by senior Israeli defense analysts
- publishes and distributes articles on defense related topics
- analyses American Jewish opinion, and articulates a security-focused, pragmatic position on the peace process.

In the peace process, Israel's security needs must come before all else. Project Nishma supports the view of most senior Israeli defense experts that, as long as a threat remains, Israel must retain the crucial military advantages of strategic depth and demilitarization in the West Bank and Gaza, but this does not require Israeli political sovereignty over all of this area. Further, it would serve Israel's security interest to rid itself of the burden of ruling over 1.7 million Palestinians against their will, provided that extensive, Israeli enforced security arrangements and substantial transition periods are part of any negotiated agreement.

## Radical Zionist Alliance

1. The unity of the Jewish people in the world over and the indispensable role of the State of Israel in the future development of the Jewish people.
2. As the ingathering of the Jewish people in its historic homeland, Eretz Israel, through aliya is the solution to the contradiction of a diaspora existence and the beginning of a constructive process of building a Jewish socialist egalitarian society based on the prophetic vision of justice

and peace, aliya is the imperative for all Zionists.

3. The improvement and intensification of all facets of Jewish and Hebrew education in the diaspora in order to bring about a heightening of Jewish cultural, social and political awareness.

4. The defense of civil rights and human dignity of the Jewish people wherever they may be.

5. National self-determination is the most fundamental principle underlying Zionism. It follows that Zionists must recognize these very same rights for all peoples of the world, including the right of national self-determination.

6. We view the above principles not as an impersonal general political dictum, but as a basis for self-realization.

We believe that no just and lasting solution to the Arab-Israel conflict can occur without the mutual recognition of the right to self-determination of the Jewish people and the Palestinian-Arab people.

We call for the cooperation and solidarity of all people who subscribe to the same principles for both themselves and for others.

## The Road to Peace
Co-Existence Between Israelis and Palestinians
Sponsored by:
*Al-Fajr:* Jerusalem Palestinian Daily
*New Outlook:* Israel Monthly and
Friends of Peace Now & American Council for Palestine Affairs
Eight Points Agreed On by Conference Initiators:
*Al-Fajr* and *New Outlook*

1. That a just and permanent peace should be established in the Middle East, where all peoples of the region, including Palestinians and Israelis, will enjoy equal rights and opportunities.

2. That the reaching of a settlement is contingent on putting an end to the occupation of the 1967 war.

3. That the settlement of the Israeli-Palestinian conflict should be based on mutual recognition of equal national rights to self-determination and on peaceful coexistence.

4. That a comprehensive settlement should include a solution to the problem of Palestinian refugees in all its aspects.

5. That all peoples of the region are entitled to live in their own States within secure and recognized borders free from threats and violence.

6. That all differences should be resolved through negotiations between

legitimate representatives of all parties, the PLO for the Palestinians, and the Government of Israel for the Israelis, with the aims of reaching a permanent solution.

7. That in order for the peace process to be advanced, a moratorium on all acts of terrorism should be declared. The called for moratorium also requires refraining from establishing new facts by the occupying authorities with the intention of making a negotiated settlement impossible or more difficult.

8. That negotiations among all parties should be concluded under the auspices of an International Peace Conference.


## Socialist Zionist Union
## (1976)

The Socialist Zionist Union is a nation-wide membership organization established in New York after a recent week-end conference. Among its members are activists in Zionist youth movements, including Habonim and Hashomer Hatzair, and in local groups such as the Radical Jewish Union in Berkeley.

The SZU stands for democratization of the American Jewish community, aliya (immigration to Israel), and socialism.

The SZU position on the Middle East is that the Israelis and Palestinian Arabs each constitutes a nation with a right to self-determination. The conflicting legitimate claims of each nation to the same homeland can be solved, the SZU holds, by the Palestinians' having a state of their own alongside Israel.


## US/Israel Women to Women

At the dawn of political Zionism, Theodore Herzl made an historic pronouncement: a declaration of equality for the daughters of Israel. On the strength of Herzl's promise, women pioneers came to Palestine, bringing with them expectations of equality. They did not find it. From that day to this, Israel women have been struggling to achieve it. US/Israeli Women to Women is part of that continuing history.

US/Israel Women to Women was born in response to news of a battered women's shelter in Israel about to close for lack of $200 for the rent. Its program was enlarged to include a wider purpose: support of women's struggle for justice and equality in the land of Israel.

US/Israel Women to Women is a volunteer organization dedicated to raising money for women's projects in Israel that need help in getting started, or, sometimes, in just staying alive. These projects include rape crisis centers, battered women's shelters, women's studies courses and public lectures, a women's health hotline, leadership development programs, feminist publications, antidiscrimination lawsuits, and other activities whose purpose is to enhance the quality of life for Israeli women by working to achieve their full and equal participation in every aspect of Israeli society.

# Organizational Glossary

**The Abraham Fund**: Supports, educates about, and fund-raises on issues concerning coexistence and reconciliation between Jews and Arabs in Israel. It has published the *Directory of Institutions and Organizations Fostering Coexistence Between Jews and Arabs in Israel* in which nearly three hundred organizations have been identified.

**Amcha for Tsedakah**: Founded in 1990; a progressive foundation supporting Jewish organizations in the United States and in Israel that embrace pluralism and reject bigotry. It encourages donors to direct the distribution of their contributions and pledges to send 100 percent of the contributions to the beneficiaries designated.

**American Friends of RATZ**: Founded in 1988 as an American support group for the Israeli civil rights and peace party RATZ.

**American-Israel Public Affairs Committee**: The hegemonic pro-Israel lobby in Washington, D.C., supporting the Israeli government. Founded originally in 1954 as the American Zionist Council of Public Affairs, which changed its name to AIPAC in 1959.

**American-Israeli Civil Liberties Coalition**: Does civil and human rights work in Israel and the occupied territories.

**American Jewish Committee**: Nationally and with chapters in various cities, tends to work behind the scenes to influence policy and attitudes. Conducts dialogues with other ethnic groups and the Catholic Church; publishes research, and a magazine, *Commentary*.

**American Jewish Congress**: A professionally-run organization focusing primarily on church-state separation and Israel.

**American Zionist Council of Public Affairs**: A lobby group founded in 1954 to advocate on behalf of Israel; in 1959 changed its name to AIPAC.

**American Zionist Emergency Council**: First popular lobbying effort on behalf of the Zionist cause, founded in 1943.

**Americans for Peace Now**: A development of the friends of the Israeli Peace Now that began organizing in the United States in 1981. It is the only national, not-for-profit organization in the United States that works in partnership with Israel's Peace Now movement. APN does educational work and established the CIPS to help its advocacy efforts.

**Americans for a Progressive Israel**: Formed originally as the Progressive Zionist League in 1946, becoming API in the 1950s, it is a socialist Zionist movement working for peace and the kinship of all peoples. It is affiliated with the World Union of MAPAM, is associated with the Kibbutz Artzi Federation, and is working within the American Zionist movement. Publishes *Israel Horizons*.

**Americans for a Safe Israel**: An ultra-right-wing pro-Israel group formed in a split from Meir Kahane's JDL. Occasionally publishes pamphlets on progressive Jewish organizations such as Breira, NJA, and NIF.

**Amy Adina Schulman Memorial Fund**: Funds service/study in Israel, and activities in the United States to educate youth and adults in a variety of aspects of Israeli life. Works in other areas such as building a just and egalitarian society, working toward a nuclear-free world, enhancing understanding among peoples, and Zionist youth movement activities.

**Anti-Defamation League (of B'nai B'rith)**: A professionally-run organization monitoring and reporting on anti-Semitism with files on both left-wing and right-wing figures and activities.

**Avukah**: Progressive student Zionist group organized on American college campuses in the 1930s supporting a Jewish homeland in Palestine, democracy in the American Jewish community, and peace and social justice issues generally.

**B'nai B'rith**: A social service organization that sponsors the ADL and originally Hillel Foundations. B'nai B'rith Women, doing advocacy work on women's issues and social service, has declared itself a separate and independent organization.

**B'not Esh**: Begun in 1981, a yearly gathering of Jewish women begun to revision Judaism using the insights of feminist theology and their own experiences as Jewish feminists.

**Breira**: Founded in 1973 after the Yom Kippur War to support peace and social justice issues in Israel, democracy in the American Jewish community, and a more egalitarian Israel-American Diaspora relationship based on Jewish commitment and responsibility. The organization was smeared by the organized establishment, and closed by 1978.

*Bridges* **Magazine**: Founded by feminists working with NJA; provides a forum for Jewish feminists and their friends combining analysis based on traditional Jewish values of justice and repair of the world with insights honed by the feminist, lesbian, and gay movements.

**Center for Israeli Peace and Security**: Founded by APN in 1990 to coordinate its U.S. advocacy efforts in Washington, D.C.

**Coalition for Alternatives (now Advancement) in Jewish Education**: Publishes alternative Jewish educational materials and holds national and regional conferences.

**Conference of Presidents of Major Jewish Organizations (also known as Presidents' Conference)**: Includes most mainstream organizations including community relations, women's, Zionist, religious, and umbrella (such as CJF) groups. Focuses on the executive branch with respect to Israel issues and is taken as the authoritative voice of the Jewish community, representing 80 percent of Jewish organizational leadership.

**Council of Jewish Federations**: The umbrella and service group for the network of local federations; the main communal organizational structure of the North American Jewish community. Many federations own or control their local Anglo-Jewish press. The CJF organizes the annual General Assembly where Jewish professionals meet and exchange information.

**The Dialogue Project**: Initiated at the start of the Intifada in order to build a working relationship between mainstream women leaders from both the American Jewish and American Arab communities. The women engage in dialogue, present joint speaking programs, and hold regional conferences.

**Education Fund for Israeli Civil Rights and Peace**: Founded in 1990 as a nonprofit organization working to educate Americans on topics of civil rights and peace in Israel. It is allied with the Israeli political party RATZ/MERETZ.

**Emergency Jewish Peace Coalition**: Organized actions such as the public mourning and fast day during the Gulf War; cosponsored by the Shalom Center, *Tikkun*, NJA, JPL, and JPF.

**Friends of Labor Israel**: An American-based fund-raising and support group for the Israeli Labor Party, advocating on its behalf in the Jewish community and in Washington, D.C.

**Friends of *New Outlook***: American support for the Israeli progressive magazine.

**Friends of Yesh Gvul**: A group of Israelis and Americans—Jews and non-Jews—who work for peace in the Middle East by educating about and supporting jailed Israeli soldiers and officers (and their families) who refuse to serve in the occupied territories.

**Habonim-Dror**: Labor Zionist youth movement affiliated with the Israeli Labor Party.

**Hashomer Hatzair**: Socialist Zionist youth movement affiliated with Israel's MAPAM Party.

**Havurah**: Movement to create small, intimate congregations without hired functionaries; they are egalitarian fellowships seeking Jewish renewal.

**Hillel**: Staff-run national organization for Jewish students; originally under the auspices of B'nai B'rith.

**Human Rights Rapid Response Network (for Palestinian and Israeli Political Prisoners)**: Organized by IJPU-NY, NJA-Manhattan, and JWCEO in coordination with Palestinian and Israeli human rights organizations. Sends telexes in the names of its subscribers on behalf of political prisoners, and is particularly sensitive to the cases of Palestinian women prisoners.

**International Center for Peace in the Middle East**: Working for peace and human rights in the Middle East. ICPME recently closed its New York office, but retains an office in Tel Aviv.

**International Jewish Peace Union**: A Jewish organization founded in Paris in 1982 to work for a peaceful resolution to the Palestinian-Israeli conflict. Active in North America, it also has affiliations in Western Europe.

**JAC-PAC**: Joint Action Committee for Political Affairs, an all-women pro-Israel Political Action Committee. One of the wealthiest of the approximately seventy-five pro-Israel PACs. Also considers candidates' positions on women's issues such as abortion rights.

**Jewish Agency**: Deals with fund-raising, leadership training, and support for emigration and resettlement (including building new settlements for immigrants within the Green Line) to Israel for Jews from around the world.

**Jewish Committee for Israel-Palestine Peace**: Founded in the early 1980s; a Washington, D.C., area Jewish peace group working with both Jewish and Arab communities locally to further discussion of a two-state solution to the Israeli-Palestinian conflict. It is affiliated with IJPU and publishes the *Israeli-Palestinian Digest*.

**Jewish Defense League**: Begun by Rabbi Meir Kahane; supports armed resistance to anti-Semitism.

**Jewish National Fund**: Raises money through regional councils to plant and maintain trees and forests in Israel. Money is supposed to be used only within the Green Line.

**Jewish Peace Conference**: Coordinated in 1989 in New York City; a coalition of Zionist, non-Zionist, and not expressly Zionist groups active on issues of Israeli and Middle East peace. It dissolved in 1991 during the Gulf War.

**Jewish Peace Fellowship**: Founded in 1941, JPF unites those who believe that Jewish ideals and experience provide inspiration for nonviolent commitment to life. Drawing upon the traditional roots of Judaism and upon its meaning in the world today, the Fellowship maintains an active program of draft and peace education and aids and supports those who, in a spirit of nonviolence, address themselves to the remaking of our society.

**Jewish Peace Lobby**: Established in May 1989 to promote constructive U.S. foreign policy vis-à-vis the Israeli-Palestinian conflict. JPL acts as a voice on Capitol Hill for American Jews who support both Israel's right to peace and security and the Palestinian right to self-determination. Although it supports the work of the Israeli peace movement, it has no formal ties to any Israeli organization.

**Jewish Peace Network**: Founded in 1991 during the Gulf War as a coalition of Jewish groups working on issues of Middle East Peace. Constituent groups were IJPU, NJA, JWCEO, JPF, and Road to Peace.

**Jewish Students' Network**: Originally an umbrella group for various student organizations; formed to promote dialogue and action. Although there still exists a group with this name, the original group was taken over by the WZO and right-wing students in 1977, ending the period of its original mandate.

**Jewish Students' Press Service**: A national press clearinghouse and programming organization.

**Jewish Welfare Board**: Services Jewish community centers.

**Jewish Women's Committee to End the Occupation of the West Bank and the Gaza Strip**: Founded in New York in April 1988 in solidarity with Israeli Women in Black and other Israeli and Palestinian women's groups working for peace in the Middle East. It worked to promote dialogue within the American Jewish community, held regular monthly vigils, organized educational programs, and published *The Jewish Women's Peace Bulletin*, and *Jewish Women's Call for Peace: a Handbook for Jewish Women on the Israeli/Palestinian Conflict*. (The collective disbanded in the fall of 1992, though the vigils continued and materials are being archived in the Swarthmore College Peace Collection.)

**Jewish Women's Consultation**: A venue for Jewish women to engage in dialogue and activities toward moving the peace process in Israel forward. It distributes educational packets, sponsors the Dialogue conference between American Jewish and Palestinian women, and sent a delegation to the Occupied Territories in 1993.

**Jews Against the War**: A New York–based coalition of Jewish groups and individuals who came together in opposition to the Gulf War.

**Labor Zionist Alliance**: The North American branch of the World Labor Zionist Movement affiliated with Israel's Labor party. Supports its youth group, Habonim-Dror, and publishes *The Jewish Frontier*.

*Lilith*: A Jewish women's/feminist magazine.

**Mishkan Shalom**: A progressive Reconstructionist congregation in Havertown, PA, that integrates a creative approach to Jewish spiritual life with a commitment to social activism.

**National Council of Jewish Women**: Does educational and social service projects within the Jewish community and more broadly on domestic issues such as prochoice, day care, hunger, and needs of the elderly. Supports the Jewish Women's Resource Center in New York.

**National Jewish Community Relations Advisory Council**: Composed of over one hundred local community relations councils and eleven national community relations organizations. Works on issues between the Jewish and other communities and puts out recommendations for consensus positions on various domestic and foreign issues.

**New Israel Fund**: A joint effort by Jews in North America, Europe, and Israel to strengthen democracy in Israel through fund-raising and technical assistance to projects working toward civil and human rights, the bettered status of women and gays and lesbians, bridging the social and economic gaps, furthering Arab-Jewish coexistence, and fostering tolerance and religious pluralism.

**New Jewish Agenda**: A multiissue American Jewish organization with a progressive agenda; it was begun in 1980 out of the ashes of Breira.

**North American Jewish Students' Appeal**: A fund-raising source for Jewish campus projects that are student run, and innovative, as well as for grassroots initiatives.

**Passover Peace Coalition**: The first coalition of Zionist, non-Zionist, and not expressly Zionist groups that came together in New York in 1988 to organize a peace rally and celebration, calling for an end to Israel's occupation of the West Bank and the Gaza Strip.

**Progressive Jewish Students Union**: The name of a progressive Jewish student group at the University of California at Santa Cruz. It is affiliated with PZC in its Israel-oriented work.

**Progressive Zionist Caucus**: Founded in 1981; a grassroots organization comprised of students in North America and Israel concerned with questions currently facing the Zionist movement.

**Project Nishma**: Working within the establishment of the American Jewish community, combines support for the peace process with a concern for Israel's security needs.

**Radical Zionist Alliance**: Founded in 1969 by North American college students as a vehicle for participation in progressive politics generally, and toward a progressive agenda within the Jewish community.

**Religious Action Center:** Connected to the Reform movement; educates and mobilizes the Jewish community on legislative and social justice concerns ranging from Israel and Soviet Jewry to economic justice, civil rights, international peace, and religious liberty.

*Response* **Magazine:** A contemporary Jewish review put together by students and committed to publishing new and student writers.

**Road to Peace:** Set up to organize the *New Outlook–Al-Fajr* conference, at Columbia University in New York, on coexistence between Israelis and Palestinians. Co-sponsored by Friends of Peace Now and the American Council for Palestine Affairs. Palestinians from the Occupied Territories, North America, and the PLO, as well as Israeli Knesset members from various Zionist parties and other Israeli political figures participated.

**Shalom Center:** An environmentalist Jewish educational and social action organization.

**Shefa Fund:** Founded in 1988; organizes North American Jews to use money, wealth, and resources to benefit the Jewish community and the wider society. Provides funding and technical support for organizations that work on various aspects of Jewish communal change, and social and economic justice; committed to a communitarian organizational model.

**Socialist Zionist Union:** Founded in 1976; a student organization calling for democratization of the American Jewish community, aliya (immigration to Israel), socialism, and supporting a Palestinian state alongside Israel as a solution to the Israeli-Palestinian conflict.

**Soviet Jewry Organizations:** The independent National Conference on Soviet Jewry, Union of Councils for Soviet Jews, and the Student Struggle for Soviet Jewry (now defunct, though local activities are supported by NAJSA); work toward human rights and emigration issues of Jews in the former Soviet Union.

**Tiferet:** A progressive Jewish student newspaper and organization at Oberlin College. PZC is organized separately on this campus.

*Tikkun* **Magazine:** an intellectual bimonthly journal providing Jewish critique of politics, culture and society. *Tikkun* is a Hebrew word meaning "to repair." The traditional Jewish concept *tikkun olam* ("the repair [mending] of the world") has come to have connotations of healing and transformation.

**Two Peoples Two States**: A dialogue and activist group on Israel-Palestine peace organized at Wesleyan College; affiliated with PZC.

**Tzedekh**: A progressive Jewish student group organized at U.C. Berkeley. PZC is organized independently on this campus and has closer ties to the Hillel.

**United Jewish Appeal**: The central fund-raising organization of the American Jewish community; coordinated by the Council of Jewish Federations.

**U.S./Israel Women to Women**: Founded in 1979 to help Israeli women achieve full equality in Israeli society. The group does educational projects on the women's struggle in Israel and funds projects toward equality in Israel.

**Washington-PAC**: A pro-Israel political action committee headed by Morris Amitay, previous head of AIPAC.

**World Jewish Congress**: Founded by Nahum Goldman; in recent years the American section has been active on anti-Semitism and Soviet Jewry.

**World Zionist Organization**: Mechanism to realize the goals of the Jewish Agency; responsible for educational programming.

**Yugentruf (Youth for Yiddish)**: A cultural, educational, and activist Yiddishist student group.

# Notes

## Introduction

1. The author was in attendance at the 1989 event described here. Special thanks go to Tom Smerling and Project Nishma for providing documents and details. In addition, Leonard Fein, one of the leaders who helped to draft the Letter of Forty-One, had organized a similar effort in 1980 that ended in a dispute among the signers, following a press conference. Despite the controversy, many consider this earlier letter one of the significant turning points in the pro-Israel politics that this book documents. The differences between the ways in which the two letters were handled has much to do with the lessons and developments of the interim decade.

2. Zionism is the liberation movement of the Jewish people through statehood. Traditionally it has been associated with the view that Jewish fulfillment is truly possible only through the communal life made possible in a politically independent Jewish homeland. Thus, although Zionism itself also is in transition, it remains connected, however loosely, to a commitment to live in this homeland.

3. Certain policy issues that accompanied this definition were: increased U.S. aid to Israel, nonrecognition of the PLO, antiterritorial compromise, anti-Palestinianism and anti-Arabism, noncriticism of Israeli foreign affairs.

4. The terms "hegemony" and "counterhegemony" come from Gramsci (1971), who suggests that a society's dominant economic and organizational structure exists within a related ideological framework. Change occurs through the development and rise of counter ideas reflecting the experience and aspirations of nonruling classes.

In fairness to the organized community, much of its organizational structure has been devoted to bridging gaps and to finding a way for the many to speak with one voice in a nonsilencing way. Organizations that receive a lot of criticism as constituting an oppressive hegemony within the American Jewish community, such as the President's Conference and NJCRAC, are actually boards, or coalitions, that can only take stands on issues about which the many organizations represented agree. In this way, these organizations do speak for a wide array of their constituents. However, the fact that they speak for the leadership of 80 percent of the organized community gets confused with the idea that they speak for the entire community. The leaders of these organizations are not democratically elected by their memberships, and most of the community at large does not even hold membership in the constituent organizations of these coalitions.

5. For example, see Findley (1985). Many Jewish activists also have commented on their experience of the intolerance of dissent from the mainstream communal line. See for example I. F. Stone's "Confessions of a Jewish Dissident," in his *Underground to Palestine and Reflections Thirty Years Later*, and Adrienne Rich's "If Not With Others, How?" in *Blood, Bread and Poetry*.

6. Although the American Jewish community will long be dealing with identity issues and inclusion, the 1980s emerged as the decade of Middle East peace work, just as the 1970s have become known for feminist activism and the 1990s for issues of gay and lesbian inclusion within the community.

7. With a feminist/multiculturalist orientation and a background in dialectical methodology, I undertook a study of the groups involved in the changing pro-Israel identity of the American Jewish community. Using a research design partly developed with the participation of activists themselves (to ensure that the work would be relevant to the concerns of real people), I conducted in-depth interviews with leadership of over twenty organizations, more formal detailed interviews with a range of staff/leadership/rank-and-file members of four others, four group interviews, and less formal interviews with key players of close to thirty other organizations. These interviews were conducted in key cities across the United States (New York, Chicago, Washington, D.C., Los Angeles, San Francisco) and in Israel. Formal reflections on my methodology, as praxis, were presented as a paper to the Midwest Women's Studies Conference (1993).

8. For example: *New York Times*, 17 November 1989, and 9 December 1989; *Los Angeles Times*, 29 November 1989; *Northern California Jewish Bulletin*, 24 November 1989; *Jerusalem Post*, 25 November 1989.

9. The polls of Jewish leaders who share these views support the claim that "by any definition of Israel commitment, this is a group deeply and broadly committed to Israel" (S. M. Cohen, 1989a, 25). Surveys of leaders and the rank and file of more progressive Israel-oriented Jewish groups conducted in the research for this work (as far as I know, the only surveys of this kind) demonstrate the same level of commitment. It is thus inaccurate to paint a picture of these activists as outsiders, unknowledgeable, or self-haters.

10. See Annual Report, Conference of Presidents of Major Jewish Organizations 1977, cited in Tivnan (1987, 119).

11. Although I am much indebted to postmodernism for its discussion of identity in terms of multiplicity, power and interpretation, this books is not a postmodernist text. Given that identity exists as part of oppressive discourses of power, postmodernists suggest liberation through the negation of identity discourse itself. (See, for example, Butler 1990.) I, on the other hand, am situating

myself in an emerging democratic tradition that looks to liberation precisely through concrete engagement with identity in its multiplicity and contradiction.

12. For a theoretical rendering of much of the more activist multicultural literature on this point, see Fraser's (1991) discussion of multiple publics. In this work I take the Jewish community in the United States as an example of a polity and the hegemony/counterhegemony dynamic of its changing pro-Israel identity is an aspect of its political process. Furthermore, the notion of a polity is understood dialectically: At the same time that the Jewish community is understood as a whole unto itself, it is also a polity related to and/or part of other polities, such as the broader polity of which it is but a part in the United States generally. Finally, in my discussion of the American Jewish community, I do not pretend to be addressing the identity questions of each Jew, but rather of shifting group identities and processes.

13. I will at times distinguish between dovish groups that would refer to themselves as pro-Israel and some that might self-identify as Middle East peace groups. Overall, however, I consider all these groups to have contributed to the changing pro-Israel identity politics within the Jewish community in the United States, and I thus often refer to them more simply as new pro-Israel groups.

14. The term "pluralism" has many meanings in common speech. When used in this work, pluralism names a particular type of democratic theory. I use terms such as "diversity" and "multicultural" to distinguish aspects of contemporary multiculturalist theory from more traditional pluralist theory. For a broader discussion of the development from melting pot theory, through pluralism, to multiculturalism in the American political imagination, see my introduction to *The Narrow Bridge: Jewish Perspectives on Multiculturalism.*

15. Contrary to popular usage of the term "liberal" in the United States, "Liberal" as used here will refer to a specific philosophic tradition, dating back to the writings of Thomas Hobbes and John Locke, to be explicated within the course of the work. As Jane Mansbridge reminds me, certain concepts I name here will surely be found in other ideologies as well. I focus on the ways these concepts converge in Liberalism, however, because of the dominant role Liberalism has played in the political life of the United States.

16. When gendered language is used, it should be read literally. The use of terms such as "man" and "men" is not intended to be universal. They are employed here either when they are used in the original, or because I am elaborating a theory that has only men in mind.

17. Hobbes was very clever adding this additional feature of human nature. The same essentialist position that gets man into a state of war, because its root is human nature itself, will now get man out of this dystopic state.

18. See Merchant (1980).

19. See Marx (1969).

20. See Macpherson (1962).

21. Hobbes does lament the lack of industry and arts in the state of nature that

could be interpreted as his concern for quality of life issues. It seems to me, however, that everyday life in the kind of society Hobbes sets up, where citizens fearfully obey the awesome sovereign, and setting the stage for the cutthroat relations of free market capitalism, remains just as nasty as his dreaded state of nature.

22. These Hobbesian ideas were imported to the New World by political strategists and framers of the United States Constitution such as James Madison and John Adams. When Bentley wrote *The Process of Government* (1908), Madisonian democracy formed the dominant theoretical paradigm for political process in the United States. David Truman (1951) picked up where Bentley left off, more recent group-based democratic theorists such as Robert Dahl (1961) perpetuated the framework, and collective action thinkers such as Olson (1971) write directly out of this tradition. Thus, Balbus has written that for those attending to the role of groups in democratic theory, "Pluralism both as normative doctrine and as behavioral analysis has often been correctly diagnosed as a modern version of Classical Liberalism which substitutes the groups of contemporary industrial orders for the atomized individual of early Capitalism as its basic unit of social interaction yet otherwise conforms in fundamental respects to the Liberal model of political behavior" (1971, 154).

23. See Zeigler and Peak (1972, 36–43).

24. The emerging multiculturalist democratic idea is a group-based conception of politics and therefore has specific intellectual roots within the discipline of political science. The role of nongovernmental and non-class-based groups in the United States has increased tremendously throughout this nation's history (Berry 1984). Such a development spurred a new avenue of research in the academy (Easton 1953; Zeigler and Peak 1972; and Garson 1978). In 1908 A. F. Bentley wrote that the study of formal institutions of government would teach us very little about the "process of government." Moving away from individualism, and rejecting the class-based political analysis that he admired from Marx but that he felt was an overly crude understanding of groups (Manley 1983), Bentley argued that we must study these other types of nongovernmental groups if we want to shed light on the real political process in the United States. Despite my critique, Bentley's work opened the way toward acknowledging an important mode of group-based political participation and interaction, broadening the scope of the political analysis of his day and forming the basis for the later torrent of research on political groups.

25. My intent in developing an alternative theoretical approach to the study of groups is not to be blind to behavior that falls into a Liberal paradigm. I seek to develop an approach that enables analysis of groups beyond such a framework. Thus, the alternative approach enables me to identify examples of Hobbesian behavior, such as distorted individuation, the perception of needs in terms of narrow self-interest, and competitiveness, while also considering a broader range of group characteristics. Considering evidence of both Liberal and non-Liberal aspects of group experience will not only help the results of this study to be more reflective of the actual world of political groups, but will also contribute to a more transformative theory.

26. Man's natural condition of negative freedom is carried over from the state of nature into civil society, and the chaos remains, only now in miniature version. (As is said often in Liberal theory, each self is a personal sphere of anarchy.)

27. Here, as elsewhere in Rousseau's writings, readers will find some apparently contradictory ideas. Some commentators point to *The Social Contract*, Book IV chapter 2, and more pointedly to *The Government of Poland*, to show that Rousseau does not deserve credit for this notion of a dialectical self. See, for example, Herzog (1986, 486). Berman (1970) treats the confusions within Rousseau's thought in a manner most relevant to this work. Given the ambiguity, I am one who will continue to credit the interpretation of Rousseau as also elaborating a theory of the self as changing and connected.

28. See *The Social Contract*, Book I chapter 8.

29. See Ollman (1993).

30. See Hinckley (1978) for comments.

31. For a summary of the feminist literature here, see Ackelsberg (1991, 164–66).

32. I am inclined to answer in the affirmative the query whether Jewishly grounded multiculturalist theory would also be considered a form of Jewish political philosophy, though I am aware that others remain skeptical. My numerous conversations on the topic lead me to conclude that as post-Emancipation Jewish political thinkers we do not yet fully understand our dual roles as *Jewish* theorists and Jewish *theorists*. I would particularly like to thank Michael Walzer for discussing with me his interest in questioning Jewish political philosophy.

33. Two appendices, presenting 1) representative group mission statements and 2) an organizational glossary of the nearly one hundred organizations involved, serve as documentary resources as well as a guide for readers.

## 1. Unity

1. Sections of this and the following chapter appear in *Commonwealth* (1994–1995). A condensed version of this chapter was presented at the Northeast International Studies Association Conference in Providence, RI, November 12–14, 1992.

2. Bentley wrote that although groups are "knitted together in a system," they are seen as individual only when they are "abstracted out" from the system (1908, 218). In keeping with their Liberal legacy, many group scholars can only see individuality as the abstraction from relation (Wilson 1973, 263; Becker 1983, 372; Browne 1990, 499).

3. See, for example, Dahl (1961); Browne (1990); Hertzke (1988, 56).

4. See, for example, Truman (1951); Dahl (1961); Uslaner (1986).

5. See Herzog's critique on this point (1986, 480), and Gauthier (1987), as examples of contemporary Liberals engaged in such a project. Gutmann (1985) and Kymlicka (1989) in particular represent newer Liberal thinking on the nature of the self, which is emerging from the Liberal-Communitarian debate.

6. As cited in Benhabib (1987, 84). See DiStefano's discussion (1991).

7. Like the vision of the independent adult male, the concept of an indepen-

dent group rests on its well-defined distinctiveness (Bentley 1908, 209). G. K. Wilson defines an autonomous group as "clearly demarcated," and as "having an exclusively served clientele or membership," and "undisputed jurisdiction over a function or service" (1981, 263). In the common understanding, a group must answer to its own boards, and must make its own decisions. The boundaries of demarcation that denote its autonomy are found in the sources of and power over its budget, and the extent to which it need not rely on the aid of other groups. In the form of the rugged individual on the American frontier, a group is more autonomous or independent the more self-reliant and separated from others it is.

8. See, for example, Salisbury (1969, 3–4); Olson (1971, 15); Cigler and Loomis (1983, 8).

9. A prime example is found in Olson (1971, 8); see also Truman (1951, 156). Here Olson acknowledges that groups will be divided into subgroups. However, he says,

> Any organization or group will of course usually be divided into subgroups or factions that are opposed to one another. . . . The approach used here does not neglect the conflict within groups and organizations, then, because it considers each organization as a unit only to the extent that it does in fact attempt to serve a common interest, and considers the various subgroups as the relevant units with common interests to analyze the factional strife.

10. For example, see Wilson (1973, 119–142); Hertzke (1988, 137); Herring (1990). An exception may be found, for example, in the treatment of women's interests in Costain and Costain (1983). See also Balbus (1971, 155–156).

11. As Hinchman has written, the individual in Liberal philosophy is nearly always "abstracted from context and equipped with certain *de facto* desires, interests and needs" (1990, 759).

12. In their treatment of the American Jewish community, Zeigler and Peak (1972, 271–274) focus on the differences between some of the well-known mainstream organizations. This much attention to the difference in the Jewish perception of its community's interests is rare, although it was written in 1972 and does not address the pro-Israel issues. However, even under these circumstances, the authors' emphasis is that this difference signifies disunity and lack of cohesion and promotes ineffectiveness. The Congressional Quarterly publication *The Washington Lobby* (1987) is one of the few sources to identify change and diversity within the Jewish and pro-Israel lobbies without such judgment (see especially pp. 80–84.)

13. This perspective is an example of Walter Benjamin's conception of memory and its use in a communal historical dialectic. It is used here in keeping with Fred Dallmayr's (1992) suggestion that Benjamin's "memory" can be a redemptive tool.

14. The Talmud is an authoritative biblical commentary containing the Mishna (compiled in the first five centuries A.C.E.) and the Gemara.

15. This post-emancipation debate focused on three main paths toward the so-

lution of the Jewish problem. Bundists formed Jewish socialist political parties within a dominant diaspora political arena, such as in Poland in the early 1900s. Some Jews, such as those associated with Simon Dubnow and his Folkspartei, saw Jews as an extraterritorial spiritual nation and worked for the creation of a network of autonomous Jewish communities around the world federated together in a general Jewish council. Zionists sought to create an autonomous Jewish center, which ultimately became the state of Israel.

16. See Waskow (1983).

17. Other minority and working-class women have similar experiences. For example, Chicana American Cherríe Moraga writes that "the concept of betraying one's race through sex and sexual politics is as common as corn" (1983). Caribbean American June Jordan writes in a chapter entitled "Wrong or White" (1994, 145): "The sexist double standard that would have us accept that we should not wail aloud and storm the streets on behalf of our own safety, our own womanly, our own female self-determination, well, to hell with that, from Montreal to Rumania, to hell with that. I am not 'a divisive issue.' " African American bell hooks told an audience of one thousand at the High School of the Fashion Industries in New York City on June 21, 1994, that the question of her dual loyalty to sex and race remains the question she is most commonly asked (her comments came as part of a Breaking Bread dialogue with Cornel West as the kickoff event for a new multicultural coalition originally organized by the African-American section of Democratic Socialists of America). This is the fundamental problem of assuming narrow and monolithic American subcommunal identities.

18. Klutznick reminds us of a number of other "small rebellions" that changed the face of the American Jewish community over the years. Around 1825, with only six thousand Jews here, the Ashkenazis (Western Jews) broke away from the Sephardic-dominated organizations. (Eastern Jews, many who came to the European world through Spain, are referred to as Sephardi. Today, other Eastern Jews are referred to as Mizrachi, if they come from the Middle East and North Africa.) By 1917, the creation of the first American Jewish Congress (a different body than the present AJCongress) "represented a successful revolt of the Eastern European wing of American Jewry from the dominant leadership of the . . . German wing" (1961, 30–32).

19. This is similar to Buber's discussion in *Between Man and Man* concerning the need for a politics with the courage to stand its test which is inherently bound with the responsibility of the person/community to explore and dissent (1947, 82).

20. See also Waxman (1993) for an example of other applications of such a Plaskow-type/non-Millian conception.

21. For Hobbes, such a situation is an anarchy to be feared and avoided at all costs. Hobbes cannot allow for the possibility of change/revolution because any such change carries within it the danger of violent chaos. Locke's thesis differs slightly from Hobbes's as it is based upon the notion that the people (or at least the wealthy men) have the right to change their government. However, a strong

argument can be made that such a Lockean premise is but a gloss on a rougher Hobbesian base. There is no real evidence that Locke accepts changing the government after its initial constitution. A modern version of the Lockean vision is found in the primary documents of the United States. Although the Declaration of Independence asserted the people's right to overthrow tyranny and organize themselves anew, the Constitution gives express power to the new government to suppress any further revolt. In this brand of Liberal philosophy, change is dangerous, and the idea of fluid, changeable men suggests chaos.

22. See Keller's discussion of the difference between the separate self and the separative self (1986, 9). She prefers the term "separative" as it implies "an activity or intention rather than any fundamental state of being." It is the ego's "sense of itself as separate, as over and against the world, the Other, and even its own body [that] endows it with its identity. It is 'this' not 'that'."

23. See Berman (1970) and Taylor (1991) for discussion of this term.

24. See Waskow (1978).

25. I owe thanks to Brenda Gevertz for our many conversations concerning NAJSA, Jewish student politics in general, and the developments of the late 1960s and early 1970s in particular.

26. NAJSA's constituent organizations at the time of this writing are the Progressive Zionist Caucus, Jewish Student Press Service, *Response: A Contemporary Jewish Review*, Yugentruf (Youth for Yiddish), and it includes special projects for *batim* (communal Jewish homes) and activities concerned with Soviet Jewry.

27. In addition, while it was under the auspices of B'nai Brith, less than 2 percent of Hillel's billion-dollar-plus budget went to the campuses (Abramowitz 1992). B'nai Brith no longer sponsors the organization.

28. See for example, Heschel (1983), Kaye/Kantrowitz and Klepfisz (1986), Beck (1984), Balka and Rose (1989), and also Klepfisz (1990).

29. See, for example, Prell (1989) and Kaminetz (1994).

30. In 1990 the *A* was changed to stand for Advancement.

31. See Tivnan's discussion, for example (1987, 252).

32. Some notable, yet recent, exceptions are Tivnan (1987), Organski (1990), and Gross (1983). It may be said that the impetus for writing these books came about only in connection with and response to the changes discussed in this work. Chapters in larger works that begin to look at this issue may be found in Ellis (second edition with an additional section on the Palestinian Uprising, 1987), Pogrebin (1991), Klepfisz (1990), and in Boyarin's treatment of this issue outside the American context (1991 and 1992). In terms of philanthropy, see chapters on Jews and Israel in Goldin (1976) and Odendahl (1990). For the more political science–oriented literature see Hertzke (1988). In addition, a number of polls have been published that have been essential to the political battle, but have not received much additional scholarly attention (see the S.M. Cohen surveys for AJCommittee, the Israel-Diaspora Institute, and [with Lipset] the Wilstein Institute).

33. Examples abound; see Wilson (1981, 142); Greenwald (1977, 106–109); Uslaner (1986); Hertzke (1988, 39–40); Organski (1990).

34. This equation was originally stated by Bentley (1908, 211).

35. See Avineri (1981) and also Hertzberg (1959).

36. Much later in the 1940s, with the Nazi Holocaust of European Jewry, most Jews came to support the idea and development of a Jewish state. However, despite the Holocaust and the communal manipulation by the pro-Israel lobby, Bundist organizations and culture remain alive, and we can still find examples of Jewish autonomy within a host country, such as is found today in India. In addition, there are still many non-Zionist Jews like those who predominated in the early Reform movement (Greenstein 1981, 4–5). Non-Zionists may work for a healthy Israel more because there are so many Jews there, rather than because they are committed to the idea of a Jewish state per se. Since the rise of the pro-Israel hegemony, these Jews have been silenced and caricatured as self-hating Jews, lumped together with anti-Zionists, a politically different breed. Many of these committed and Jewish-identified Jews may be found active in other Jewish organizations in the United States. See also Knee's (1979) perspective on such activity.

37. See Tivnan (1987, 15) and Greenstein (1981, 2).

38. See Tivnan (1987, 16), for a critical analysis of the AJCommittee's non-Zionism. See also N. Cohen, for more of an emphasis on how AJCommittee actually ended up contributing to the creation of the state of Israel, despite its strong non-Zionist perspective (1975, 293–331).

39. See Tivnan (1987, 23).

40. See N. Cohen (1975, 293–331), especially comments such as Blaustein's (which are reported on 312–313). See also Klutznick (1961, 125).

41. Pro-Israel hegemonic forces have succeeded in confounding the terms and distorting history in order to create the impression of their loyalty. See also Kronish (1994).

42. Of the 35,000 Americans and Canadians who immigrated during the first decade of the state of Israel, only 5,400 stayed (Urofsky 1978, 271).

43. The *Hofjude* or *shtadlan* approach came in the form of "intercession with the authorities by a Jew who enjoyed government favor or had the ear of the powerful. When necessary, the mediator would approach leaders and molders of public opinion and, if required, would seek to galvanize the Jewish community into action" (N. Cohen 1975, 5–6).

44. On the AJCommittee's dislike of Brandeis see N. Cohen (1972, 27–28).

45. See Kenan (1981, 66–67) and Tivnan (1987, 34–35).

46. Groups often thought to be lobby groups such as the Religious Action Center, which is the political arm of the Reform movement, APN's Washington Center for Peace and Security, and Project Nishma are in fact advocacy, not registered lobby, groups.

47. Tivnan (1987, 82).

48. See Tivnan's (1987, 88–89) and Findley's (1985, 100–101) discussion of the "letter of 76" and the killing of Breira (Tivnan, 94–96; Findley, 266–267).

49. One can understand an organization's keeping files on individuals' and groups' statements or positions on issues of concern to it. However, a number of

exposé articles published in the early 1990s critically discussed AIPAC's filing system. The authors claim that the organization overstepped boundaries in distorting information and distributing lists of people deemed threatening. The problem is exacerbated by the fact that AIPAC equated dissent from its pro-Israeli government position with anti-Israel, anti-Semitic, pro-Arab, and pro-Arab-terrorist positions. Many have condemned these tactics as McCarthyite: see, for example, Slabodkin (1992) and Robert Friedman (1992a; 1992b). See also Twersky's critique of Friedman (1994).

50. Jewish lobby interest groups such as AIPAC are often characterized as enormously powerful. Scholars such as A.F.K. Organski (1990), however, have explored the successes and many failures of the Jewish lobby and conclude that, in U.S. policy terms, these groups are often unable to wield the influence they seek. Although Jewish political actors to whom I presented Organski's findings continued to claim their own importance, Organski's work suggests an interesting challenge to our understanding of the relationship between Jewish politics and U.S. interests.

51. Slabodkin discusses AIPAC's monitoring of and engagement (through plants) in campus politics concerning the Middle East (1992, 90).

52. Despite the fact that these conservative groups disagreed with the Jewish communal stance on all other key issues—including prayer in school, abortion, and civil rights, for example—these groups were courted by AIPAC because they supported aid to Israel. In 1994 there was a surge in Jewish conservatism aligned with the radical and Christian right in the United States. The Christian right's "support" of Israel continues to be offered as a defense for this bizarre relationship. (See, for example, the exchange in *Moment* 19:5 (October 1994).

53. JAC-PAC, the Joint Action Committee for Political Affairs, began to do some work with the Women's Dialogue Project in the late 1980s. I would like to thank Reena Bernards for providing me with an opportunity to meet with JAC-PAC members through the Women's Dialogue Project.

54. See Greenstein (1981, 101–126).

55. See Tivnan (1987, 23) and N. Cohen (1975, 257–260).

56. See Tivnan (1987, 31) and N. Cohen (1975, 310–315).

57. See Tivnan (1987, 48–49). N. Cohen's presentation of the issue, (1975, 323) is vague, but essentially supports Tivnan's assertion that the AJCommittee and others in organized American Jewry were upset by Israel's invasion but were won over by Eban into a position of active support.

58. See also Tivnan (1987, esp. 129, 215, and 136).

59. Some of the following individuals are also mentioned in Findley (1985) as well as the organizations Breira and New Jewish Agenda. To my knowledge, however, no other work has more fully explored the actual level of dissent within the community and especially not in organized form.

60. This story was generated by a report in *New York* magazine of 1978. See also Findley (1985, 274) and Tivnan (1987, 121).

61. See Tivnan (1987, 121 and 214) and also Klutznick (1961).

62. Examples were Alexander Schindler of the Reform movement, Theodore Mann, Jacqueline Levine, and Henry Seigman. The disproportionate number of men on this list reflects the disproportionate representation of men in mainstream Jewish leadership positions. According to a study released by the CJF and its new Women's Advocacy Department, women continue to remain absent from leadership roles. See Blustain (1995).

63. As to the importance of the role of student politics in the shifting pro-Israel identity, it must be stressed that the college campus is a focal point in the lives of most modern North American Jews. According to the 1990 CJF Survey, 90 percent of the community's university-age members are actually in college. It is often noted that college is traditionally a time of exploration and finding direction, and it is felt by Jewish leaders that the university is the community's last major opportunity to reach out (with assimilation and intermarriage at all-time highs, this is a communal priority). In addition, the campus enjoys high levels of activism and political participation, and Israel and the debate over Middle East peace played central roles in the campus political environment. It is also commonly noted by Jewish activists that Jewish students are on the front lines of a battle in the formation of a new politics in the United States based on identity and multiculturalism. As was asserted by a student activist at the 1988 Council of Jewish Federations–General Assembly in New Orleans, Jewish students are not only the "future" of the community, they are also essential to its "present." An interesting and self-critical discussion can be found in *Response* 62 (Winter 1995).

64. I would like to thank Sylvia and Oscar Ackelsberg for providing the documentation and background on Avukah.

65. Thanks to Stefi Kirschner for ideas about and documentation on this period and API.

66. I would like to thank Mark Seal and Ken Bob for their help in clarifying for me some of the RZA and 1970s progressive Zionist student organizing history.

67. For a history of this movement, see Goldberg (1993).

68. For a history of this movement in the United States and Canada, see Hurwitz (1994).

69. For example, in the period after RZA and before the SZU, the left-Zionist youth movements staged a counterdemonstration against the JDL, whose right-wing politics, they said, were "foreclosing any chance for peace [for Israel]." The counterdemonstrators were called anti-Jewish for demonstrating against another Jewish organization. The flyer passed out by the seventy-five counterdemonstrators stated, "It is with a great deal of reservation that we have brought ourselves to the point of openly criticizing another Jewish organization . . . but our commitment to the State of Israel leaves us no choice" ("Labor Zionists Picket JDL as Peril to Israel").

70. The SZU was even mentioned in the New York press for counterdemonstrating against a Zionist rally supporting settlements in the occupied territories ("Zionists in Clash Near UN," *New York Post* 1976, and "30,000 Israelis Parade in Claim to the West Bank," *New York Times* 1976).

71. For published material on NIF, see for example, Nesvisky (1984).

72. See S. M. Cohen (1989a,b).

73. I first heard Gary Tobin discuss this issue when he spoke at a salon for NAJSA at the 1988 CJF-GA in New Orleans. He spoke of the crisis of the American Jewish establishment fund-raising focus on the Holocaust and then more exclusively on Israel. See also Tobin (1990 and 1992). It is my assertion that, unfortunately, out of a fear that Jews no longer relate to their Jewish identities in any meaningful way, mainstream fund-raisers have exploited these two phenomena. Despite the importance of the Holocaust and Israel and their centrality in modern Jewish identity, such exploitation twists these experiences into what has been termed a "problematic obsession." Many Jewish commentators have noted this situation. For example, commenting on the fund-raising crisis in the Los Angeles Jewish Federation, Leonard Fein (1992) wrote that as the traditional buzzwords—Holocaust and Israel—have proven less and less lucrative, new words have recently been substituted—intermarriage and anti-Semitism—rather than a new approach explored. Fein writes, "It all comes down to survival . . . an obsession that derives from our destabilizing historical experience—and that is encouraged and sustained by the myopic timidity of our institutions." He continues, however, "Survival is not something to stand for; survival is the result of standing for something. Until we can persuasively complete the following sentence, we shall be in trouble, and our survival will remain iffy: 'It is important that the Jews survive in order that ———.' " Fein's own suggested ending to that sentence can help begin the dialogue: He offers, " . . . in order to help mend the world, a task they are assigned and for which their texts and their memories and their situation have prepared them."

74. See Alisa Solomon's piece on Jews during the Gulf War (1991, 28–29).

75. Of special note for this work is that the main difference between PZC and earlier attempts at progressive Zionist student organizing—such as Avukah, RZA, or SZU—was that rather than forming to confront students' alienation from the general left (although this certainly remained an important aspect of the Jewish campus experience and a motivator for students joining PZC), PZC was specifically formed to confront the growing alienation from Zionism in response to a right-wing Israeli government and a limited (what is referred to here as the hegemonic) American Jewish pro-Israel attitude. I owe thanks to Ken Bob for clarifying this point.

76. A support group for the Israeli Peace Now movement began locally in Chicago in 1981.

77. This information was gathered from interviews with APN staff. For published sources, see, for example, Twersky (1992b).

78. See early S. M. Cohen surveys for the American Jewish Committee.

79. It is interesting to note that as early as 1949 a group of Orthodox Jews demonstrated in the streets of New York against the Israeli government (for what the group perceived to be its neglect of those with religious needs). The ultraorthodox right continues to be an outspoken critic of Israel and is able to remain anti-Zionist,

yet it receives support from the Israeli government. However, criticism from the dovish camp has never been tolerated. Criticism even from establishment Jewish leaders who leaned toward the left remained in house and was severely discouraged through the 1980s.

80. Samuelson (1978). See also S. M. Cohen's survey, which shows that some Jews "may feel a commitment to free speech within the confines of organized Jewry, or they may believe it to be simply more prudent to keep dissent within the Jewish family rather than forcing it outside" (1989a, 34–35).

81. See Tivnan (1987, 171 and 247–248).

82. Interview with Michael Berenbaum, January 1993.

83. A number of peace groups further to the left, or taking a more pacifist stance, also existed in Israel. Most of Israel's mainstream peace movement traditionally has not been pacifist, not objecting to any killing or all wars, but specifically wars and military actions deemed unjust and unnecessary such as those to defend Israel's occupation of the West Bank and the Gaza Strip. As another example, although in dialogue with the group, Peace Now distinguished itself from Yesh Gvul (meaning literally "There is a limit," which is a play on the Hebrew word *gvul*, also meaning "border" which is used in Israel to refer to the Green Line, the border between Israel proper and the territories it occupies). Yesh Gvul members claimed conscientious objector status, refusing to perform military service, while Peace Now's official policy was to protest but to continue to serve when called.

84. Steven M. Cohen also cites the 1984 election of Meir Kahane to the Israeli Knesset, the 1987 Pollard affair, and the often violent religious-secular conflicts in the mid-1980s as examples of events that provided a background for the changes found by his surveys in American Jews' relationships to Israel during the course of the decade (1989a, 12).

85. The change in the pro-Israel attitude during the 1980s may be noted in this interesting phenomenon. Previously, an attitude that was openly critical of Israeli government policy and did not see the strength of Israel and the Arab states and the Palestinian people as mutually exclusive categories was considered to be on the fringe left wing. Groups such as PZC and APN have succeeded in one measure to the extent that they have created space on the spectrum further to the left than they are. By the early 1990s there was a viable place on the Jewish political spectrum that considered groups such as PZC and APN as rather conservative (on the student level, for example, were the Progressive Jewish Student Union at the University of California at Santa Cruz, Tzedekh at U.C. Berkeley, Tiferet at Oberlin College, and Two Peoples Two States at Wesleyan; on the nonstudent level there were some elements in NJA, the IJPU, JWCEO, and JPF, to name but a few). On the other hand, groups emerged with ideological positions similar to that of APN, for example, but that were purposely mainstream. The successful activity of such groups as NIF and APN have made the above positions more legitimate within the community. Groups such as Project Nishma, the Dialogue Project, and the Jewish Women's Consultation exist, in part, for people who basically share the political

perspective, but are concerned with APN's previous reputation as marginal or radical.

86. The Shefa Fund and the Jewish Fund for Justice also emerged, but they focus their energy domestically.

87. This group was active in Minneapolis. For a discussion of this and other affiliates see Falbel, Klepfisz, and Nevel (1990).

88. *Bridges*, a newer Jewish feminist journal, began publishing soon after the establishment of *Tikkun* in order to meet the needs left unmet by the older Jewish feminist magazine, *Lilith*.

89. S. M. Cohen's (1989a) survey of Jewish communal leaders found that 72 percent would contribute to AIPAC if asked (29). What is significant is that 19 percent would not, and 9 percent were not sure (31). It is also important to note that his survey revealed that 76 percent would support NIF, and even 58 percent would support Peace Now (45). Such numbers suggest that by the end of the 1980s groups such as AIPAC and UJA no longer controlled American Jewish philanthropic dollars and ideology the way they once did.

90. It also should be noted that Cohen's survey of Jewish leaders found that 57 percent rejected the statement "American Jews should not publically criticize the policies of the government of Israel" (1989a, 34).

91. The results of the Wilstein poll were deliberately released the day before the 1991 CJF-GA in Baltimore. Also, APN circulated a letter signed by 250 rabbis, and *Tikkun* sponsored an op-ed piece in the *Baltimore Sun* published the day of Shamir's speech. Although this activity attracted much attention and could not have happened even a few years before, its impact remained outside the official framework of the GA. The program of the GA still called for unity behind Shamir. A November 1991 *Tikkun* editorial states: "Not to exaggerate the importance of what happened—the GA and the institutions of Jewish life remain officially committed to supporting Shamir and will not publically oppose his policies. These institutions are 'not' organized democratically, so it was no surprise that the conference did not produce any open debate about loan guarantees or Israeli policy in the Occupied Territories."

92. The connected, concrete self has been a central aspect of feminist philosophy. See, for example, Gilligan (1982), C. Keller (1986), and the work of Seyla Benhabib, particularly her article on the Gilligan-Kohlberg debate (1987).

93. For example, J. Q. Wilson's notion of "clearly demarcated" groups (1973, 263), and Browne's vision of groups with "specific recognizable boundaries" (1990, 477) do not reflect the sense of self of these case study groups.

94. Cohen's survey of American Jewish leaders shows that the idea still exists that "criticism detracts from the image of world Jewish unity that, they claim, is so important for influencing the American government" (1989a, 33). This is probably not without foundation. Tivnan reports that "legend has it" that John Foster Dulles was the one who actually suggested the creation of a second Jewish lobby. Henry Byroade, assistant secretary of state to Dulles, told Goldman, who was then head of the World Jewish Congress, that American Jewry would be more effec-

tive if it could address the State Department "with one voice" (1987, 40). The challenge to the Jewish community is, therefore, how to fulfill its commitment to a living diverse community in an environment of such heavy pressure towards monism.

95. In Selsam and Martel (1963, 182).

96. See Martin Buber *I and Thou* (1958, 81), and Mary Daly (1978).

97. See Selsam and Martel (1963, 132–134).

98. See also Arnett's chapter "Freedom: The Unity of Contraries" (1986, 111–126).

## 2. Diversity

1. Sections of this chapter concerning the relationship of interests to needs were presented to the APSA (American Political Science Association) Meeting, 1993. A feminist reading was presented to the Women as Social Conscience Conference 1994 and a multiculturalist reading presented at the NYSPSA (New York State Political Science Association) 1994.

2. Jeffrey Berry opens his work on *The Interest Group Society*, with the following observation: "people will pursue their self-interest even though the policies they advocate may hurt others, and may not be in the best interest of the nation" (1984, 1). See also Bentley (1908); Truman (1951); Latham (1965); Hershey and Levine and Thurber (in Cigler and Loomis eds 1986); Aberbach and Rockman (1978); and Fritschler (1983).

3. Madison wrote in *Federalist* 10, "By faction I understand a number of citizens, whether amounting to a majority or minority of the whole, who are united and actuated by some common impulse of passion, or of interest, adverse to the rights of other citizens, or to the permanent and aggregate interests of the community." Although this work will analyze the term "interests" critically, it should be noted that by the seventeenth century interest was viewed favorably by thinkers as a rational improvement over motivation by irrational passions (see Holmes, in Mansbridge 1990).

4. For an intellectual history of self-interest see Mansbridge (in Mansbridge 1990). The collection of essays in the Mansbridge anthology provide a much-needed contribution to the debate over self-interest in democratic theory by focusing on the tension between self-interest and altruism. This work, however, will treat the assumptions and obfuscations related to self-interest itself.

5. In 1963 Norman Jacobson wrote of the link (and its implications) between the political education of the founding fathers and the political science of contemporary groups scholars. He argued that the authors of the Constitution framed a political system that would effectively mold citizens into the perfect specimens of contemporary political science. The following pages build on and develop Jacobson's thesis by more closely analyzing the Liberal roots of group-based theory, especially in light of the developments of the past thirty years of groups scholarship in American democratic theory.

6. Others have suggested that we understand "interests" as "preferences"

(Mansbridge 1983; Young 1990). Marxists often discuss the difference between subjective and objective interests (Balbus 1971; Lukes 1974), or need in biological terms, and interest as the situation created to satisfy those needs.

7. One of Marx's major contributions has been to remind us of the concrete material conditions that actually form the social base. Marx points out that in bourgeois society this concrete material base becomes "estranged" in the "illusory forms in which the real struggles" occur within the State (*The German Ideology* in McLellan 1979, 161). (Marx makes a similar, though more deterministic, argument in the Preface to *The Critique of Political Economy*.)

In *The German Ideology*, Marx writes of the problem of commodities:

A commodity appears, at first sight, a very trivial thing, and easily understood. Its analysis shows that it is, in reality, a very queer thing, abounding in metaphysical subtleties and theological niceties. So far as it is a value in use, there is nothing mysterious about it, whether we consider it from the point of view that by its properties it is capable of satisfying human wants, or from the point that those properties are the product of human labour. (In Tucker 1978, 319)

Using the example of a table, Marx continues,

For all that, the table continues to be that common, every-day thing, wood. But, so soon as it steps forth as a commodity, it is changed into something transcendent. It not only stands with its feet on the ground, but, in relation to all other commodities, it stands on its head, and evolves out of its wooden brain grotesque ideas, far more wonderful than 'table-turning' ever was. (Ibid., 320)

8. Even in Liberal theory, human needs as needs are incontestable (Locke 1980, 18), but when our needs are seen as interests, they can be negotiated.

9. Young further helps us to see how this subordination has been achieved in our functioning political system. Young writes that subordination is possible within our system because "a general will that transcends the particular differences of group affiliation, situation, and interest has in practice excluded groups judged not capable of adopting that general point of view" (in Sunstein 1990, 118). This was achieved, as Young writes, through early American republicans' defining "moral, civilized republican life in opposition to this backward looking, uncultivated desire that they identified with women and nonwhites" (ibid., 122) and the nonpropertied class.

10. In *The Second Treatise*, Locke wrote that "men are biased in their interests" (1980, 66), and even Rousseau felt, as he wrote in *Social Contract*, that "the particular will tend, by its very nature, to partiality, while the general will tends to equality" (1973, 182).

11. Although fear plays a part in various political philosophies, note, for example, Hobbes's well-known appeal: "If a man does not believe me let him therefore consider with himselfe, when taking a journey, he arms himself and seeks to go accompanied. . . . Does he not there as much accuse mankind by his actions, as I do by my words?" (1983, 187).

12. Thus, contemporary Liberal philosophers continue to work within the same paradigm. Rawls, for example, is also criticized for positing a theory of justice that is blind to difference with the same actual effect of ignoring the difference of women and other nondominant groups. See Young in Sunstein (1990, 124); and Okin in Sunstein (1990). See also Gilligan's (1982) feminist critique, and Dietz (1985) and Ackelsberg and Diamond (1987) for a discussion of some of the problems with this type of feminist critique. Although I utilize Rousseau's critique of Hobbes and Locke, it also should be noted that he too has a tendency to ignore the particular in discussions of the general will. See Young's critique, in Sunstein (1990, 119), and her critique of later participatory democrats such as Barber, in Sunstein (1990, 123–125).

13. For a view of difference and diversity in this vein see feminist works such as Starhawk (1982).

14. Rousseau writes in *The Discourse on the Origins of Inequality* that "the rich, in particular must have felt how much they suffered by a constant state of war, of which they bore all the expense; and in which, though all risked their lives, they alone risked their property" (1973, 88).

15. Hobbes and Locke had slightly different understandings of the role of property and class with respect to the formation of the common good. For Locke there is already an inequality of property before we form the social contract, whereas one could argue that there can be no property at all in the Hobbesian state of nature (it is too unstable). That government is instituted for the protection of private property, thus institutionalizing inequality, is made more explicit therefore in Locke but is implicit in Hobbes's theory. Although Hobbes noted a kind of equality in precivil society, he did not perceive it as a good thing, for it contributed to the chaos. In the effort to regain stability through the social contract, similarly to Locke, Hobbes sought to legitimize and protect the ruling class. Rousseau's arguments apply to both Hobbes and to Locke.

16. The vast majority of Jews living in the United States are Ashkenazi (of European descent). Many thus often have "white skin privilege." Jews usually cannot consider themselves "simply white," however, as the cultural and religious differences between (even Ashkenazi) Jews and white ethnics (who are usually Christian) are large, and anti-Semitism in response to those differences remains all too common. Melanie Kaye/Kantrowitz in particular has written with sensitivity and insight about issues of class, color, and Jews (1992).

17. Bentley began in 1908 to develop the pluralist paradigm which, by basing itself on "special interests," would make it very difficult to see the points of contention experienced by the varieties of people and groups, whose appropriate place to be figured out is the political realm. See also Hale (in Connolly 1969), Dahl (1961), Polsby (1963), and Banfield (1963). For an excellent critique, see Balbus (1971). A number of critical scholars have attempted to rectify this bias of group-based theory. See, for example, Cobb and Elder (1972), Bachrach and Baratz (1962), Steven Lukes (1974), and Fraser (1987 and in Sunstein 1990).

18. See also Bachrach and Baratz (1962) and Balbus (1971, esp. 153).

19. See N. Fraser (in Sunstein 1990, 162).

20. See *The German Ideology*, in Tucker (1978, 172).

21. I would like to thank Rabbi Gerry Serotta for providing me with much of the background for this section and much of the documentation from his own files. Jonathan Birnbaum also made his files on Breira available to me. A lengthy interview and follow-ups with Serotta and private conversations with a number of those who had been involved with the organization added to the following presentation and corroborated the validity of the written material cited.

22. The process of organization building, as reported in the *Proceedings of Breira's First Annual Membership Conference* (p. 6), continued. "In the spring of 1975 the Advisory Council met in New York and laid the groundwork for more direct participation by its membership in Breira decision-making. This led in September 1975 to the formation of an expanded Board of Directors replacing the Working Committee of young people who had founded the organization with a group more broadly representative of Breira's growing constituency. For the first time, Breira was set up as a membership organization and chapters began to form."

23. On choosing the name Breira, the editor of *The Jewish Week and the American Examiner* (week of 13–19 February 1977) wrote that "Breira was trapped at its birth by its founders into betraying that role [the role of 'an organization critical of the Establishment and devoted to dialogue, dissent, and constructive criticism of Israel's policies']." It claimed that the name was chosen "to refute the consensus in Israel that Arab hatred and intransigence had created an 'ain Breira' situation for Israel." It was claimed that Breira sought an "alternative" to Zionism. In the *Proceedings of Breira's First Annual Membership Conference* it was explained, "For decades the slogan "ain breira"—there is no alternative—symbolized the commitment of the Zionist movement to armed struggle to achieve the creation of the State of Israel. There was no alternative but for Jews to fight in their own behalf; to act rather than be acted upon. . . . Today, after 30 years of war following the creation of the state of Israel, there may still be no alternative to ongoing armed struggle. But to deny the possibility of other solutions undercuts the entire vision of the Zionist movement and in effect ensures the continuation of the status quo. What was once a positive call to action—ain breira—is becoming a defensive strategy devoid of vision or hope for the future" (3).

24. See the Breira mission statment reprinted in Appendix A.

25. In October of 1974 a demonstration was held with the participation of many Jews who were also active in Breira. The efforts of a group of progressive Jews were rebuffed when they tried to make an appointment with Israeli officials at the embassy. Later, an action was planned that began with a demonstration at the Israeli Consulate, and proceeded with a march to the PLO office calling on the two sides to begin talking with one another. This action was the first of its kind, at least on the East Coast, and brought out one hundred to one hundred and fifty progressive Jewish activists. As Breira was not a demonstrating organization, this action was not, however, organized under its auspices.

26. The *New York Times* received an interesting response to its 30 December 1976,

article, "American Jewish Leaders Are Split Over Issue of Meeting With P.L.O.," which came out after five American Jews met with two top PLO representatives on November 15, 1976. The next day (31 December 1976), the paper printed a correction: "The article should have said that the dispute had arisen among 'some members of the American Jewish community'," rather than "among the leaders." The "correction" continues, "The accepted leaders of the community, who make up the Conference of Presidents of Major Jewish Organizations . . . oppose contacts with the P.L.O." Although the article reports that in most cases those in attendance came as individuals and not as representatives of their organizations, this "unacceptable leadership" was comprised of (with their affiliations at that time) Herman Edelsberg, former director of the B'nai Brith International Council; David Goren, Washington Director of the American Jewish Congress; Olya Margolin, Washington Representative of the National Council of Jewish Women; Rabbi Max Ticktin, national director, department of field services and leadership training, B'nai B'rith Hillel Foundation; and Arthur Waskow, Jewish writer.

27. Interview with Rabbi Gerry Serotta, August 1992.

28. Foer (1983, 22) cites this quote from *The Jewish Transcript* of Seattle.

29. For example, the editor of *The Jewish Week and The American Examiner* (13–19 February 1977) criticized I. F. Stone's support of Breira, even as "an eminent non-member," as "nothing less than home-grown anti-Semitism."

30. In January of 1977 the dismissal of Hillel rabbis who had been associated with Breira was demanded from various parts of the B'nai B'rith structure. *The Jewish Week and The American Examiner* ran a story in the week of 13–19 February 1977, entitled "Views of Breira said to dominate Student Network." Quoting from the *American Zionist*, the article charged that "Hillel Foundations have developed into something like incubators for Breira's perspectives and activators of its programs," which were charged with deceitfully luring young Jews "and us[ing] them as funnels for their pro-PLO information to the masses of unknowing students." The article condemned the entire Jewish student movement of the decade by implicating the Jewish Students' Network, an umbrella group for Jewish organizations outside Hillel, in the aid and comfort of these traitor groups. The antidovish heat was on in Hillel and generally in the Jewish student movement. In May of that year B'nai B'rith devoted time and resources to forming a committee of prestigious Jewish leaders to study the situation (See "B'nai B'rith opens Breira study session in 2–day sessions.") The outcome was, under the circumstances, relatively positive: Staff members could join Breira, but could not hold office or endorse Breira policy as representatives under the name of B'nai B'rith (see also Foer 1983, 22).

31. Tivnan quotes Arthur Samuelson, past editor of Breira's magazine *interChange*, from an interview in 1983, as saying that the attacks "felt like an orchestrated campaign. . . . We heard rumors that the Israelis were behind it, but we could never be sure" (1987, 95).

32. However, Foer (1983, 18–19) dates the first evidence of anti-Breira activity back to early 1975 with a paper distributed in the Washington Jewish community.

Congressman Larry McDonald, an ultraconservative, submitted his first testimony against Breira to the *Congressional Record* on 7 June 1975 (he would submit another in February 1977). David Tulin, a Philadelphia-based Zionist leader associated with Breira, came under pressure to resign and was summoned to the Israeli consulate in early 1976. Articles in the Jewish press began appearing by that spring.

33. See also the pamphlet author's article, "The Rabbis of Breira," in *Midstream*, April 1977.

34. In retrospect, it becomes clear that dissent from the left was perceived as far more perilous to the pro-Israel hegemony than was dissent from the right; the JDL and AFSI, though not in agreement with the Labor government, had not come under such intense attack. See also Kornberg's analysis (1978, 112).

35. The original formulation in the American context can be found in *Federalist Papers* 10 by James Madison. Later examples can be found in Truman (1951, 57), Salisbury (1969, 3–4), J. Q. Wilson (1973, 154), and Greenwald (1977, 305).

36. The woman writing under this pseudonym was Eleanor Lester, a niece of the publisher of *The Jewish Week and The American Examiner*. Others writing under pseudonyms were "Jeremiah" in the *Seattle Jewish Transcript* and "Daniel Charles" in the *American Zionist* (see also Foer 1983, 19).

37. In response to the question "But why did *The Jewish Week* choose the issue of Jan. 9–15 to explode the Breira issue?" the editor wrote, "What triggered our article on Breira was a front-page story in the *New York Times* last Dec. 30, reporting that a virtual civil war, ideologically, had broken out in the American Jewish community over Breira's activity in promoting meetings of Jews and PLO people. The following day, the *Times* 'corrected' its sensational exaggeration of Breira's dimensions with an inconspicuous one-paragraph note stating that there had been an 'error in editing' and that the Jewish civil war was limited to a lesser area. *The Jewish Week* then decided to focus some light on Breira's harmful role in the great national media, to expose the hollowness of its pretensions and to prove to Breira's innocent sponsors and supporters that they were being 'used'."

38. The debate over Breira raged in organizations such as the World Jewish Congress, the New York Federation/United Jewish Appeal, the National Jewish Community Relations Advisory Council, the Executive of the World Zionist Organization, B'nai B'rith, the Rabbinical Assembly (of the Conservative Movement), and the Reform movement.

39. For example see articles, editorials and letters in *The Jewish Week and The American Examiner* from January through June 1977. See also the exchange of letters published in *Commentary* of June 1977. Foer (1983) cites a series of pieces in a chain of West Coast Jewish weeklies published by Brin.

40. See also Foer (1983, 21).

41. Foer (1983, 18).

42. See, for example, Tivnan's report on the Rabin meeting (1987, 94) and an internal memo written by Steven Shaw, then director of a New Jersey–based Jewish Community Relations Council, to the executive vice president of the National Jewish Community Relations Advisory Council.

43. See, for example, Tivnan (1987, 96).

44. For a concrete example, Ackelsberg writes that the women of B'not Esh seemed to have achieved a living community that is "not only accepting of, but thriving on, diversity" (1986, 118).

45. Breira reprinted some of these comments, for example from a World Zionist Organization report, in its conference proceedings (1977).

46. A more recent example of community silencing during crisis occurred during the Gulf War. As soon as the war started, the Jewish press and major Jewish organizations claimed that the American Jewish community was united in its support of the United States government. This became the popular call, despite the fact that the national press, such as the *Washington Post*, reported that Jews comprised a substantial 14 percent of antiwar organizers and activists. Specifically Jewish antiwar organizations (such as Jews Against the War in New York City) sprang up around the country but were shunned by the larger, more mainstream organizations.

47. Although there are, of course, no guarantees, the invitation of an open political space is also less likely either to require the normalization of radical claims, or to necessitate a Liberal-type negotiation in which some voices are subordinated; this politics is, instead, an ongoing dialogic process.

48. See Kornberg for an elaboration on the position of this organization (1978, 110).

49. There have been a number of peace talks or mediated peace negotiations between Israel and various Arab states in the past. I am referring here to the peace talks beginning in the fall of 1991, which are distinguished from all previous talks in their multiple, public, international, and direct format, and by their the inclusion of Palestinians and their depth.

50. Material for this section was compiled from lengthy interviews with APN's Political Director Mark Rosenblum and Cochair Peter Edelman. Other confidential interviews were conducted with high-ranking representatives from another dovish pro-Israel group and from AIPAC. Amanda Josephs of APN provided some of the written sources utilized in the case study. In addition, the author was in attendance at three Jewish events during the Democratic National Convention in New York in July 1992: the AIPAC delegates' briefing, APN's delegate breakfast briefing, and *Tikkun* magazine's event. I had the opportunity at these three convention events to talk to many delegates and campaign workers concerning the role of Jewish pro-Israel groups in the year's campaign.

In addition to appearing in *Commonwealth* (1994–1995), portions of this section have been published in *Israel Horizons* 40:4 in an article by the author entitled "Behind Clinton's Middle East Platform: A Progressive Shift in American Jewry."

51. I have chosen to focus on an example of specific policy deliberations to demonstrate a concrete example of more authentic politics. Such a choice runs the risk of leaving the impression that politics is only about policy. However, given the attention paid above to philosophical visions of an open public space, choosing a less concrete example ran the risk of leaving the impression that more inclusive

interactive understandings of the common good exist only in theory. For one of the best articles that begins to explore how the community might look if it were more inclusive and supportive of difference, in the case of women see Ackelsberg (1986). There has not been an equivalent of the process undertaken by B'not Esh and other women's groups in the pro-Israel part of the community. The closest experience was the (only half-jokingly called) Conference of Presidents of Minor Jewish Organizations, which grew out of the Passover Peace Coalitions of the late 1980s (which are discussed in more detail in the next chapter).

52. For example, that sponsored by the Wilstein Institute of Jewish Policy Studies at the University of Judaism in Los Angeles and funded by Project Nishma (Cohen and Lipset, 1991).

53· From the 1990 Jewish Public Opinion Survey sponsored by three institutes of Brandeis University.

54. The Cohen surveys, for example, which report overwhelming popular Jewish support for these positions, began coming out in the early 1980s.

55. See Twersky (1992a).

56. In fact, after the Israeli Labor victory, AIPAC leadership came under enormous attack for having been more pro-Likud than pro-Israel. Top AIPAC officials eventually resigned their posts.

57. This phenomenon continued into the political wrestling over positions in the new Clinton Administration. In early January the *New York Times* (See T. Friedman 1993) headlined an article "Clinton Nominees Disturb Some Jews: Cabinet Would Lack Voice for Israel and Be Too Close to Carter, Groups Say," but the article continued: "The real worry of the Jewish groups, transition aides contend, is that their monopoly on representing Jewish positions is being broken. Many top Clinton aides—Sara Ehrman, community liaison advisor; Peter Edelman, legal affairs advisor for the transition, and Eli Segal, who was the campaign chief of staff—are associated with Jewish groups like Americans for Peace Now that have often been at odds with the traditional groups which are less inclined to criticize Israeli policy." Such a politics was also at work in the controversy over APN's joining the Presidents' Conference (see "Row Over Peace Now Embroils Jewish Bigs").

58. It must be stated clearly that most interest group scholars, particularly pluralists such as Dahl and Greenwald, write from the perspective that group activity is actually a sign of a healthy political system. However, for the most part, those who think group activity is good still tend to assume that groups themselves are narrowly self-interested. It is through the political process with the help of government that these groups, given the threat such narrow selfish interests pose to the common good, are kept in check and out of danger of toppling the system as a whole.

59. In her critique of the maternalist strain of social feminism, Dietz rightly sensitizes us to the potential conservatism of political theory based on "traditional bonds of kinship, the web of relationships that emerge from a respect for and remembrance of past generations and a sense of rootedness" (1985, 22). However,

as both Dallmayr (1992), drawing on Walter Benjamin, and Plaskow (1991), sounding like Martin Buber, suggest, such a base also has radical and transformatory potential.

60. As discussed in the previous section, I do not intend to imply a homogeneity within communities when I posit subcommunities as loci of the heterogeneity of a larger polity. See also Riley (1988) and Bourdieu (1985) for a discussion of this problem.

61. This stipulation reminds us to be attentive to the individuals who comprise communities (as Buber is), as well as to the idea that it is only through the incorporation of many subcommunities that this process will be transformative. See, for example, Ackelsberg (1991, 178).

62. This consideration stems from the awareness that in naming subcommunities such as women, African Americans, Jews, and so on, we are in danger of continuing an oppressive mode of discourse. Such lists tend to suggest that these communities are mutually exclusive, and thus stifle people's multiple identities and obscure the deeper and more complex roots of their positions and outlooks within society. See, for example, Fraser (1987) and Lorde (1984).

63. Thus, following chapter 1, I do not assume here that needs are in any way natural, unalienated, or static. I am suggesting only that they are real and inviolable, even as they are ever being reinterpreted. The process of politics as an open public space thus must be one that affirmingly facilitates this reinterpretation over time.

64. This form of tentative acknowledgement of a common good is similar to a strong strain in group theory that takes a process oriented perspective on this point. For thinkers such as Bentley (1908), Banfield (1963), and Schumpeter (1962), for example, the common interest can only be said to be whatever emerges from the group process. However, the study of groups from an egalitarian perspective, seeking to overcome oppression in and through politics, provides critical insight into the obfuscation of bias in the traditional group perspective. Faith in process in the context of traditional group theory has a tendency to result in or ignore inequality in three ways. By focusing on existent groups, based in interest rather than need, and without grounding in democratic/egalitarian norms by which to judge the process, an inegalitarian bias of group theory—even given this process-oriented strain—is achieved and obscured. Due to these three facets of group theory, even the Bentleyan process-type common good will end up with class biases similar to a more independent common interest found elsewhere in our Liberal assumptions about the common good, which I discuss in this section in Hobbesian/Lockean terms.

## 3. Relationships

1. Although they went through a few permutations, common Darwinian concepts such as the "survival of the fittest" and the "struggle for existence" became what is called the "conflict theory," upon which Bentley relied (Ward 1978 and

Garson 1978, especially 24–30). This conflict theory has come to characterize much of the modern scholarship on political groups (Zeigler and Peak 1972, 8). Although in his introduction to Schattschneider's *The Semi-Sovereign People* (1960) Adamany points to Schattschneider's moral concerns to show that "conflict theory" is not a monolith, even Schattschneider makes many of the same assumptions about conflict and the nature of power as do other conflict theorists, such as describing politics as "the domination and subordination of conflicts" (1960, 64).

Thus, what is interesting for the purposes of this work is that as much as Bentley drew on Darwinian thought, Darwin drew on Hobbesian thought. In general, what we call natural and social sciences are not so separate, as earlier Hobbes aimed to utilize the methodology of mathematics and the natural sciences in his exploration of society (Macpherson 1962, 30; see also Merchant 1980).

2. On this point, there is only a slight development from Bentley and Truman into the more recent pluralist discussion of conflict. This difference is found in the more direct discussion of the socializing aspect of conflict (Dahl 1956 and Garson 1978, 94). For example, Schattschneider writes, "The socialization of conflict is the essential democratic process" (1960, 138). Thus, Latham writes that the task of the government is to "referee" this conflict, not to seek to alter it or move beyond it (1965, 35). Drawing directly on the Madisonian response to the threat of such conflict in society, Schattschneider writes that "the most powerful instrument for the control of conflict is conflict itself" (1960, 65).

Interest group scholars actually attend to the inadequacies of such a philosophy without fully acknowledging the implications for the theory. Much attention has been given to what has been called the problem of "too much democracy": "solving conflict with conflict" (Schattschneider 1960) has resulted in an "advocacy explosion" (Berry 1984 and Walker 1983). Many perceived the result of such an "explosion" to be the "ungovernability" (Huntington 1975) of government, or the "inefficiency" (Olson 1971) of the interest representation system. Thus, in contrast to the Madisonian encouragement of factionalization as a guarantee of democracy, some have suggested limiting group activity (Cigler and Loomis 1986, 27). However, that this contradicts interest group theories of conflict is not addressed.

3. See also chapter 5 of Locke's *Second Treatise on Government*. On Hobbes, see Macpherson's discussion (1962, 36).

4. For example, the "exchange theory of interest groups," which became popular in the 1960s, remains a common conceptualization (see Salisbury 1969; Olson 1971; Bauer et al. 1963; Hayes 1981; Browne 1990). Here, the relationships between groups and government are seen as based on the principles of markets and exchange.

5. See Lukes's comment on the subtle differences in Dahl's early attempts to formulate a definition of power (1974, 11–15).

6. As an original example, in *The Elements* Hobbes writes that "power is simply no more, but the excess of the power of one above that of another" (1969, part 1, ch. 8 sec. 4). G. K. Wilson also writes that in the pluralist account "the power of

groups could be assessed by a comparison of their resources" (1981, 133). We thus find Schattschneider writing of an issue's strength as measured in terms of its ability to "overwhelm, subordinate and blot out a multitude of lesser ones" (1960, 65). Banfield, as another prominent example, defines power as "the ability to establish control over another" (1963, 348 n4).

7. This power-over notion is fundamental to Hobbes's thought, forming the basis of his theory of equality: that everyone has enough of some sort of power over others that they can kill the other (1983, 183). Here in Hobbes's statement of equality, power-over gets reduced to its zero-sum nature in the most extreme way.

8. The zero-sum nature of power is also assumed by contemporary democratic theorists attending to the role of groups. One may choose to take issue with this assertion by noting that pluralists, and even some of its critics, see that everyone gets a little of something in a pluralist democracy. See Becker (1983, 372); Dahl (1961); Lowi (1969). However, this has not really translated into a refutation of zero-sum thinking. What these thinkers assume is that no one will lose the overall "war." On the level of each "battle," however, these writers utilize the zero-sum paradigm. The prevailing conception is that some groups lose and some groups win. This is also a premise of disequilibrium theory (Salisbury 1969 and Truman 1951; 57), which suggests that organizations will form in response to a disturbance in the political arena where the attainment of goals for some is simply a setback for others.

9. As in Hobbes, an element of scarcity is also assumed by contemporary group scholars. For example, Banfield writes that "an actor has a limited stock of power" (1963, 312). In incentive theory, similar assumptions are made: Clark and Wilson write that "the competition usually centers on conflicting claims for scarce incentives" (1961, 156). See also Browne (1990, 500); Salisbury et al. (1987, 1218); J. Q. Wilson (1973, 261).

On the one hand, there is some discussion in the literature which attributes the advocacy explosion, in part, to increased affluence and the rise in individuals' discretionary funds (Wilson 1973, 201). In addition, a few scholars have pointed to the rise in the use of foundation money as aiding groups avoid free-rider problems (Berry 1977, 72; Walker 1983; Hayes 1983). On the other hand, however, these scholars still tend to fall back on assumptions of scarcity in continuing their discussion based on the possibility that such support will end or pointing to other new expenses.

10. Other than scarcity, greed is the only other possible cause for man's having to acquire more to assure his ability to live well. If he were inherently greedy, whatever social conditions were, man would always want more. This is not the case, says Hobbes. He writes in The Leviathan that man has a "perpetual and restless desire of Power after power that ceaseth only in death." This may sound like inherent greed, but Hobbes follows: "The cause of this, is not always that a man hopes for a more intensive delight, than he has already attained to; or that he cannot be content with a moderate power." If this is not "always" the case, then it is not inherent in man's nature. Macpherson (1962) also takes the position that

Hobbes is not implying that man is naturally greedy. (See pp. 42–43 for his argument against Strauss. In *The Political Philosophy of Hobbes*, pp. 8–12, Strauss argues that Hobbes does assume natural greed.)

11. As I am still in the midst of an Hobbesian argument, I continue using the male-gendered language.

12. Lindbloom (1959, 174). See also Bentley (1908) and Truman (1951) for the origins of this assumption in pluralist thought. For more recent versions see Greenwald (1977, 305), and Clark and Wilson (1961). Outside the pluralist paradigm, this assumption is also often made explicit. In *The Semi-Sovereign People*, Schattschneider writes, "The assumption made throughout is that the nature of political organization depends on the conflicts exploited in the political system, which is ultimately what politics is all about" (1960, v). Later he defines democracy itself as a "competitive political system" (1960, 138). Collective action theorists and others make the same assumption (see Olson 1971 and Becker 1983).

13. Ninety percent of the organizations interviewed by Lehman Schlozman and Tierney (1983) report entering into coalition as a technique of exercising influence.

14. For example, Salisbury writes that coalitions do not outlast the issues (1983, 1984). See also Cigler and Loomis (1986) and Browne (1990, 494–496).

15. Clark and Wilson (1961) assert that the more organizations share things such as issues, markets, members and resources, the more they will compete with one another. See also J. Q. Wilson (1973, 264).

16. It is interesting to note that Madisonian and pluralist promises for representative democracy rest on the notion that there will be "issue overlap." The system will balance out competing forces only if there are forces that are actually competing on the same issue. This idea that many sides are represented in the competition over issues has been challenged empirically (Rose 1967; Lauman and Knoke 1987; McConnel 1966). Kingdon (1973, 40) showed that on 30 percent of key issues in Congress, there was no relevant group activity. On 35 percent of the decisions there was only one group active (see also Hinckley 1978, 52–54). See also Cigler and Swanson (1981), Salisbury et al. (1987), and Browne (1990).

17. In contrast to the Liberal base of traditional group theory, it is interesting to compare such an understanding of group relations with a feminist understanding. Johnson Reagon's "Coalition Politics: Turning the Century" (in B. Smith 1983) and Rich's "If Not With Others, How?" (in Rich 1986) present a very different relational imperative for groups based in cooperation through coalition.

18. I would like to thank Donna Nevel, Marilyn Neimark, and Alisa Solomon for refreshing my memory of this period, and Neimark and Solomon for making their files available to me.

19. The cosponsors included groups such as Holocaust Survivors Association USA, and the Generation After (children of Holocaust survivors). Americans for Peace Now, the Israeli Zionist political party affiliates, and the Progressive Zionist Caucus were participating overtly Zionist groups, and the International Jewish Peace Union, the Jewish Peace Fellowship, and New Jewish Agenda were involved as non-Zionist, or not specifically Zionist, groups.

20. Some newspapers reported 2,000 participants (such as New York City's *The Westsider* 28 April–4 May 1988, 1), and others reported about 4,500 (such as *Boston Globe* 25 April 1988).

21. Many of the participants in this conference are the same leaders who are now at the official negotiating tables of the Middle East peace process.

22. See Cohen in *Jewish Women's Call for Peace*; Falbel, Klepfisz, and Nevel 1990.

23. See, for example, Power 1991.

24. See, for example, *New York Times* 11 January 1991.

25. Henry Schwarzschild, Director Emeritus of the Capital Punishment Project of the American Civil Liberties Union, and board member of Jewish Peace Fellowship, offered an interesting comment on NJA's dilemma during this period. In a private fax to Marilyn Neimark on 23 January 1991 (which I found in Neimark's file and quote here with permission from Schwarzschild), commenting on NJA's inability to come out clearly against the Gulf War, Schwarzschild wrote, "Tell NJA to go to hell: They have the courage to criticize the likes of Bush and Saddam Hussein, but not the Am.[erican]-Jewish balabatim [literally "lords of the house," referring to mainstream leadership]. They want to avoid the fate of B'reira [sic] (assassination by the Establishment) at the cost of their soul and their usefulness."

26. See, for example, Larry Yudelson, "Left Proposes a Day's Fast for Peace," and Stephen Burd, "Anti-War Groups Galvanizing." in *Forward*, 1 February 1991.

27. See, for example, Neimark, 1992.

28. Hinckley quotes from Jewell and Patterson (1966, 297–298): "Lobbying activity is, in the main, directed at legislators who sympathize with the policy positions of the group or groups involved; lobbyists depend very substantively on their friends—those who sympathize with their cause."

29. See Matthews (1960, 178). Jewell and Patterson write about "reinforcement and activation" rather than conflict (1966, 298).

30. See Segal 1989.

31. T. Friedman's (1992) characterization of JPL's activity in the Clinton camp could suggest the group as adopting a more competitive stance.

32. Nor has the New Israel Fund, or the many other alternative Jewish fund-raising organizations, ever characterized itself as "anti-United Jewish Appeal" (the UJA is the long-established fund-raising organization of the American Jewish community). More recently a new foundation called Amcha for Tsedakah formed that is very close to NIF, in its Israel focus, and to the Shefa Fund and the Jewish Fund for Justice, in its American focus. None of these groups, however, see Amcha as in any way a threat; instead, the new fund is welcomed. Jeffrey Dekro of the Shefa Fund noted that these groups are consciously communitarian, rather than Liberal ideologically, and function according to values of collaboration and synergy, rather than fear and competition (personal interview, December 1992).

33. Social critique based on power is the hallmark of the anarchist perspective. Many feminists have drawn on this anarchist analysis of power, pointing to the connection between patriarchal political philosophy (that which fundamentally assumes, perpetuates, and/or justifies the inequality of men and women) with the

power-over understanding of power. They see power-over as supporting a system of domination generally, rather than a system of equality (see, for example, Starhawk 1982, 5–6).

34. See, for example, Foucault's *Power/Knowledge.*

35. See Starhawk, (1982, especially chapter 1, and 1990, especially 8–20) and Hartsock (1983).

36. An exception to the expectation of outright competition comes from scholars who write about organizations that choose to stay utterly disconnected from other groups. Being so separated, these groups neither cooperate nor compete. In discussing such a phenomenon, J. Q. Wilson (1973), Latham (1952, 396–397), and Browne (1990) assume Liberal standards of autonomy as discussed in chapter 1. The discussion of differentiation that I present here, which I claim contributes to the relative lack of competition among case study groups, is similar to that of these scholars. It differs significantly, however, because I am not claiming the differentiation of these groups in a Hobbesian sense. These groups overlap in many ways and are intimately connected to one another. Thus, conflict is minimized not because they have no contact at all, but because of the non-Liberal nature of their contact.

37. An interesting connection between a competitive understanding of the relationship between political groups and a silencing politics was made, for example, in the spring of 1981. At that time Rabbi Gerry Serrota was a cochair of the national steering committee of New Jewish Agenda, and he was told that he would therefore have to resign from his post on his local Hillel board. However, due to at least the pretense of academic freedom within Hillel, this action could not be taken against him officially for political reasons. Instead, it was couched in competitive terms: Serrota was informed that he could not expect to go on working for "Ford in the daytime and General Motors at night." (This story was related to me by Serrota in an interview in July 1992.)

38. See Truman (1951, 510).

39. Truman (1951); and Hayes (1983, 120).

40. Wright and Hyman (1958, 284–292); and Verba and Nie (1972, 176).

41. Hayes (1983, 120). In addition, Hayes points to the predominance of staff-run organizations, in contrast to membership-focused group relations, to reconfirm the conflict theory.

42. I am aware of the contradictory usage of the concept of scarcity in Liberal thought. Despite the presumption of scarcity elaborated above, bourgeois society relies on the exact opposite approach at times in its never-ending exploitation of resources and in the expansion of its markets. The ecologist's response to this is not only to point to the limited nature of many resources but—perhaps more importantly—to highlight the dominating nature of the power relationships engaged in. The varied manner and consequences of the invocation of claims to scarcity are thus complex, and need to be further explored. (I thank Susie Tanenbaum for helping me to clarify my ideas on this topic.) Thus, the assertion here that groups do not necessarily proceed from the assumption of scarcity is but the beginning

of such an exploration which is beyond the scope of this present work.

43. National NJA eventually closed down, although numerous local chapters continue to operate.

44. Interview with Michael Lerner, July 1992.

45. The central organizing committee of JWCEO disbanded in the fall of 1992, though the monthly vigils, at least in New York City, continued for some time under the generic solidarity name Women in Black.

46. See, for example, "Shaking Up Old Ways of Benevolence," *New York Times*, 15 September 1992, B1.

47. Interview with Simcha Weintraub, December 1992.

## 4. Success

1. AFSI had printed a few booklets, during the 1980s, on such organizations as New Jewish Agenda, for example. None of these interim reports, however, garnered the attention of the ones on Breira or NIF.

2. For example, NJCRAC adopted a national resolution calling the AFSI tactic "McCarthyite" and called for the right of dissent. Slabodkin (1992) notes this also as an example of a changing pro-Israel politics, though he calls on the community to stand up to more mainstream Jewish groups than the ultraright AFSI.

3. Fowler and Shaiko (1987); Malecki and Mahood (1972, 207); Cigler and Loomis (1983).

4. Some studies focus on the city (Dahl 1961; Crenson 1978), state (Malecki and Mahood 1972; Browne 1985), or national (Denzau and Munger 1986) levels of government. Further variations are found in the study of success in the legislative (Gelb and Palley 1977; R. A. Smith 1984), executive (Heclo 1978; McGlennon and Rapoport 1983), or judicial (Epstein and Rowland in Cigler and Loomis 1986; Stewart 1987) branches or in the bureaucracy (Aberbach and Rockman 1978; Gormley, Hoadley, and Williams, 1983; Romzeck and Hendricks 1982; Berry 1981).

The most popular evaluation of success, however, is legislative influence at the national level in the United States Congress (Poole 1981; Herndon 1982). This level of influence gets measured in various ways. For example, some scholars have commented on the structure of influence in terms of the provision or exchange of information (Matthews 1960, 178; Hinckley 1978, 51–54). A common standard of success becomes "access" to legislators (Wright 1989; Truman 1951, 264–270). By far, the most common evaluation is performed in terms of legislative victories. These are either examined in terms of single issues at one point in time (Ornstein and Elder 1978), or in quantitative terms according to such things as roll call votes (Fowler and Shaiko 1987).

5. See, for example, Elshtain (1981) and Brown (1988), and on minorities see (Matsuda et al. 1993).

6. Rousseau's thesis has other problems that feminists have been quick to point out. See for example Young (in Sunstein 1990).

7. Madison, like Hobbes, sees the principle problem of society, factionalism, as "sown in the nature of man." Madison identifies two main methods of solving

this problem, "the one, by removing its causes; the other by controlling its effects." After arguing against a solution that gets at the root of the problem, he concludes that relief can only be found in the second. Madison's solution, following the classic Liberal formula, is therefore the social contract known as the Constitution of United States of America, and the formation of a federal republic.

8. A. F. Bentley's *The Process of Government* (1908) also begins with "the private" in his "Feelings and Faculties as Causes." He moves, however, to the discussion of the "group" as the "solid and substantial part of all interpretations of history" and discusses the political in terms of government and its sphere (which includes these political groups).

9. Banfield, for example, writes that "a political situation may be viewed as one in which a proposal is to be adopted or not adopted" (1963, 6).

10. For example, see Malecki and Mahood (1972); Greenwald (1977); Lehman Schlozman and Tierney (1983).

11. Although Kavka (1986) challenges the importance of the fear of death in Hobbes's theory, Johnston (1986) also holds the view that attention to the fear of death is central to understanding Hobbes in *Leviathan*.

12. Actually, this conception is not only found among pluralist group theorists. In *Party Government*, Schattschneider assumes a certain level of governmental passivity when he writes that, "the sovereign, moreover, can speak only when spoken to" (1942, 52).

13. Latham, for example, refers to the role of government as a "referee" (1965, 35–36). Actually, there is a slight inconsistency here. State theorists (see, for example, King 1989) and others (Schattschneider 1942) have shown that the pluralist conception of the government is that which balances the competing forces in society as represented by interest groups (see Latham 1952, 36). This understanding follows Hobbesian and Madisonian views of the role of the sovereign/government. However, one also finds in the literature the idea that it is the role of groups to act as watchdogs of the government (Cigler and Loomis 1983, 15; Langton 1978, 7; Walker 1983; Greenwald 1977).

14. Such a conception is employed regularly, for example see Schattschneider (1979, 47). For an interesting case study that exists within this "playing by the rules" framework, but is critically conscious of such a requirement, see Gelb and Palley (1979).

15. It is also Madison's argument for the fact that other forms of government (in *Federalist Papers* he actually is referring to democracies) "have in general been as short in their lives, as they have been violent in their deaths."

16. E. E. Schattschneider's criticism of pluralism is expressed in this well-known line: "The flaw in the pluralist heaven is that the heavenly chorus sings with a strong upper-class accent" (1960, 35). See also Lowi (1969).

17. Hobbes proposes that men "confer all of their power and strength upon one man or upon one assembly of men" (1983, part 2, ch. 17, 227).

18. This is the justification for the situation in which the government has the sole legitimate right to use force.

19. Hobbes writes that "a man cannot lay down the right of resisting them that assault him by force, to take away his life" (1983, part 1, ch. 14, 192). For Hobbes, "a covenant not to defend myself from force, by force, is always void" (1983, 199).

20. To make matters worse, from the perspective of the citizen, the sovereign is arbitrary (for to what higher power could a sovereign be loyal?).

21. If you are not sure about this, ask Rodney King and the thousands of others like him. In addition, although Kavka (1986) does not find this a fundamental challenge to Hobbes's theory, he does discuss the fact that the sovereign often cannot fully protect us.

22. For discussions of the persistence of pluralism see Garson (1978, 110–111) and Browne (1990, 479).

23. See, for example, Greenwald (1977); G. K. Wilson (1981); Salisbury et al. (1987).

24. There is some justification for performing this translation. In Hobbes's great statement on equality we really might have the sense that he is including women in the discussion. When he addresses the issue that individuals have various strengths and weaknesses, particularly in a society with gender divisions, we can think of the various strengths and weaknesses men and women have when compared to one another. We are led to accept Hobbes's assertion, granted in his negative fashion, that in the end everyone is fundamentally equal. Later, Hobbes actually states that man is not necessarily "the more excellent Sex . . . " (1983, part 2, ch. 20, 253); "for there is not always that difference of strength, or prudence between the man and the woman, as that the right can be determined without war."

25. Hobbes wrote in *Leviathan* that "there be always two that are equally parents: the Dominion therefore over the Child, should belong equally to both; and he be equally subject to both."

26. See, for example, Cobb and Elder (1972).

27. As J. Q. Wilson writes, "organizations tend to persist. That is the most important thing to know about them" (1973, 30). See also Olson (1971, 6); Clark and Wilson (1961); J. Q. Wilson (1973).

28. See for example, Salisbury (1969); Smith (1985, 132); Clark and Wilson (1961).

29. Discussion of the benefits and drawbacks of a large membership was found within the Progressive Zionist Caucus, New Jewish Agenda, and many of these other newer counterhegemonic groups studied.

30. For example J. Q. Wilson (1973, 266); Salisbury (1983, 363); Smith (1985, 132).

31. For discussions of this level of politics see Young's discussion of the Five Faces of Oppression (in 1990) and Taylor (1992).

32. Although Biale has shown that historically it may be said that Jewish communities actually have been more autonomous when they have not been politically independent (1987).

33. Although many have pointed out, of course, that by assuming the role of statehood, Israel has had to assume the responsibility for oppressive mechanisms of the modern nation state such as supporting a military (see, for example, Schwarzschild 1982).

34. In the contemporary period, this is mostly expressed in Holocaust imagery. For analysis and critique, see, for example, Ellis (1987) and Klepfisz (1990).

35. This term as used here is meant to refer to a tendency in Zionism to see Israel as not only a Jewish center but somehow as more important than the diaspora. From this hubris, some Israelis and Zionists have tried to subordinate the concerns of, and challenges from, diaspora Jewish communities.

36. From an interview with Mark Rosenblum conducted by Alisa Solomon, 1 April 1988.

37. See Jacoby (1989).

38. This story was first related to me by Mishkan Shalom member Natalie Gorvine during the workshop I gave on relating theory and practice at the 1992 National Havurah Institute in Bala Cynwyd, PA. Rabbi Brian Walt agreed to talk with me concerning the issue in January 1993.

39. From Mishkan Shalom's Statement of Purpose; see Appendix C. See also Balka (1991) and Lenel (1989).

40. Confidential interview, January 1993, with the Hillel director, who also provided written documentation.

41. During the research for this work, innumerable individuals and group representatives from around the country shared their stories (or recommended that I follow up on stories that they had heard), good and bad, of their participation in American Jewish pro-Israel politics. Thus, in the course of my research, many people agreed to tell me their stories of how they had experienced the community's silencing of pro-Israel politics because of their dissenting or dovish views. These people requested various levels of confidentiality depending on how current the story was, the stature of the individual or group in the community, how painful the experience was, or for various other reasons. In the years during which I conducted this research, the most extreme request was from some well-known establishment Jewish leaders that I not use some particular stories at all, though those involved had always agreed to discuss incidents off the record for my general background. Unfortunately, this person, a student activist, could not even break the silence confidentially. Despite the fact that, as always, I made clear who had recommended that I contact him, and that I explained my personal organizational affiliations, the nature of my work, and the various levels of confidentiality that I could respect, this student remained silent.

42. The American Jewish organizations represented included AIPAC, B'nai B'rith, the Anti-Defamation League, AJCongress, AJCommittee, the National Council of Jewish Women, UJA, the Jewish National Fund, the U.S. Holocaust Museum, NJCRAC, and APN. The meeting was cosponsored by the National Association of Arab Americans. Briefers included Michael Shiloh, the deputy chief of the Israeli embassy, Marwan Muasher, spokesperson for the Jordanian negotiating team at the peace talks, and Hanan Ashrawi, spokeswoman for the Palestinian delegation to the talks.

43. Since the election of Labor, many who had used the argument against dissent to support unity behind Israel's right-wing policies are now advocating pub-

lic dissent, in forums from *Midstream* to *Long Island Jewish World*. The most recent challenge has been changes at the Zionist Organization of America. ZOA's national executive committee no longer refers simply to its commitment to the "security of Israel," but now "oppose[s] dismantling any settlements in the West Bank and Gaza." In addition, the Conference of Presidents of Major Jewish Organizations is troubled by the sudden and questionable ascendancy of Morton Klein, a right-wing maverick, to the ZOA presidency. Klein's criticism of the peace accords are seen as competing with AIPAC's stance, which is still deemed the "official" American Jewish position. (See Cohler, 1994.)

44. See Rosenblum 1993 and positions taken by the organization through the mid-1990s.

45. In 1993 extremist right-wing Jewish groups placed bombs outside the offices of both NIF and APN in New York City. In addition, the Jewish settler's massacre of Muslims in Hebron on Purim of 1994 was vociferously condemned.

46. In such an uncertain world, it can be difficult to feel assured while promoting the creation of a sphere in which, as Berman writes, "for the politics of authenticity, any final solution would be a dissolution" (1970, 318).

47. See Taylor (1992).

48. N. Fraser (in Sunstein 1990, 180) suggests a combination of procedural considerations ("reached by means of communicative processes that most closely approximate ideals of democracy, equality, and fairness" and inclusiveness) and consequentialist considerations ("those that do not disadvantage some groups of people vis-à-vis others"). Benhabib suggests "procedural constraints of universal respect and egalitarian reciprocity aimed at "continuing and sustaining the practice of the moral conversation among us" (1990, 345–346).

49. Seyla Benhabib writes that "by allowing that the presuppositions of the moral conversation can be challenged within the conversation itself, they are placed within the purview of questioning. But insofar as they are pragmatic rules necessary to keep the moral conversation going, we can only bracket them in order to challenge them but we cannot suspend them altogether" (1990, 340). In two ways here, she is saying that "the shoe is really on the other foot" (ibid.).

## Conclusion

1. From *Pirkay Avot (Ethics of the Fathers)*, Birnbaum, trans., (1949, 6).

2. In Rich (1986).

3. From "Rift," in *A Wild Patience Has Taken Me this Far*, (1981).

# Bibliography

Aberbach, J. D., and B. A. Rockman. 1978. "Bureaucrats and Clientele Groups: A View from Capitol Hill." *American Journal of Political Science* 22, no. 4 (November): 818–832.

Abramowitz, Yosef. 1992. "The Ongoing Abandonment of Jewish Students." *Response* 59 (spring): 14–24.

Ackelsberg, Martha. 1986. "Spirituality, Community, and Politics: B'not Esh and the Feminist Reconstruction of Judaism." *Journal of Feminist Studies in Religion* II, no. 2 (fall): 109–120.

———. 1991. *Free Women of Spain*. Indianapolis: Indiana University Press.

Ackelsberg, Martha, and Diamond, Irene. 1987. "Gender and Political Life: New Directions in Political Science." In *Analyzing Gender: A Handbook of Social Science Research*, edited by Myra Mary Ferree and Beth B. Hess. Beverly Hills, Calif.: Sage.

Arnett, R. C. 1986. *Communication and Community: Implications of Martin Buber's Dialogue*. Carbondale, Ill.: Southern Illinois University Press.

Avineri, Shlomo. 1981. *The Making of Modern Zionism*. New York: Basic Books.

Bachrach, M., and M. S. Baratz. 1962. "Two Faces of Power." *American Political Science Review* 56 (December): 947–952.

Balbus, Isaac D. 1971. "The Concept of Interest in Pluralist and Marxian Analysis." *Politics and Society* 1, no. 2 (February): 151–177.

Balka, Christie. 1991. "In Search of the Ideal Shul." *Lilith* (fall): 10.

Balka, Christie, and Andy Rose. 1989. *Twice Blessed: On Being Lesbian, Gay, and Jewish*. Boston: Beacon Press.

Banfield, Edward C. 1963. *Political Influence*. Glencoe, Ill.: Free Press.

Bauer, Raymond Augustine et al. 1963. *American Business and Public Policy*. New York: Atherton Press.

Beck, Evelyn Torton. 1984. *Nice Jewish Girls*. Freedom, Calif.: Crossing Press.

Becker, G. S. 1983. "A Theory of Competition Among Pressure Groups for Political Influence." *Quarterly Journal of Economics* XCVIII, no. 3 (August): 371–400.

Benhabib, Seyla. 1987. "The Generalized and the Concrete Other: The Kohlberg-Gilligan Controversy and Feminist Theory." In *Feminism as Critique*, edited by

Seyla Benhabib and Drucilla Cornell. Minneapolis: University of Minnesota Press.

———. 1990. "Afterword: Communicative Ethics and Contemporary Controversies in Practical Philosophy." In *The Communicative Ethics Controversy*, edited by Seyla Benhabib and Fred Dallmayr. Cambridge, Mass.: MIT Press.

Benjamin, Walter. 1969. *Illuminations*. New York: Schocken Books.

Bentley, A. F. 1908. *The Process of Government*. Evanston, Ill.: Principia Press of Illinois.

Berman, Marshall. 1982. *All That Is Solid Melts Into Air: The Experience of Modernity*. New York: Penguin Books.

———. 1970. *The Politics of Authenticity: Radical Individualism and the Emergence of Modern Society*. New York: Atheneum.

Bernstein, Phillip. 1983. *To Dwell in Unity: The Jewish Federation Movement in America 1960–1980*. Philadelphia: Jewish Publication Society.

Berry, J. M. 1977. *Lobbying for the People: The Political Behavior of Public Interest Groups*. Princeton: Princeton University Press.

———. 1981. "Beyond Citizen Participation: Effective Advocacy Before Administrative Agencies." *Journal of Applied Behavioral Sciences* 17 (October): 463–477.

———. 1984. *The Interest Group Society*. New York: Little, Brown.

Besser, James D. 1992a. "American Jews, Arabs Meet to Break the Ice." *Baltimore Jewish Times*, 18 December.

———. 1992b. "Diplomatic Momentum." *New York Jewish Week*, 18–24 December, p. 5.

———. 1992c. "Jews and Arabs Break the Ice." *Detroit Jewish News*, 18 December.

———. 1992d. "A Lively Exchange." *Jewish Journal of Greater Los Angeles*, 18–24 December.

Biale, David. 1987. *Power and Powerlessness in Jewish History*. New York: Schocken Books.

Birnbaum, Philip, trans. 1949. *Pirkay Avot (Ethics of the Fathers)*. New York: Hebrew Publishing Company.

Blustain, Rachel. 1995. "Women Found Absent from Top UJA Posts: Men Direct Federations in All Large U.S. Cities." *Forward*, 6 January, 4.

"B'nai B'rith Opens Breira Study in 2–day Sessions." 1977. *The Jewish Week–American Examiner*, 1 May, 14.

Bourdieu, Pierre. 1985. "The Social Space and the Genesis of Groups." *Social Science Information* 24: 195–220.

Boyarin, Jonathan. 1991. *Polish Jew in Paris: The Ethnography of Memory*. Indianapolis: Indiana University Press.

———. 1992. *Storm from Paradise: The Politics of Jewish Memory*. Minneapolis: University of Minnesota Press.

Brettschneider, Marla. 1994–1995. "Re-thinking Ideological Diversity in Group Theory: Implications of Clinton's Middle East Policy." *Commonwealth: A Journal of Political Science* 7: 19–32.

———. Forthcoming 1996. *The Narrow Bridge: Jewish Perspectives on Multiculturalism.* New Brunswick, N.J.: Rutgers University Press.

Brod, Harry. 1988. *A Mensch Among Men.* Freedom, Calif.: Crossing Press.

Brown, Wendy. 1995. *States of Injury: Power and Freedom of Late Modernity.* Princeton: Princeton University Press.

Browne, W. P. 1976. "Benefits and Membership: A Reappraisal of Interest Group Activity." *Western Politics Quarterly* 29: 258–273.

———. 1985. "Variations in the Behavior and Style of State Lobbyists and Interest Groups." *Journal of Politics* 47, no. 2 (May): 450–468.

———. 1990. "Organized Interests and their Issue Niches: Search for Pluralism in a Policy Domain." *Journal of Politics* 52, no. 2 (May): 477–509.

Buber, Martin. 1947. *Between Man and Man.* London: K. Paul.

———. 1949. *Paths in Utopia.* New York: Macmillan.

———. 1958. *I and Thou.* trans. Ronald Gregor Smith, New York: Macmillan.

———. 1966. *The Way of Response.* New York: Schocken Books.

———. 1973. *On Zion: The History of an Idea.* New York: Schocken Books.

Burd, Stephen. 1991. "Anti-War Groups Galvanizing." *Forward,* (1 February), p. 8.

Butler, Judith. 1990. *Gender Trouble: Feminism and the Subversion of Identity.* New York: Routledge, Chapman and Hall.

Carroll, B. 1979. "Political Science, Part I: American Politics and Political Behavior." *Signs* 5, no. 2 (winter): 289–306.

Chamberlain, J. 1974. "Provision of Collective Goods as a Function of Group Size." *American Political Science Review* 68: 707–716.

Chamberlin, J.R.A. 1978. "A Collective Goods Model of Pluralist Political Systems." *Public Choice* 33: 97–113.

Cigler, A. J., and B. A. Loomis, 1983 and 1986 editions. *Interest Group Politics.* Washington, D.C.: Congressional Quarterly.

Cigler, A. J., and Cheryl Swanson, 1981. "Politics and Older Americans." In *The Dynamics of Aging,* edited by Forrest J. Berghorn et al. Boulder, Colo.: Westview Press.

Clark, P. B., and J. Q. Wilson, 1961. "Incentive Systems: A Theory of Organizations." *Administrative Science Quarterly* 6 (June): 129–166.

Cloward, R. A., and F. Fox Piven. 1979. "Hidden Protest: The Channelling of Female Innovation and Resistance." *Signs* 4, no. 4 (summer): 651–669.

Cobb, Roger W., and Charles D. Elder. 1972. *Participation in American Politics: the Dynamics of Agenda Building.* Boston, Mass.: Allyn and Bacon.

Cohen, Naomi. 1972. *Not Free to Desist: The American Jewish Committee 1906–1966.* Philadelphia: Jewish Publication Society.

———. 1975. *American Jews and the Zionist Idea.* New York: Ktav.

Cohen, Steven M. 1989a. *Israel-Diaspora Relation: A Survey of American Jewish Leaders.* Tel Aviv: Israel-Diaspora Institute.

———. 1989b. "Ties and Tensions: An Update—The 1989 Survey of American Jewish Attitudes Toward Israel and Israelis." New York: American Jewish Committee.

Cohen, Steven M., and Seymour Martin Lipset. 1991. "Attitudes Toward the Arab-Israeli Conflict and the Peace Process among American Jewish Philanthropic Leaders, 1991." Los Angeles: The Wilstein Institute of Jewish Policy Studies of the University of Judaism. (November).

Cohler, Lawrence. 1994. "One-Man Lobby." *Jewish Week*, 24–30 June, 22–24.

Connolly, W. E. 1969. *The Bias of Pluralism*. New York: Atherton Press.

Crenson, M. A. 1978. "Social Networks and Political Processes in Urban Neighborhoods." *American Journal of Political Science* 22, no. 3 (August): 578–594.

Dahl, R. 1956. *A Preface to Democratic Theory*. Chicago: University of Chicago Press.

———. 1961. *Who Governs?* New Haven: Yale University Press.

Dallmayr, Fred. 1992. "Redemptive Remembering: Ethics and Recollection." Paper for 1992 Annual American Political Science Association, Chicago, 4 September.

Daly, Mary. 1978. *Gyn/ecology: The Metaethics of Radical Feminism*. Boston, Mass.: Beacon Press.

Davis, A. 1983. *Women, Race and Class*. New York: Random House.

Denzau, A., and M. Munger. 1986. "Legislators and Interest Groups: How Unorganized Interests get Represented." *American Political Science Review* 80, no. 1 (March): 89–106.

Di Stefano, Christine. 1991. *Configurations of Masculinity: A Feminist Perspective on Modern Political Theory*. Ithaca: Cornell University Press.

Dexter, L. A. 1969. *How Organizations Are Represented in Washington*. Indianapolis: Bobbs-Merrill.

Dietz, Mary. 1985. "Citizenship With a Feminist Face." *Political Theory* 13, no. 1: 19–37.

Easton. 1953. *The Political System*. New York: Knopf.

Elazar, D. J. 1980. *Community and Polity*. Philadelphia: Jewish Publication Society.

Eliav, Arie Lova. 1988. *New Heart, New Spirit*. Philadelphia: Jewish Publication Society.

Ellis, M. H. 1987. *Toward a Jewish Theology of Liberation*. New York: Orbis Books.

Elshtain, Jean Bethke. 1981. *Public Man, Private Woman: Women in Social and Political Thought*. Princeton: Princeton University Press.

Ethical Jewish Giving Project, Ann Arbor New Jewish Agenda. 1991. *Ethical Jewish Giving and Israel*. Second edition. Ann Arbor, Mich. Ethical Jewish Giving Project (March).

Evans, S. 1979. *Personal Politics*. New York: Knopf.

Falbel, Rita, Irena Klepfisz, and Donna Nevel, eds. 1990. *Jewish Women's Call for Peace: A Handbook for Jewish Women on the Israeli/Palestinian Conflict*. Ithaca, N.Y.: Firebrand Books.

Fein, Leonard. 1988. *Where Are We? The Inner Life of American Jews*. New York: Harper and Row.

———. 1992. "Language of Crisis." *Forward*, 6 November, 7.

Findley, Paul. 1985. *They Dare to Speak Out: People and Institutions Confront Israel's Lobby*. Westport, Conn: Lawrence Hill Books.

Foer, Paul M. 1983. "The War Against Breira." *The Jewish Spectator* (Summer): 18–23.

Foucault, Michel. 1977. *Discipline and Punish*. New York: Pantheon Books.

———. 1984. *Foucault Reader*. Edited by Paul Rabinow. New York: Pantheon Books.

Fowler, L., and R. Shaiko. 1987. "The Grassroots Connection: Environmental Activists and Senate Roll Calls." *American Journal of Political Science* 31, no. 3 (August): 484–510.

Fraser, Nancy. 1987. "Women, Welfare and the Politics of Need Interpretation." *Hypatia: A Journal of Feminist Philosophy* 2: 103–121.

———. 1991. "Rethinking the Public Sphere: A Contribution to the Critique of Actually Existing Democracy." *Social Text* 25/26: 56–80.

Freedman, J. 1975. *The Politics of Women's Liberation*. New York: David McKay.

Freeman, J. 1980. "Women and Urban Policy." Whole (spring) supplement of *Signs*.

Friedman, Maurice. 1974. *The Hidden Human Image*. New York: Delacorte Press.

Friedman, Robert. 1992a. "A PAC with McCarthy: New Revelations About AIPAC's War on Liberal Jews." *Village Voice*, 25 August, 19.

———. 1992b. "The Israel Lobby's Blacklist: Exposing AIPAC's Activities." *Village Voice*, 4 August, 25.

Friedman, Thomas. 1992. "Behind Appointments, Quiet Warning." *New York Times*, 13 December, 36.

———. 1993. "Clinton Nominees Disturb Some Jews." *New York Times*, 5 January, A11.

Garson, David G. 1978. *Group Theories of Politics*. Beverly Hills, Calif.: Sage.

Gauthier, David. 1987. *Morals by Agreement*. Oxford, England: Clarendon Press.

Gelb, J., and M. Leif Palley. 1977. "Women and Interest Group Politics: A Case Study of the Equal Credit Opportunity Act." *American Politics Quarterly* (July): 331–352.

———. 1979. "Women and Interest Politics: A Comparative Analysis of Federal Decision-Making." *Journal of Politics* 41, no. 2 (May): 362–392.

Gilligan, Carol. 1982. *In a Different Voice*. Cambridge, Mass.: Harvard University Press.

Goldberg, J. J. 1993. *Builders and Dreamers: Habonim Labor Zionist Youth in North America*. New York: Herzl Press.

Goldin, M. 1976. *Why They Give*. New York: Macmillan.

Goldscheider, C., and A. S. Zuckerman. 1984. *The Transformation of American Jews*. Chicago: University of Chicago Press.

Gopian, J. D. 1984. "What makes PAC's Tick? An Analysis of the Allocation Patterns of Economic Interest Groups." *American Journal of Political Science* 28, no. 2 (May): 259–281.

Gormley, W., J. Hoadley, and C. Williams. 1983. "Potential Responsiveness in the Bureaucracy: Views of Public Utility Regulation." *American Political Science Review* 77, no. 3 (September): 704–717.

Gramsci, Antonio. 1971. *Selections from the Prison Notebooks*. New York: International Publishers.

Greenberg, Blu. 1981. *On Women and Judaism*. Philadelphia: Jewish Publication Society.

Greenstein, Howard R. 1981. *Turning Point: Zionism and Reform Judaism*. Brown Judaic Studies no. 12. Chico, Calif.: Scholars Press.

Greenwald, C. 1977. *Group Power*. New York: Praeger.

Grenzke, Janet. 1989. "PAC's and the Congressional Supermarket: the Currency is Complex." *American Journal of Political Science* 33, no. 1 (February): 1–24.

Gross, Peter. 1983. *Israel in the Mind of America*. New York: Knopf.

Gutmann, Amy. 1985. "Communitarian Critics of Liberalism." *Philosophy and Public Affairs* 14, no. 3 (summer): 308–322.

Gwertzman, Bernard. 1976. "American Jewish Leaders Are Split Over Issue of Meeting With P.L.O." *New York Times*, 30 December, A1.

Hansen, J. M. 1986. "The Political Economy of Group Membership." *American Political Science Review* 79, no. 1 (March): 79–96.

Hardin, R. 1982. *Collective Action*. Baltimore: Resources for the Future.

Harding, Sandra, ed. 1987. *Feminism and Methodology*. Bloomington: Indiana University Press.

Hartsock, Nancy. 1983. *Money, Sex and Power*. Boston: Longman.

Hayes, M. T. 1981. *Lobbyists and Legislators*. New Brunswick, N.J.: Rutgers University Press.

———. 1983. "Interest Groups: Pluralism or Mass Society." In Cigler and Loomis 1983.

Heclo, H. 1978. "Issue Networks and the Executive Establishment." In *The New American Political System*, edited by A. King. Washington, D.C.: American Enterprise Institute.

Henry, Sondra, and Emily Taitz. 1988. *Written Out of History: Our Jewish Foremothers*. New York: Biblio Press.

Herndon, J. F. 1982. "Access, Record and Competition as Influences on Interest Group Contributions to Congressional Campaigns." *Journal of Politics* 44, no. 4 (November): 996–1019.

Herring, Mary. 1990. "Legislative Representativeness to Black Constituents in Three Deep South States." *Journal of Politics* 52, no. 3 (August): 740–758.

Hertzberg, Arthur. 1959. *The Zionist Idea*. New York: Jewish Publication Society.

———. 1979. *Being Jewish in America: The Modern Experience*. New York: Schocken Books.

———. 1989. *The Jews In America*. New York: Simon and Schuster.

Hertzke, A. D. 1988. *Representing God in Washington*. Knoxville: University of Tennessee Press.

Herzog, Don. 1986. "Civic Republicanism and Its Critics: III. Some Questions for Republicans." *Political Theory* 14, no. 3 (August): 473–493.

Heschel, Susannah. 1983. *On Being a Jewish Feminist: A Reader*. New York: Schocken Books.

Hinchman, Barbara. 1990. "The Idea of Individuality: Origins, Meaning and Political Significance." *Journal of Politics* 52, no. 3 (August): 759–81.

Hinckley, Barbara. 1978. *Stability and Change in Congress*. New York: Harper and Row.

Hirschman, A. O. 1970. *Exit, Voice and Loyalty*. Cambridge, Mass.: Harvard University Press.

Hobbes, Thomas. 1949. *De Cive*. New York: Appelton-Century Crofts.

———. 1969. *The Elements of Law, Natural and Political*. London: Cass.

———. 1983. *The Leviathan*. New York: Penguin Books.

Hochstein, Philip. 1977. "Why All the Fuss About Breira?" *Jewish Week–American Examiner* 13–19 February, 25.

hooks, bell. 1984. *Feminist Theory from Margin to Center*. Boston: South End Press.

Huntington, S. P. 1975. "The Democratic Distemper." *Public Interest* 41 (fall): 9–38.

Hurwitz, Ariel. 1994. *Against the Stream: Seven Decades of Hashomer Hatzair in North America*. Givat Havira, Israel: Yad Ya'ari.

Isaacs, Rael Jean, and Erich Isaacs. 1977. "The Rabbis of Breira." *Midstream* (April): 3–17.

Isaacs, Stephen. 1974. *Jews and American Politics*. New York: Doubleday.

"Israel's Dilemma." 1976. *New York Times,* 11 May, 32.

ITON, AYSHET. 1977. "Pamphlet Tells of Israel Backers Snared into Alliance for PLO." *Jewish Week–American Examiner* 16–22 January, 1.

Jacobson, Norman. 1963. "Political Science and Political Education." *American Political Science Review* LVII, no. 3 (September): 561–569.

Jacoby, Tamar. 1989. "A Family Quarrel: Once American Jews loved Israel blindly. Now they're learning to ask hard questions." *Newsweek,* 3 April, 58.

Jaggar, Alison M., and Susan R. Bordo, eds. 1989. *Gender/Body/Knowledge*. New Brunswick, N.J.: Rutgers University Press.

Jewell, Malcolm E., and Samuel C. Patterson. 1966. *The Legislative Process in the United States*. New York: Random House.

"Jewish Students Under Siege." 1992. *Forward,* 31 January, 4.

Johnston, David. 1986. *The Rhetoric of Leviathan: Thomas Hobbes and the Politics of Cultural Transformation*. Princeton: Princeton University Press.

Jordan, June. 1994. *Technical Difficulties: African-American Notes on the State of the Union*. New York: Vintage Books.

Kaminetz, Roger. 1994. "Has the Jewish Renewal Movement Made It Into the Mainstream." *Moment* 19, no. 6 (December), 42.

Kaplan, Mordechai. 1967. *Judaism as a Civilization: Toward a Reconstruction of American-Jewish Life*. Philadelphia: Jewish Publication Society.

Kavka, Gregory. 1986. *Hobbesian Moral and Political Theory*. Princeton: Princeton University Press.

Kaye-Kantrowitz, Melanie. 1992. *The Issue Is Power: Essays on Women, Jews, Violence and Resistance*. San Francisco: Aunt Lute Books.

Kaye-Kantrowitz, M., and I. Klepfisz. 1986. *The Tribe of Dina*. Sinister Wisdom 29/30. Reprint 1989. Boston: Beacon.

Keller, B. 1982. "Computers and Laser Printers Have Recast the Injunction: 'Write Your Congressman.'" *Congressional Quarterly Weekly Report*, 11 September, 2245–2247.

Keller, Catherine. 1986. *From a Broken Web: Separation, Sexism and Self*. Boston: Beacon Press.

Kenan, I. L. 1981. *Israel's Defense Line*. New York: Prometheus Books.

Key, V. O. 1952. *Political Parties and Pressure Groups*. New York: Thomas Y. Crowell.

———. 1961. *Public Opinion and American Democracy*. New York: Knopf.

King, Desmond S. 1989. "Political Centralization and State Interests in Britain: The 1986 Abolition of the GLC and MCC'c." *Comparative Political Studies* 21, no. 4 (January), 467–494.

Kingdon, John. 1973. *Congressmen's Voting Decisions*. New York: Harper and Row.

Klatch, R. 1988. "Coalition and Conflict among Women of the New Right." *Signs* 13, no. 4 (summer): 671–694.

Klepfisz, Irena. 1991. "Peace Still." *Village Voice*, 19 February.

———. 1990. *Dreams of an Insomniac: Jewish Feminist Essays, Speeches and Diatribes*. Portland, Ore.: Eight Mountain Press.

Klutznick, Philip. 1961. *No Easy Answers*. New York: Farrar, Straus and Cuday.

Knee, Stuart. 1979. *The Concept of Zionist Dissent in the American Mind 1917–1941*. New York: Robert Speller and Sons.

Knoke, David, and James R. Wood. 1981. *Organized for Action*. New Brunswick, N.J.: Rutgers University Press.

Koltun, E. 1978. *The Jewish Woman*. New York: Schocken Books.

Kornberg, Jaques. 1978. "Zionism and Ideology: The Breira Controversy." *Judaism* 105: 27, no. 1 (winter): 103–114.

Kronish, Ronald. 1994. "Is Zionism Still Relevant?" *Sh'ma*, 30 September, 3–5.

Kropotkin, Peter, n.d. *Mutual Aid: A Factor of Evolution*. Boston: Porter Sargent Publishers.

———. 1987. *Anarchism and Anarchist Communism*. London: Freedom Press.

Kymlicka, Will. 1989. *Liberalism, Community and Culture*. Oxford, England: Clarendon Press.

"Labor Zionists Picket JDL as Peril to Israel." 1975. *American Examiner–Jewish Week*, 1 February, 7.

Langton, S. 1978. *Citizen Participation in America*. Boston: D. C. Heath.

Laswell, Harold D. 1936. *Politics: Who Gets What, When, How?*. New York: McGraw-Hill.

Latham, E. 1952. *The Group Basis of Politics*. New York: Octagon Books.

Lauman, Edward O. and David Knoke. 1987. *The Organizational State*. Madison: University of Wisconsin Press.

Lawson, R., and S. E. Barton. 1980. "Sex Roles in Social Movements: A Case Study of the Tenant Movement in New York City," *Signs* 6, no. 2 (winter): 230–247.

Lehman Schlozman, Kay, and John T. Tierney. 1983. "More of the Same: Washington Pressure Group Activity in a Decade of Change." *Journal of Politics* 45, no. 2 (May): 351–377.

Lehman Schlozman, Kay. 1984. "What Accent the Heavenly Chorus?" *Journal of Politics* 44 (November): 1006–1032.

Lenel, Jane. 1989. "Palestinian and Israeli Talk Peace at Center." *Chestnut Hill Local*, March, 160–179.

Lindbloom, Charles. 1959. "The Handling of Policy Norms in Analysis." In Moses Abramowitz ed. *Allocation of Economic Resources*. Stanford, Calif.: Stanford University Press.

———. 1977. *Politics and Markets*. New York: Basic Books.

Lipset, S. M. 1960. *Political Man: The Social Basis of Politics*. New York: Doubleday.

Lloyd, Genevieve. 1984. *The Man of Reason*. Minneapolis: University of Minnesota Press.

Locke, John. 1980. *Second Treatise of Government*. Indianapolis, Ind.: Hackett.

Lorde, Audre. 1984. *Sister Outsider*. New York: Crossing Press.

Lowi, T. J. 1964. "American Business, Public Policy, Case studies and Political Theory." *World Politics* (July), 677.

———. 1969. *The End of Liberalism: Ideology, Policy and the Crisis of Public Authority*. New York: Norton.

———. 1976. *Incomplete Conquest: Governing America*. New York: Holt, Rinehart and Winston.

Lukes, Steven. 1974. *Power: A Radical View*. London: Macmillan.

Luttberg, N. R., and H. Zeigler. 1966. "Attitude Consensus and Conflict in an Interest Group." *American Political Science Review* 60 (September): 655–666.

McConahay, J. B. 1982. "Self-Interest vs Racial Attitudes as Correlatives of Anti-Busing Attitudes in Louisville: Is It the Buses or the Blacks?" *Journal of Politics* 44, no.3 (August): 692–720.

McConnell, G. 1966. *Private Power and American Democracy*. New York: Knopf.

McFarland, A. S. 1976. *Public Interest Lobbies*. Washington, D.C.: American Enterprise Institute.

———. 1984. *Common Cause*. Chatham, N.J.: Chatham House.

McGlennon, J., and Rapoport, R. 1983. "The Party Isn't Over: Incentives for Activism in the 1980 Presidential Nominating Campaigns." *Journal of Politics* 45, no. 4 (November): 1006–1015.

MacIver. 1932. "Interests." *Encyclopedia of the Social Sciences* VII. New York: Macmillan.

McLellan, David. 1987. *Karl Marx: Selected Writings*. New York: Oxford University Press.

Macpherson, C. B. 1962. *The Political Theory of Possessive Individualism: Hobbes to Locke*. New York: Oxford University Press.

Madison, James, Alexander Hamilton, and John Jay. 1961. *The Federalist Papers*. Edited by Clinton Rossiter. New York: Penguin Books.

Malecki, Edward S., and H. R. Mahood. 1972. *Group Politics: A New Emphasis*. New York: Scribner.

Manley, J. F. 1983. "Neo-Pluralism: A Class Analysis of Pluralism I and Pluralism II." *American Political Science Review* 77, no. 2: 368–383.

Mansbridge, Jane. 1983. *Beyond Adversary Democracy*. Chicago: University of Chicago Press.

———, ed. 1990. *Beyond Self-Interest*. Chicago: University of Chicago Press.

Marsh, D. 1976. "On Joining Interest Groups." *British Journal of Political Science* 6: 257–271.

Marx, Karl. 1969. *The Communist Manifesto*. New York: Penguin Books.

———. 1977. *Capital: Volume One*. New York: Vintage Books.

Matsuda, Mari J. et al. 1993. *Words that Wound: Critical Race Theory, Assault Speech, and the First Amendment*. Boulder: Westview Press.

Matthews, Donald R. 1960. *U.S. Senators and Their World*. New York: Vintage Books.

Melone, A. P., and Jones, J. H. 1982. "Constitutional Convention Delegates and Interest Groups: a Panel Study of Elite Socialization." *Journal of Politics* 44, no. 1 (February): 183–192.

Merchant, Carolyn. 1980. *The Death of Nature*. San Francisco: Harper and Row.

Messinger, S. 1955. "Organizational Transformation: A Study of a Declining Social Movement." *American Sociological Review* 20: 3–10.

Milbrath, L. W. 1963. *The Washington Lobbyists*. Chicago: Rand McNally.

Moe, T. A. 1980. "A Calculus of Group Membership." *American Journal of Political Science* 24: 593–632.

Moe, T. M. 1980. *The Organization of Interests*. Chicago: University of Chicago Press.

———. 1981. "Toward a Broader Range of Interest Groups." *Journal of Politics* 43, no. 2 (May): 531–543.

Moraga, Cherríe. 1983. *Loving in the War Years*. Boston: South End Press.

Muller, E., and Opp, K. D. 1986. "Rational Choice and Rebellious Collective Action." *American Political Science Review* no. 2 (June): 471.

Neimark, Marilyn. 1992. "American Jews and Palestine: The Impact of the Gulf War." *Middle East Report* No. 175, Vol. 22, no. 2 (March–April): 19–23.

Nesvisky, Matthew. 1984. "Unlimited Partnership." *Moment* (May), 30.

Odendahl, Teresa. 1990. *Charity Begins at Home: Generosity and Self-Interest Among the Philanthropic Elite*. New York: Basic Books.

Ollman, Bertell. 1993. *Dialectical Investigations*. New York: Routledge.

Olson, Mancur. 1971. *The Logic of Collective Action: Public Goods and the Theory of Groups*. Cambridge, Mass.: Harvard University Press.

Orbell, John M., Peregrine Schwartz-Shea, and Randy T. Simmons. 1984. "Do Cooperators Exit More Readily than Defectors?" *American Political Science Review* 78, no. 1 (March): 147.

Organski, A.F.K. 1990. *The 3.6 Billion Dollar Bargain*. New York: Columbia University Press.

Ornstein, N. J. and S. Elder. 1978. *Interest Groups, Lobbying and Policymaking*. Washington, D.C.: Congressional Quarterly.

Pateman, Carole. 1988. *The Sexual Contract*. Stanford: Stanford University Press.

Pertschuk, M. 1933. *Giant Killers*. New York: Norton.

Plaskow, Judith. 1991. *Standing Again at Sinai: Judaism from a Feminist Perspective.* New York: HarperCollins.

Pogrebin, Letty Cottin. 1991. *Deborah, Golda, and Me: Being Female and Jewish in America.* New York: Crown.

Polsby, N. 1963. *Community Power and Political Theory.* New Haven: Yale University Press.

Poole, K. T. 1981. "Dimensions of Interest Group Evaluation of US Senate, 1969–1978" *American Journal of Political Science* 25, no. 1 (February): 49–67.

Porter, J. 1965. *The Vertical Mosaic.* Toronto: University of Toronto Press.

Power, Michael. 1991. "Iraq's Attacks Put Jewish Doves at Odds." *New York Newsday,* 25 January, 21.

Pratt, H. J. 1976. *The Gray Lobby.* Chicago: University of Chicago Press.

Prell, Riv-Ellen. 1989. *Prayer and Community, The Havurah in American Judaism.* Detroit: Wayne State University Press.

*Proceedings of Breira's First Annual Membership Conference: February 20–22, 1977.* 1977. New York: Breira.

Putnam, R. D. 1976. *The Comparative Structure of Political Elites.* Englewood Cliffs, N.J.: Prentice Hall.

Rawls, John. 1971. *A Theory of Justice.* Cambridge, Mass.: Harvard University Press.

"Reform Judaism Defends Breira from Its Critics." 1977. *Jewish Week–American Examiner* 29 April, 14.

Rich, Adrienne. 1981. *A Wild Patience Has Taken Me This Far: Poems 1978–1981.* New York: Norton.

———. 1986. *Blood, Bread and Poetry.* New York: Norton.

Riley, Denise. 1988. *Am I That Name? Feminism and the Category of Women in History.* Minneapolis: University of Minnesota Press.

Romzek, B. S., and J. S. Hendricks. 1982. "Organizational Involvement and Representative Bureaucracy: Can We Have It Both Ways?" *American Political Science Review* 76, no. 1 (March): 75–82.

Rose, A. M. 1967. *The Power Structure.* New York: Oxford University Press.

Rosenau, J. 1974. *Citizenship Between Elections.* New York: Free Press.

Rosenblum, Mark. 1993. "Rabin's Test: Be Strong, Seek Peace." *Boston Sunday Globe,* 3 January, 71.

Rosenthal, A. M. 1992. "The Special Interests." *New York Times* 15 December, A23.

Roth, S. 1977. *The Jewish Idea of Community.* New York: Yeshiva University Press.

Rousseau, Jean-Jacques. 1973. *The Social Contract and the Discourses.* Translated by G.D.H. Cole. London: Everyman's Library.

"Row Over Peace Now Embroils Jewish Bigs." 1993. *Forward,* 12 February, 1.

Ruddick, Sara. 1989. *Maternal Thinking: Toward a Politics of Peace.* Boston: Beacon Press.

"RZA Zionist Platform." *Jewish Radical,* spring 1970.

Salisbury, R. H. 1969. "An Exchange Theory of Interest Groups." *Midwest Journal of Political Science* 13 (February): 1–32.

———. 1984. "Interest Representation: The Dominance of Institutions." *American Political Science Review* 78, no. 1 (March): 64.

Salisbury, Robert H., John P. Heinze, Edward O. Laumann, and Robert L. Nelson. 1987. "Who Works with Whom?: Interest Group Alliances and Opposition." *American Political Science Review* 81, no. 4 (December): 1217–1234.

Samuelson, Arthur. 1978. "The Dilemma of American Jewry." *Nation*, 1 April, 359–365.

Schattschneider, E. E. 1942. *Party Government*. New York: Rinehart.

———. 1975. *The Semi-Sovereign People*. Hinsdale, Ill.: Dryden Press.

———. 1979. *Two Hundred Million Americans in Search of a Government*. Hinsdale, Ill.: Dryden Press.

Schumpeter, Joseph A. 1962. *Capitalism, Socialism and Democracy*. New York: Harper and Row.

Schwarzschild, Henry. 1982. "On Withdrawing from Sh'ma." *Sh'ma*, 3 September.

Sears, D. O., and R. R. Lau. 1983. "Inducing Apparently Self-Interested Political Preferences." *American Journal of Political Science* 27, no. 2 (May): 223–252.

Segal, Jerome M. 1989. "Why We Need a Second Jewish Lobby." *Washington Jewish Week*, 14 September, 16.

Selsam, H., and H. Martel, eds. 1963. *Reader in Marxist Philosophy*. New York: International Publishers.

Setel, T. Drorah. 1986. "Feminist Reflections on Separation and Unity in Jewish Theology." *Journal of Feminist Studies in Religion* 2 (spring): 113–118.

Shapiro, Yonathan. 1971. *Leadership of the American Zionist Organization 1897–1930*. Urbana: University of Illinois Press.

Silberman, Charles. 1985. *A Certain People: American Jews and their Lives Today*. New York: Summit Books.

Slabodkin, Gregory. 1992. "The AIPAC Politics of Smear: The Secret Section in Israel's U.S. Lobby that Stifles American Debate." *Washington Report on Middle East Affairs* (July).

Smith, Barbara, ed. 1983. *Home Girls: A Black Feminist Anthology*. New York: Kitchen Table/Women of Color Press.

Smith, R. A. 1984. "Advocacy, Interpretation and Influence in the US Congress." *American Political Science Review* 78, no. 1 (March): 44–63.

Smith, V. K. 1985. "A Theoretical Analysis of the 'Green Lobby'." *American Political Science Review* 79, no. 1 (March): 132–147.

Solomon, Alisa. 1991. "Between Iraq and a Hard Place, Jews Against the War." *Village Voice*, 5 February: 28–29.

Starhawk. 1982. *Dreaming the Dark*. Boston: Beacon Press.

———. 1990. *Truth or Dare*. San Francisco: Harper and Row.

Stein, Barry. 1977. "Views of Breira Said to Dominate Student Network." *Jewish Week–American Examiner*, 13–19 February, 40.

Stewart, Jr., J. F. 1987. "Does Interest Group Litigation Matter? The Case of Black Political Mobilization in Mississippi." *Journal of Politics* 49, no. 3 (August): 780–800.

Stone, I. F. *Underground to Palestine and Reflections Thirty Years Later.* New York: n.p., 1978. Originally published as *Underground to Palestine.* New York: Boni and Gaer, 1946.

Strauss, Leo. 1952. *The Political Philosophy of Hobbes: Its Basis and Its Genesis.* Translated by Elsa M. Sinclair. Chicago: University of Chicago Press.

Sunstein, Cass R., ed. 1990. *Feminism and Political Theory.* Chicago: University of Chicago Press.

Taylor, Charles. 1991. *The Ethics of Authenticity.* Cambridge, Mass.: Harvard University Press.

————. 1992. *Multiculturalism and "The Politics of Recognition."* Princeton: Princeton University Press.

"30,000 Israelis Parade in Claim to the West Bank." 1976. *New York Times*, 20 April, 1.

Tivnan, Edward. 1987. *The Lobby.* New York: Simon and Schuster.

Tobin, Gary. 1990. *Israel and American Jewish Philanthropy.* Policy and Planning Paper 5. Mass.: Maurice and Marilyn Cohen Center for Modern Jewish Studies at Brandeis University.

————. 1992. *Trends in American Jewish Philanthropy: Market Research Analysis.* Mass.: Maurice and Marilyn Cohen Center for Modern Jewish Studies at Brandeis University.

Truman, D. B. 1951. *The Governmental Process.* New York: Knopf.

Tucker, Robert C. 1978. *The Marx-Engels Reader.* 2nd ed. New York: Norton.

Twersky, David. 1992a. "Democrats Seek Unity, Back Israel." *Jewish Forward*, 17 July, 1.

————. 1992b. "Hatikva in New Key is Song of Peace Now." *Forward*, 31 January, 1.

————. 1994. "The Conspiratorial World of an Investigative Reporter." *Moment* 19, no. 5 (October): 52ff.

Uhlaner, Carole J. 1989. "Rational Turnout: The Neglected Role of Groups." *American Journal of Political Science* 33, no. 2 (May): 390–422.

"U. of Wisconsin Repeals Ban on Hate Speech." *New York Times*, 14 September, A10.

Urofsky, Urovsky. 1978. *We Are One!: American Jewry and Israel.* New York: Anchor Press/Doubleday.

Uslaner. "One Nation, Many Voices: Interest Groups in Foreign Policy Making." In Cigler and Loomis 1986.

Verba, Sidney, and Norma H. Nie. 1972. *Participation in America.* New York: Harper and Row.

Walker, J. 1966. "A Critique of the Elitist Theory of Democracy." *American Political Science Review* 60 (June): 285–295.

————. 1983. "The Origins and Maintenance of Interest Groups in America." *American Political Science Review* 77, no. 2 (June): 390–406.

Ward, J. F. 1978. "Arthur Bentley's Philosophy of Social Science." *American Journal Of Political Science* 22, no. 3 (August): 595–608.

*The Washington Lobby.* 1987. Washington, D.C.: Congressional Quarterly.

Waskow, Arthur. 1978. *God-Wrestling*. New York: Schocken Books.

——. 1983. *These Holy Sparks: The Rebirth of the Jewish People*. San Francisco: Harper and Row.

Watkins, J.W.N. 1955. "Philosophy and Politics in Hobbes." *Philosophical Quarterly* no. 19: 125–146.

Waxman, Chaim. 1983. *American Jews in Transition*. Philadelphia: Temple University Press.

——. 1989. *American Aliya: Portrait of an Innovative Migration Movement*. Detroit: Wayne State University Press.

Waxman, Deborah. 1992. "Symposium on the Nature of Diaspora." *Response* 60 (fall): 21–23.

Wechsler, James A. 1976. "Dove With Talons." *New York Post*, 28 April, 37.

Weidman Schneider, S. 1985. *Jewish and Female*. New York: Simon and Schuster.

Welch, Susan, and Fred Ullrich. 1984. *The Political Life of American Jewish Women*. New York: Biblio Press.

Wilson, Graham K. 1981. *Interest Groups in the United States*, Oxford, England: Clarendon Press.

Wilson, James Q. 1973. *Political Organizations*. New York: Basic Books.

Wright, Charles R., and Herbert H. Hyman. 1958. "Voluntary Association Memberships of American Adults." *American Sociological Review* 23, no. 2 (June): 284–294.

Wright, John R. 1989. "PAC Contributions, Lobbying, and Representation." *Journal of Politics* 51, no. 3 (August): 713–729.

Yudelson, Larry. 1991. "Left Proposes a Day's Fast for Peace." *Forward*, 1 February, 8.

Young, Iris Marion. 1990. *Justice and the Politics of Difference*. Princeton: Princeton University Press.

Zeigler, L. Harmon, and G. Wayne Peak. 1972. *Interest Groups in American Society*. Englewood Cliffs, N.J.: Prentice Hall.

"Zionists in Clash Near UN." 1976. *New York Post*, 19 April, 15.

## American Jewish Journals

*Bridges*
*Commentary*
*Congress Monthly*
*Forward*
*Hadassah Magazine*
*Israel Horizons*
*interChange*
*Jewish Currents*
*Jewish Frontier*
*Jewish Spectator*
*Jewish Week*

*Jewish World*
*La'Inyan*
*Lilith*
*Midstream*
*Moment*
*New Outlook*
*Response*
*Sh'ma*
*Tikkun*

# Index

## About the Author

Dr. Marla Brettschneider earned her B.A. in political science at SUNY-Binghamton and her M.A. and Ph.D. degrees in political philosophy in the Politics Department of New York University. She is author of numerous articles and editor of *The Narrow Bridge: Jewish Perspectives on Multiculturalism* (forthcoming from Rutgers University Press). She is a longtime political activist and is currently Assistant Professor of Political Theory at Bloomsburg University in Pennsylvania.

**DATE DUE**

| | | | |
|---|---|---|---|
| | | | |
| | | | |
| | | | |
| | | | |
| | | | |
| | | | |
| | | | |
| | | | |
| | | | |
| | | | |
| | | | |
| | | | |
| | | | |
| | | | |